Barak & Deborah United

Love, Freedom, and Spirituality

Mary L. Windsor
and
Dr. Rudolph R. Windsor

PublishAmerica
Baltimore

First printing

PublishAmerica has allowed this work to remain exactly as the authors intended verbatim, without editorial input.

Publisher's Cataloging-in-Publication
(*Provided by Quality Books, Inc.*)

Windsor, Mary L.
Barak and Deborah United: love, freedom, and spirituality / Mary L. Windsor and Rudolph R. Windsor.
--Rev. ed
p. cm
Previous ed.: Deborah and Barak / by Mary L. Windsor and Rudolph R. Windsor. Windsor Golden Series, 2001.
ISBN-13: 978-1-4626-5300-3
ISBN-10: 1-4626-5300-6

1. Deborah (biblical judge)--Fiction. 2. Barak (Biblical judge) -- Fiction. 3. Bible. O.T.-- Biography--Fiction. I. Windsor, Rudolph R.,1935- II. Title.

PS3623.I6245B37 2011 813□.6
QBI11-600124

Softcover 9781462653003
mcCover Paperback 9781462679331
PUBLISHAMERICA, LLLP
www.publishamerica.com
Baltimore

Printed in the United States of America

To

Leatta Jones
and
Sam Davis,
the
mother
and
step-father
of
Dr. Rudolph R. Windsor

and

Edward
and
Eva Robinson,
the
parents
of
Mary L. Windsor

Acknowledgements

First of all, we would like to give special gratitude to the Most High God who guided us through every step of this book. Without His assistance, this book would not have been possible.

I want to acknowledge my uncles and aunts of the Clark family for their inspiration and support over the years.

A special recognition goes to my brother, Cole Windsor, my first wife, Mary Ellen Windsor, and my sisters who brought joy to our family.

A heart of sincere gratitude goes to Maurice Kennedy, Jr. whose knowledge and expertise in computer science was invaluable.

A special thanks to Thais Sherell J for her many hours of discussion about the cover design of our book.

Other Books by the Author

From Babylon to Timbuktu

The Valley of the Dry Bones

Judea Trembles Under Rome

When Is the Next War?

Deborah and Barak

Within these pages, there is an important message for our generation.

The need for excellent leadership is paramount in our neighborhoods. However, in order to acquire this good leadership, certain qualities are essential such as love and service. These are the words of **Dr. Cornel West** and **Tavis Smiley**. Because of the terrible situations that face our nation and our people today, good leaders must display a lot of love, dedication, and service. This means that the would-be good leaders must come down off their ivory towers and get their feet muddy and scared in the battlefield of life if we really intend to reduce improper guidance, poverty, crime, and ignorance among our youth. It is too dangerous to wait for others to solve our problems; the responsibility devolves upon us. This book helps to point us in the direction of how this can be accomplished.

Cast of Characters

Deborah Lapidoth	A beautiful, well-known, middle-aged widow is the heroin of this novel
Barak Ben Abinoam	The handsome prince, as well as a freedom fighter, is the hero of this novel who pursues Deborah
Demetrius Lysimacus	A Greek surgeon who studied in Egypt
Isis Lysimacus	The Egyptian wife of Demetrius
Hapshepsut	The daughter of Demetrius by his deceased Greek wife
Medical Assistants	Greek junior doctors
Samuel	The prosecutor during the trial of Zekekiyah
King Jabin	Steaming with hatred, Jabin is the shrewd and ruthless leader of the Canaanite nations
General Sisera	The callous diabolical general responsible for the oppression of the Hebrews

Mashchit	Grand Vizier under King Jabin
Elder Ariel	The wise, senior chief judge of the Supreme Court who guides Barak on the road to success
Prince Zaken	One of the princes from the tribe of Issachar
Elder Ram	Head elder in the City of Daberath
Sarah	Deborah's handmaid and confidant
Rachel	The spokeswoman for a group of ladies who came to meet with Deborah
Azuv	The beggar at the marketplace who meets Deborah
Elder Tamim	Chief elder of the Hebrew village near the City of Nahalol
Lieutenant Abrams	Officer of the perimeter guard
Abinoam	The father of Barak
Ophrah	House servant of Caleb
Madreech	The supervisor of Deborah's factory workers
Shemurah	The mother of Adam

Eli	The father of Adam
Adam	Son of Shemurah and Eli who wants to marry a Canaanite girl
Tamar	The Canaanite girl who wants to marry Adam
Caleb	The brother-in-law of Deborah
Yoetz	Deborah's uncle who raised her
Shallum	Chief judge of the court in Beer Sheba
Zadekiyah	The woman who is accused of adultery
Benjamin Ben Hur	Brother-in-law of Zadekiyah
Abraham	The husband of Zadekiyah
Ishamel	One of the accusers of Zadekiyah
Katan	The second accuser of Zadekiyah
Captain Enoch	Barak's first officer
Captain David	The training officer under Barak
Zaeer	A Canaanite officer captured by the Hebrews
Prince Abihu	Prince of the tribe of Judah

Jonathan	Prince Abihu's tax collector
Reuben	The leader of a band of thieves
Malcah	A teenage friend of Deborah
Dan	The teenage boyfriend of Malcah
Lieutenant Sabar	A Canaanite officer under Sisera
Eved-Baal	High Priest of Haroshet-ha-goiim
Elder Nahash	A high official of the City of Nahalol
Kahan	High Priest of the City of Nahalol
Marah	Her village and family is destroyed by Sisera
Jael	The women who slew Sisera
Joel	The nephew of Barak, who was wounded in battle
Joseph	One of the nephews of Barak, who was placed in a pit
Katurah	Barak's sister
Ben	The boy who wants Barak to be like a father to him
Leah	Ben's mother

A Few Interesting Passages From This Book

He pushed the necklace toward her, "Take it! It's yours," he urged her.

She took hold of it. "It is so thoughtful of you Barak," she said smiling. Then her countenance changed quickly; and her facial expression became serious. "Oh Barak, I can't accept it."

"Please Deborah, don't do this to me. When I am away from you, I think of you morning—noon—and night."

"There are plenty of beautiful women in Galilee. Discover them Barak—and they will help you to forget about me."

"I told you that I want only you! Can't you understand? Even if you had a twin sister, I would want only you."

"I am past childbearing age," Marah said, "What can I do?"

"There are many orphans among our people who don't have mothers or fathers," said Deborah. "Adopt a son and a daughter and give them love and joy. Then in return, they will give you love and joy."

Barak said, "Yes, but there is something else—I haven't told you. The lady Deborah, who you met earlier, is a prophetess, and she has said that we will win." (the war)

"Did she look into her crystal ball?" asked Demetrius.

Barak appeared offended and replied, "I don't know of any darn crystal ball?"

After noticing that Barak's facial expression had changed, Demetrius backed down. "Excuse me, Barak for being abrupt. I am not going to get involved in your business. However, I did detect a spiritual quality in her eyes. Whatever she told you, that is between you and her. I have said enough."

Foreword

The subject of this novel is predicated on Hebrew ancient records as the following: the fourth and fifth chapters of the book of Judges and other historical records of this time period. Some characters and events appear as they are given in this primary source; however, there are some that are the creation of the authors' imagination. This was done so that they could give the readers an absorbing and entertaining story that would come alive in their minds. In order that they could bring to you the flavor of that time, the authors consulted a variety of historical records pertaining to this period. We sincerely hope that they have fulfilled your expectations.

Social critics, including Aristotle, believe that a novel should instruct mankind in right action. The authors believe that the moral principles set forth in this novel can benefit the present generation and uplift our world.

Now sit back and relax and enjoy what the authors have shared with you. And when you have gained something worthy from these pages, let your light shine by sharing this knowledge with others.

xviii Mary L. Windsor and Dr. Rudolph R. Windsor

CHAPTER 1
Palestine (c.1350-1125 B.C.)

The lady Deborah—a spiritual woman—arose early from her bed with mixed feelings in anticipation of the arrival of an unusual visitor. She sat in her bedchamber thinking of how handsome he was with those gorgeous, seductive dark brown eyes. On this cloudy chilly morning, she thought about her late husband who was murdered by the Canaanites over three years ago. His death had caused her much emotional pain. Now, she sat there waiting for the arrival of Barak whose primary mission is to fight the Canaanites. Would the same thing happen to him, she wondered. She became troubled and chills ran down her spine.

Deborah, a woman in her late thirties, quickly got dressed in her white silk dress decorated with purple and gold borders around the neckline, bodice, and sleeves. The dress was long and loose; however, because she had a pleasing figure, it emphasized her shape in all the right places.

At that moment, Deborah felt as if she wanted some fresh air and company; therefore, she called for her handmaid who also functioned as her personal scribe. "Sarah, come here please!" Sarah was fair skin, had blue eyes, was of mixed ancestry, and she could write and speak Hebrew, Aramaic, and the Egyptian languages.

"Yes, my lady."

"I want you to walk with me outside to get some fresh air."

"Certainly," Sarah replied. "Oh, I like the way your purple linen shawl covers your long braids and shoulders." The shawl contrasted well with her white dress and pretty chestnut brown skin. "My lady, are you expecting a visitor today?"

"Yes, I am." At that moment, Deborah rubbed the prominent bridge of her nose and squeezed her nostrils which stood out slightly. "Why do you ask?"

"Because you are dressed up so special today, like—like a princess."

As they walked through the huge door made of cedar wood, Deborah said, "Well, after all, I am expecting a prince." Then they passed through the iron gate of the courtyard.

Sarah turned around to her. "I believe you are serious. Could he be a prince from Moab, Syria, or from our southern neighbor, Egypt?"

Deborah looked at her with surprise. "No, Sarah—don't be silly! He's from the Hebrew tribe of Naphtali."

They walked out to the main road which was about sixty cubits from her house. As they walked along the pebbled walkway, they passed by red and purple lilies that bloomed every spring.

"Have I ever met or seen this prince?" asked Sarah.

"I don't think …" Deborah paused and then continued. "Yes, we met him in the City of Bethel last year. At that time, one of the elders introduced him to us. His name is Barak Ben Abinoam."

"Ah—do you mean General Barak, the commander of the Hebrew army in northern Israel?"

"Yes! That's the man."

"He was devilishly handsome."

As they approached the road, Deborah could see people and caravans—no doubt—going to Jerusalem, Syria, Tyre, Egypt, and Ethiopia; but there was no Barak. This was the north-south main road that passed through the land of Canaan—later called Israel, and thereafter—renamed Palestine. This road was not far from the Jordan River and ran parallel to it. People and caravans traveled this road to go from Egypt and Arabia to Jerusalem, Shechem, Bethel, Galilee, Syria, and to other northern cities. This is the road that Barak will use when he comes to visit Deborah.

Deborah expected his arrival because she received a letter from him a week ago stating that he would arrive today after leaving Hebron. Then she closed her eyes, and she saw an image of him. He was tall, had brown skin, a thick black beard, and a turban-like rap on his head. He had broad shoulders and a strong square jaw.

"Deborah, are you all right?" asked Sarah, seeing her standing there with her eyes closed.

"Yes Sarah, all is well. I was just thinking about Barak." Deborah remained still wondering whether he was yet lean and muscular, or had he gotten fat around the belly, rump, and thighs like some other men.

As moments passed, Sarah said "Look!" Deborah looked up the road facing northward towards Bethel and saw a group of people approaching. They looked like little children in comparison to the high mountain on this side of the road.

"Sarah, I have a suspicion that those people are coming to visit us," commented Deborah, as she adjusted her purple sash around her thin waist.

"It is possible. We receive visitors at least three or four times a week. Maybe they are from the City of Bethel." Deborah and her handmaid began to walk slowly back to the house because they wanted to be there whenever anyone would arrive. Deborah turned her head and gazed at the fresh green grass growing beyond the walkway.

As Deborah walked back to her house, she thought, since the death of my husband over three years ago, I haven't been involved with any man. She concluded that Barak could possibly be the beginning of a new relationship. However, she remembered that he expressed a disinterest in spiritual matters. Nevertheless, she was still attracted to him. In view of this dilemma, the situation left her uncertain about him.

Finally, the group of people, who Deborah saw coming, turned off the road and came up her walkway. There were a few men, but most of the people were women. From the steps where Deborah stood, she could discern from the faces of the women that their hearts were full of grief, and she went back into the house. As the ladies approached the gate, they saw baskets of food along the courtyard wall. The wall was plastered with white lime which gave it a clean appearance. Then the spokeswoman of the group stepped forward briskly and greeted Nachshon, the gatekeeper.

"Peace, my brother. We come to meet with Mother Deborah, the Prophetess."

Nachshon was a very tall muscular man of almost seven feet and approximately two hundred and eighty-five pounds, with a powerful appearance. He served as a gallant warrior in the army of Shamgar, the last deliverer of Israel. "You— have a meeting with Deborah?" he asked hesitantly, stepping in front of her. "I have no knowledge of such a meeting between …"

"This matter is urgent!" Rachel interrupted him, raising her eyes glaringly. Then she placed her hands on her hips and spoke defiantly: "I am not afraid of you—you big —! I was raised with eight brothers. Now please step aside."

"I see that you are a tough lady," responded Nachshon moving slightly.

"Raising seven children by myself, I had to be tough."

"Let the ladies in, Nachshon," Deborah advised her gatekeeper, as she looked through a window. "The ladies must be tired after a long journey. Let them rest their feet, and give them some fresh water and fruit. I'll be out in a short while."

"Yes, Mother Deborah," he gave a slight bow. Immediately, Nachshon escorted the ladies into the courtyard where they sat down under the three palm trees that stood in the center. The floor of the courtyard was made from stone slabs. Also, there was a large stone table situated to the side of the courtyard. This is where Deborah sat when she listened to the complaints of disputants and gave council. In addition, the tribal leaders, elders, priests, and princes sat here with her when they convened to discuss tribal affairs.

It became a custom for Deborah to receive visitors on a regular basis. They came to seek expert advice, to obtain spiritual counseling, and to hear her interpretation and judgment on civil and criminal matters. On this particular morning, she was not expecting this group of ladies; however, Deborah was not surprised because she usually received unannounced visitors.

Besides taking care of communal matters, Deborah operated a wick factory that she inherited over three years ago from her late husband. She gave last minute detailed instructions to Madreech, the supervisor of her workers, and turned to her handmaid. "Oh Sarah, did I receive a letter from Caleb?"

"No, you did not, my lady."

"I wonder why it is taking my bother-in-law so long to write me," she muttered, as she went out to listen to the patient group of ladies.

As she walked with her handmaid into the courtyard, she looked over at the gate to see if Barak had come, but he was not there. She greeted the women with a big smile and said, "Peace be unto you." Deborah's eyes registered warmth with eager gladness. "Welcome, it is so nice to meet all of you." The anxious ladies responded in kind. After Rachel introduced everyone, Deborah asked, "What tribes are you from?"

"We are from Zebulun, Manasseh, Naphtali, and Issachar, the northern tribes."

"That is a beautiful region my sisters. How can I be of service to you today?" inquired Deborah sympathetically, as she raised her small dark brown eyes.

"This is our problem," answered Rachel, turning slowly toward Deborah. "Most of us have lost husbands who have been taken by Sisera, the evil Canaanite. We don't know if they are living or dead. Our children are growing up without fathers, and they cry and ask about them constantly. We don't know what to tell them. Also, we miss the companionship of our husbands. You understand, don't you?"

Deborah lowered her head in silence and brought her hands together. She felt the pain and loneliness of the ladies because she also could empathize with them. She thought about her own lack of companionship due to the death of her husband over three years ago. She raised her head up slowly, looked at all of them, and said, "Yes, I understand. I also lost a husband. After his death, all the responsibility fell on me just as it has fallen on you."

"But Prophetess Deborah—you can marry again," commented one of the younger ladies, with tears in her eyes.

"We can't. We don't know whether our husbands are dead or alive. We feel trapped! What can we do, Deborah?"

The vehement passionate pleading of the ladies struck Deborah like a thunderbolt. At that moment, she wanted to be very still and meditate. Her face became extremely solemn; she closed her eyes and lowered her head. The courtyard became uncommonly quiet like the stillness of the night. The only sound that was heard was the chirping of a black bird on the frond of one of the palm trees. After a short period of meditation, Deborah raised her head, opened her eyes, took a deep breath, and smiled at the ladies.

As Deborah turned her head slightly to the right, she saw a handsome, rugged looking man with a straight broad nose. He was over six feet tall, solidly built, standing by the courtyard gate near her gatekeeper, Nachshon. When he caught Deborah's eyes, the stranger smiled and nodded his head at her. She knew who he was. He was Barak, the man for whom she was waiting.

Then her thoughts returned to her female guest. "This is what the Lord has said to me ladies, 'Be patient.' Maintain your integrity and loyalty to God and to your husbands. Pray and meditate day and night. Go back to your tribes; tell your people to pour out their souls in sincerity to the Lord your God, and He will hear your cry just as He heard the cry of your ancestors in the land of Egypt."

"But, will we see our dear husbands again?" inquired another young lady.

"Yes! I am getting a strong feeling that most of you will be re-united with your husbands."

Deborah looked subtly at Barak. Then he smiled again and gave her a double nod of his head as though he was giving her his special approval for something. She couldn't help noticing his well-trimmed black beard and mustache which had gotten a little gray. He trimmed his beard the way she liked her man to wear it. Suddenly, she began to feel a little uneasy, and she became momentarily distracted. She quickly regained her composure and looked at the ladies.

"Some of us have been separated from our husbands for more than five years. Do you have any idea when we shall be reunited with them?" asked Rachel, with fluttering eyes.

Deborah continued, "Your husbands will be free next year in the sabbatical year when we let the land rest and cancel all debts. Pertaining to this, I feel very strongly, and you can be assured of this."

Rachel rose to her feet. "Deborah, when I first came through your gate earlier this morning, I saw baskets of various kinds of food. What is this food for?"

Deborah looked up. "I thought you knew. It is for the poor."

"It's for the poor?"

"Yes Rachel. It is an old custom of ours to give to the poor, to the widows, to the blind, to the orphans, and to the strangers. Have you forgotten this?"

"I guess—times are hard for us right now, and I haven't thought about it lately," replied Rachel, as she lowered her head.

At that moment, Deborah moved a few steps closer to the ladies and said, "I want all of you to give more to the poor. When you give, it will return to you many folds. This is universal law. Remember, this is what Moses meant when he said, if you keep these commandments, 'all these blessings shall come unto thee.' "

"But Mother Deborah, when I donate, I feel that I am loosing something," said a middle-aged man.

"My brother, you shouldn't feel that way. When you give today, remember," she said, "it will come back to you in the future. Do you have a barley or wheat field?"

"Yesss, I have a small barley field," the man answered slowly. "What are you getting at Deborah?"

"When you plant a field of barley seeds, the barley will multiply unto you a thousand fold at harvest time. The same thing will happen for you when you give to mankind."

"Oh Deborah, how can I receive a blessing when a poor man is not able to repay me?"

Deborah smiled and continued. "The ways of the Lord are righteous and beyond our understanding. Don't always expect your reward to come from the poor. Your blessing, quite often, may come from another source—or from another person. Remember this—when your blessings come from another source, they will be, in most cases—greater in value than if you had received it from the poor man."

The man smiled. "You give a very good answer, Mother Deborah."

Finally, Rachel asked, "How can I give what I don't have?"

At that moment, Deborah walked over to Rachel and took her by the hand. "You have good health."

"That's all I have."

"That's a lot." Deborah assured her. "There are many ways you can give, Rachel: If you have one slice of bread, then divide it and give to the poor. Another way of giving is by giving of yourself, give your time, a helping hand, your genuine interest, your conversation, and—above all—give your sincere love. This is the greatest gift you can offer. When you do this, you will bring great joy to the hearts of others. In giving joy to others, you will experience great joy for yourself."

After listening attentively, Rachel stepped forward and leaned her head on Deborah's shoulder and remarked, "Your words have very deep meaning, Mother Deborah. Where did you get all of your knowledge?"

"I received it from the Lord and from our sacred books, and traditions. Some of it I received from my Uncle Yoetz, who was a senior member of the Council of the Seventy Elders at the Tabernacle. Also some I learned from the sages who came with the caravans from India, the Nile Valley, and Ethiopia."

Rachel stood back a little and said, "We admire you so much Deborah. You are truly God sent. Thank you so much. You have been a great help to us. Now, we must be on our way."

Deborah then hugged all the ladies and kissed them on their cheeks. When Rachel turned toward the gate, Deborah asked her softly and quietly. "Have you ever seen—that tall man near the entrance?"

Rachel took one step forward and stopped. She placed her finger over her lower lip and chin as if she was in deep thought. "He—looks familiar. Oh—that's Prince Barak from the tribe of Naphtali."

"Yes, I thought you would recognize him. He is from up your way."

"Are you interested in him?" asked Rachel nonchalantly.

"That's a big question. I'm not sure," said Deborah, in a low tone. "I've met him once before."

"Put out the bait; and the fly will bite, Deborah."

"The fly has done just that."

"Well, good luck," said Rachel, as she walked slowly away.

"Have a safe return trip, and may peace be with you," commented Deborah, glancing at the entire guest.

As the women departed through the large, iron gate, they touched the mezuzah on the gate. This object was intended to remind everyone passing through the gate to remember the commandments of the Lord.

CHAPTER 2

In the mind of Deborah, the time moved quickly with a mixture of joy, uncertainty and expectation. Nachshon, the gatekeeper, introduced Barak to Deborah. Barak wore a white turban-like wrap on his head and on it was a gold braided band. Around his waist, he wore a six-inch-wide, black girdle belt with a sheath for his eighteen-inch long dagger. "It is a great pleasure to see you again, Deborah," Barak said, with an admiring smile. "You look so beautiful. And with that gorgeous bracelet, you look like a Cushite queen."

"Thank you, Barak for your kind words." She looked at his short white dashiki with the neckline and sleeves trimmed in gold, and commented, "Also, I like the tunic you're wearing."

"Thank you. By the way, I have heard many good things about you," Barak remarked, as he adjusted his girdle belt which held his white pantaloons in place.

"Oh—! Is that so," she responded. Then she led the way to the two stone benches near the wall.

As Barak walked across a small carpet, he noticed it had a picture of a green palm tree and a yellow sunset against a blue sky. "Oh! What a beautiful carpet you have. Where did you get it?"

Deborah looked down at the carpet, and said, "I purchased it from the merchant of an Egyptian camel caravan several years ago, and I'm thinking about buying another one."

Barak looked up at her with a smile on his face. "Deborah, did you know that a carpet is bought by the cubit yard and is worn out by the feet?"

Deborah chuckled with delight. "Is this your manner—to make humor?" she asked, feeling at ease.

"Yes! Sometimes—it depends upon my mood."

"Well, stay in that mood. It is pleasing in my eyesight. Barak, you were about to tell me what the people are saying about me."

"Oh yes—the reports, which I hear from my region, are that you are an excellent counselor and a good listener."

"Well! It is surely nice to hear the good tidings," she said with delight, as the warm sun shined through the moving white clouds. Then she stared again with admiration at his dark green vest trimmed with gold fringes embroidered around the borders. "Is there more, Barak?"

Barak raised his head and appeared to be in deep thought. "Recently, when I was in the City of Beer Sheba, I heard a group of people say that you could become the next ruler in Israel, like Ehud or Othniel."

"Well, that's interesting. We shall see what the Lord has in store for me. Tell me Prince Barak—may I call you just Barak?"

"Yes, I would like that; and I hope that this can be the beginning of a good friendship."

Deborah heard his words; however, she didn't want to give a comment at this time; instead, she smiled slightly. At that moment, one of the servants brought in a container of water and two goblets. "I am curious—what brings you here to the territory of the Ephraimite tribe?" Deborah asked, staring straight into his eyes.

"Because we are at war with Jabin, Sisera and the Canaanites, I have been trying to buy weapons from certain tribes in the South so that we can have some kind of defense against our enemies."

Then Deborah thought of the situation that produced the Canaanite threat:

> *It was more than one hundred years after the death of Joshua—the son of Nun—that another Jabin, the King of the Canaanites—attacked* ***the Hebrew tribes in Galilee and the*** *surrounding areas. Jabin was the king of Hazor, which was renamed Harosheth-ha-goiim, and the head of his army was Sisera. With his nine hundred chariots, Sisera took complete control of the Jezreel Valley, ravaged the countryside, taxed the Hebrews heavily, took away their blacksmiths so that they could not make any weapons, and put many of the Hebrews into hard labor. Since the regular roads were unsafe, the Hebrews had to take the longer routes around and over the mountains and hills.*

This is what Deborah remembered as she stood there in front of Barak.

"You seem to be deep in thought, Deborah," he commented. "Is anything troubling you?"

"No—no, my mind was miles away for a little while. Oh! A moment ago, you said that you were trying to buy weapons for your soldiers. Have you had any success with your contacts?" Deborah asked softly.

"Unfortunately not," he replied, as he looked a little dejected and lowered his head.

Suddenly, she felt a strong magnetic attraction to him. She moved toward him and placed her hand on top of his and said softly, "Everything will be all right."

"I thank you for the encouragement," he expressed, as he placed his other hand on top of hers. "As a matter of fact, I like a kind and understanding lady like you."

As he touched and held her hand, she felt a vibration move up her arm. She pulled her hand away quickly, stood up, and walked over to a large orange vase that had a green plant inside of it. Then she squeezed one of the green leaves between her fingers to hide her true feelings.

"Is there something wrong, Deborah?" asked Barak, paying close attention to her reactions.

"No! There is nothing wrong," she assured him. "Do you have a family?" she inquired, turning around in his direction.

At that moment, Barak took a sip of water from the goblet. "If you are asking am I married, the answer is no. My wife and son died in childbirth."

"Oh! I am so sorry to hear this, may peace be with her soul. Do you think that you will ever get married again?"

"I think about it sometime, but at other times, I'm fearful that the same thing could happen to my next wife; and this discourages me from wanting to get married again. If I get married again, it will have to wait until after the war."

"It seems that you might have someone in mind." Hoping to hear an honest comment, she waited for an answer.

"No! I have only some admirers. But I am remaining unattached to commit more time to the training and organization of our mountain fighters. In addition, I hope there will be an end to this conflict soon so that my people and I can live normal lives as other tribes."

"I have a very strong feeling, that during next year, the reign of terror of the notorious King Jabin will be terminated," Deborah intimated with confidence.

"This is really good news—better news than what I had anticipated. Thank you, Deborah. By the way, I heard about the death of your husband by the hands of the Canaanites; and I want to express my condolences to you."

"That is nice of you." Deborah sat down and pulled her purple headpiece around the front of her neck. "How long have you been fighting the Canaanites?" she asked.

"About 15 years."

"May I ask what caused you to fight the Canaanites?"

"What caused me—? I really don't want to talk about that," he snapped, turning his back to her. Then he lowered his face into the palm of his hands and sulked for a little while.

Because Deborah didn't want to be pushy, she waited a few moments then continued. "Perhaps, it must be painful, but I think that you should talk about it. It will help you feel better," she said, touching him gently on the back of the shoulders.

He turned toward her slowly, paused, placed his large hands on his hips, and looked up into the blue sky in sorrow. Finally, he took a deep breath. "It hurts too much."

Deborah could see that he wanted to shed some tears but the tears did not come. "You said to me that you like an understanding woman, and I'm trying to be just that—talk to me Barak! Tell me what's troubling you!"

"It's—it's about my dear mother," he muttered softly, looking down.

"What about your mother? Did she give up the ghost?"

"Yes, but it was not an ordinary death that happened. Now, I find myself standing here—getting ready to reveal to you my inner most feelings."

"Barak, it's all right. You don't have to feel less than a man just because you are about to pour out your heart to me. Remember, you are still mortal—and you have feelings just like other people."

Barak turned his head and glanced at her with a thoughtful look on his face. "Perhaps—you are right, Deborah."

"Continue, I'm listening," she said, as she gently touched the strong arm of his six-feet and three-inch muscular frame.

"Sisera, the evil general of the Canaanite army— murdered—" Barak paused; then he took another deep breath and gritted his teeth with anger. He choked for words and labored to speak. "He—murdered my dear mother—a kind and gentle woman," he informed her, as he pounded his fist against the wall almost hitting a gray lizard.

Deborah looked at him with concern. "Barak—I'm very sorry, so sorry, to hear this. Now I can understand how your loss has left you with so much grief."

"Grief—is not the word!" he said sharply, raising his voice.

"Well—a lot of anger, then."

"I want Sisera to pay for the murder of my mother; and I'll get him—even if it takes me ten more years."

"I can understand how you feel. Also, the Canaanites killed my husband; however, vengeance belongs to the Lord."

Turning towards her, he roared again like thunder. "I hope that heaven will grant me the chance to be the hand of God's vengeance."

"And that might very well be. Tell me Barak, what was the situation that led up to the murder of your mother?"

There was a complete silence for an entire minute; he moved not a muscle. Then Barak began to tell her what happened to his family nineteen years ago when he had just turned twenty-five. They had just completed the preparation for the Feast of Booths and had set out on their pilgrimage to the Tabernacle in Shiloh. They were traveling on the main road going south passed the Sea of Galilee. There were also many other people on that same road going to the Tabernacle. Moreover, his father and mother were traveling with him. Suddenly, they heard the hooves of camels and horses galloping toward them. The people knew that it was the Canaanite soldiers, and some tried to escape to the caves in the nearby hills. The Canaanites rushed down on them and rounded them up.

General Sisera gave orders to Lieutenant Sabar to line up the people. "Form one line over here!" commanded the lieutenant. The people moved slowly with resentment and with hatred in their eyes against the Canaanites. Next, the lieutenant pointed to one man. "You—over there, step it up—get moving!" After the soldiers lined up the people, Sisera approached ten cubits in front of his soldiers with two of his officers on both sides of him. They held their spears in their hands. Sisera was a dark brown skin man in his middle 40s with a coat of mail hanging from his broad shoulders. He wore a copper looking helmet with a purple plume extending upward.

Finally, Sisera spoke. "Now, I'll tell you why I stopped you. A group of Hebrew men have been raiding Canaanite merchant caravans and seizing their property. We have a good reason to believe that they might have come to your area. If you know of these men, or have seen them, I want you to turn them over to me."

"Turn Hebrews over to you?" shouted a young man. "Why should we?"

"Because they are sons of Belial and transgressors, and I command you."

"Transgressors?" interrupted Barak. "You place a very heavy burden of taxation around our necks, rape our women, and take our boys and girls to be burned in the fire as sacrifices to your god, Baal. Now, you have the gall to call those Hebrews transgressors!" At that moment, Barak's mother took hold of his arm in an attempt to silence him.

"Yes! They are transgressors." Sisera then raised his head seething with indignation at the defiant young man. "You ... ! Come here!" Then Barak stood still. "Don't stand there and stare at me like a darn fool," yelled Sisera. "When I give you an order, you obey—boy!"

Barak moved forward slowly. "What do you want with me?"

All of a sudden, Sisera slapped Barak hard with the back of his hand, and he recoiled backward.

"You have too much mouth boy—and if you are not careful, your mouth is going to get you in a lot of trouble!"

"Leave my son alone!" yelled his father.

Instantaneously, Barak's mother ran up to protect her son. "Keep your hands off my son, you old brute!"

"Get back—! You wench," ordered Sisera, as he jabbed her in the side of her head with his spear. As she fell to the ground, the crowd quickly rushed forward to help her; but the mounted soldiers blocked their way.

Barak fell to his knees and held his mother in his arms who was covered with blood. Then he cried. "Mother, mother, mother, don't leave me." At that moment, death snatched her life. Barak looked up slowly at Sisera with tears in his eyes sobbing. "I'll get you for this—I'll get you even if it takes me ten years," Barak cried bitterly, as his father pressed a cloth over her wound.

"You'll get me … Huh … ! Where is your army? You got your chance right now! Make your move—I want to see how stupid you are." Barak just stared at him with anger. "Either you are smarter than what I thought, or you are just a low-down sniveling coward. Let's go men and leave these wretched Hebrews to themselves."

After Barak finished telling Deborah how his mother had been murdered, he stood there before her with tears in his eyes and dried them on the sleeves of his dashiki.

"It is good that you are getting it all out. It will help you feel better."

"I … suppose so."

For a while, there was a silence. Then Deborah spoke. "Would you like something else to drink or eat, Barak?"

"Yes, I think I'll have some tea and fruit."

"Do you like your tea, dark?"

"Yes."

When Sarah passed by the courtyard entrance, Deborah called, "Oh Sarah, would you bring in some tea and fruit."

After a short while, Sarah brought in a large tray full of refreshments; and Deborah introduced Barak to her. "This is Barak, the General I mentioned to you earlier."

"It is a pleasure to meet you sire," she said, as she bowed and walked away slowly.

"I want to tell you Barak … there will come a time in battle that you will become far more successful if you will rely on the Lord and become more spiritual," she said, with a serious look.

"Spiritual? What do you mean by that?"

"I mean communing with your God by prayer, meditation, and tuning into the small subtle voice that speaks to you deep down inside," she uttered.

"Oh, I don't believe in that stuff. I rely on the number of my soldiers, the chariots which I don't have, and the number of my spears and swords. These are the things that can break the back of the enemy," he harangued, as he stood on his feet and clinched his fists to express his emotions.

"If you trust in God, He will work miracles in your life."

"I don't believe in miracles either."

"Why not … ? All creation is a miracle."

"Where was this miracle of God when Sisera stabbed my mother in the head?"

"The works of God are mysterious. We cannot judge Him. If we patiently seek Him, He will reveal the hidden things to us in due time. Moreover, if you look at your loss in the right way, from your pain will come a gain. Finally, in the process of time, you will receive a revelation so profound that it will change your entire thinking." She further explained to him: "It was by the power of God that our ancestors were saved from the Egyptians and not by the number of their soldiers and swords. This is what Moses, Joshua, and the elders taught."

"Well, if God has all this great power, why does He cause us to suffer under the harsh oppression of the Canaanites?" he asked, moistening his lips with his tongue.

"God does not cause ..." she paused and moved under the shady part of the palm tree. When Barak followed her, she smiled with unconscious delight because she relished the attention. She continued. "God does not cause mankind to suffer. Men and women cause their own suffering. Hence, they reap what they sow; this is universal law. If a person commits a crime and is punished by the court, is that person suffering for nothing?"

"No ... ! He deserved it," he answered.

"And this is the way it is with the heavenly Judge. He gave his commandments to mankind and to our people, and many rejected them and committed abominations. This is what the priests, the Seventy Elders, and the scribes report to us from the Tabernacle in the City of Shiloh: 'The people served the Lord all the days of Joshua, and all the days of the Elders that outlived Joshua, who had seen all the great works of the Lord, that He had wrought for Israel ... . And also all that generation was gathered unto their fathers; and there arose another generation after them that knew not the Lord; nor yet the works which He had wrought for Israel ... .' "

"Deborah, are we a part of this new generation?"

"Yes we are, and you will understand this after I finish." Then Deborah continued to quote the elders in the City of Shiloh. "The elders taught: 'And they forsook the Lord and served Baal and Ashtaroth ... . And the Lord gave them over into the hand of Jabin, the king of Canaan, which reigned in Hazor; the captain of whose host was Sisera, who dwelt in Ha-rosheth ... .' "

"Ahhh," Barak gushed. Then he yawned and drew both fists toward the direction of his dark brown ears. "Very interesting," he remarked, as he smiled at her with admiration. After that, he fixed his eyes upon her with a long silent stare.

"Why are you staring at me like that?" she asked.

"It is because … you are so beautiful and nice to look upon." Barak answered, in a slow mesmerized tone.

"Well, thank you, Barak!" she smiled, looking at him with a surprised glance.

At that moment, he asked her softly and slowly, "Did anyone ever tell you—that you are beautiful?"

She became flattered and lowered her head modestly. "Yes … but that was a long time ago … my late husband use to tell me this often when he was alive. But I don't think about beauty anymore," she uttered nonchalantly. Nevertheless, she enjoyed those words coming from Barak.

"Deborah, you are not just beautiful in your facial appearance, but also your inner beauty radiates."

"Beauty is just the outward appearance," she said gently, as she turned her head away feeling a sense of delight.

"When I speak of beauty, Deborah … I mean also your inward beauty … . I can feel your tenderness and the warmth of your womanly presence."

"You can?" she asked, with an enthusiastic smile on her face. "But let's not talk about me."

He became silent again. "Well, can we talk about your deceased husband?"

She hesitated, and said slowly, "Yesss."

"What was he like?"

"He was gentle and compassionate."

"In what way do you mean?"

She answered without hesitation. "He recognized my abilities, and he encouraged me to develop and use them in spite of the fact that I am a woman in a role that has been always held by men."

"Are you referring to your ability to explain the laws to our people, and to advise and speak to groups of people?" he inquired, while touching the frond of a small palm tree.

"Yes—I am!"

"But how did the people from your area know that you had these abilities?"

"Oh! That is a long story ... at first, men ... but mostly women would come to our fields to buy fruit, vegetables, and other products. When the ladies came, we would sit and talk for a long time about women's problems and the family. Slowly, the word got around that I was very helpful to many. Then more and more ladies came to seek my advice, and some skeptical men came as well."

"Deborah, it is strange to have a woman take a major role in public matters."

"Yes, but as I said, the women came to me first, and later the men because they were not getting satisfaction from some of the elders of their tribes. You must understand that the judges of the various tribes were handing down decisions according to what they thought was right in their own eyes and not according to the interpretations handed down by Moses and Joshua. Moreover, some judges and elders corrupted themselves by taking bribes, by favoring the rich and powerful, and trampling on the poor."

"Deborah, I can understand what you mean because there are some judges in my tribe who are guilty of the very same thing."

"Barak, I want your honesty. What do you think of my work?"

Barak thought a moment, "Well, I'll be honest with you Deborah. In our times, it is not the custom to have a woman doing the work of a man. However, at this time, there is no king in Israel, no unity, and very few learned men. Furthermore, our people are suffering under the oppression of the Canaanites, and most men do what they think is right in their own eyes. In view of this, your work is very helpful; and I welcome it as the need of the times."

"Thank you Barak for being very truthful with me. I needed to know this."

"Well, honesty is my policy."

"Barak, I want you to fully understand; you will never completely remove Sisera's powerful army from the northern territories until our people remove the abominations from our communities which are distasteful before God. I believe that when we make right our society, the Lord will remove the enemy right from our midst. This means that we shall be victorious in battle. Now, in order to achieve this, I need for you to help catch the lawbreakers, who run and hide among the other tribes, and bring them to justice. When we root out the bad things in our villages and cities, then we will have peace, love, prosperity, and unity. To accomplish this, it is our responsibility—not the responsibility of others. Can I get your support concerning this matter?"

Barak lowered his head and thought for a moment and then looked up. "Yes! You have my complete support. Also, I am in favor of maintaining a peaceful and orderly society. I am against all robbers and murderers whether they are Canaanites or Hebrews," Barak explained.

"Thank you. Oh Barak, I think that it would be a good idea if you would stop by the Tabernacle in Shiloh and get a Certificate of Authority from the high court. Ask for Elder Ariel; he was a close associate of my uncle. This Certificate would make you a bonafide officer of the court. With your position as prince and commander of the northern army, and my recommendation, I don't think you will have any problems obtaining it."

After that, Barak asked her a question about the war. "When do you think that the final battle will take place between King Jabin and us?"

"I …" she paused, "believe it will be about a year from now."

"Can you give me a definite month?"

"No!" she replied, "but I can definitely tell you this, as that time approaches, it will become clearer; and it will be revealed to me. When this happens, I'll send for you. I want to remind you Barak, that to defeat Sisera, you'll need more than chariots."

"We'll see," he said softly. "Well, it is time for me to leave. Oh, by the way, may I call on you again … ?" Barak waited for an answer. "Deborah, may I call upon you again … ?" he repeated louder. She remained silent. "Deborah, are you going to make a beggar out of a man of noble birth?"

They exchanged glances; she swallowed his words hard and attempted to speak. "You—you can call on me again as long as it is important business," she said, as she looked at him scantly with longing and inviting eyes.

"Important business!" he repeated. Hearing her comment, Barak seemed confused. His eyes blinked rapidly, and he continued to speak. "I know what I like and I know what I want and I want you."

"Don't be too hasty, Barak, as a widow living outside of my father's house, I think that I should have something to say about this. Barak, are you going to deny me my choice?"

He turned towards her and answered, "No … ! I am not that low … . In my desire for you, I will not violate your rights.

However, I must inform you right now that I intend to pursue and pursue and pursue until you change your mind."

She looked at him with amazement, "I see that you are a very determined man."

"Yes, I am. This is the only way I can win battles and save my nephew, Joseph from that hellhole he is in. May peace be with you Deborah," he said, as he departed with self-confidence. After he mounted his horse, Deborah waved at him with mixed feelings.

As Deborah sat on her bench, she wondered and was doubtful about a viable relationship with Prince Barak. He is a man of high social standards in his tribe and the commander of the militia in his region. As a man of considerable means, he projects a strong, handsome muscular appearance; and he has a nice smile that is magnetic. On the other hand, she had at least three reasons why not to become emotionally involved. There was still the matter of the letter that she was expecting from her brother-in-law, Caleb which could change her marital situation. Also, she had a wick business and judicial duties; her husband was killed by Canaanites; and if the same thing happened to Barak, this would only increase her emotional pain. In view of the fact that Deborah was a spiritual woman, Barak's rejection of her spiritual advice did not set well with her. Therefore, she concluded that she would not get her hopes up.

Now, Barak was on his way to the City of Shiloh to obtain the Certificate of Authority which Deborah had requested.

CHAPTER 3

On his way to Shiloh, Barak met a man who recently passed by that city. "Are you going to Shiloh?" inquired the man anxiously.

"Yes, why do you ask?"

"Criminals and robbers were fighting at the Tabernacle when I passed by," informed the stranger. "It was a terrible situation. Somebody needs to help them."

"Who were they fighting?" asked Barak, looking worried.

"They were fighting the priest and the Levites," he said.

"Did you help them?"

"No ... No ... I couldn't get involved. I have a family to support."

"How many were they?" Barak asked, with concern.

"I really don't know for sure, twenty or thirty. Shameful! Robbers fighting in the house of God," he said, shaking his head as he turned and continued on his way. Then Barak thought about the City of Shiloh:

> *It was about ten miles north of Bethel and was situated off to the right side of the same road that passed through the City of Bethel. Shiloh became the national Capitol of the Israelites. It was at Shiloh that Joshua cast*

*lots for the division of the land and sent
out spies to bring back a report on it. Here,
Joshua and Eleazar, the High Priest, gave
orders to the Levites and to the priest to set
up the Tabernacle.*

Barak could see the hills and the valleys as he traveled
that road; and he couldn't get the robbers off his mind. He
was riding through the territory of the tribe of Ephraim. He
passed by some of the people and caravans going to Megiddo,
Sidon, Tyre, Damascus, Carchemish, and other places. These
caravans included one-hump camels. Later, he noticed some
shepherds taking their sheep to new green pastures. The
bleating sound of the sheep could be heard by everyone.

As Barak rode onward thinking about the robbers, he knew
that he had to do something and do it fast; there was no time
to waste. After riding rapidly for about ten or fifteen minutes,
Barak lifted up his eyes and he saw the City of Shiloh in the
distance.

Barak was alone; he knew that there was not much he could
do by himself. There were very few people in this small city at
this time of the year. Therefore, he thought of a stratagem to
scare off the robbers. Not too far from him was a dry hill. He
rode his white horse up one side of it like a skillful equestrian
racing back and forth kicking up dust with the hooves of his
horse. With his ram's horn, he blew the sound of an attacking
army. Barak hoped that this stratagem would work. At last,
Barak rode towards the City of Shiloh with great speed to
see what damage the robbers had done. As he rode, his every
movement was replete with grace and rhythm. Bending down
closer to the white mane, pressing his knees against the side
of his horse, Barak ordered his horse onward with his neck

scarf blowing in the wind. "Faster, Laban faster," he urged him. He passed by many houses and inns constructed from baked mud and straw, and from beige stones found in the land of Israel. The owners of the inns would earn extra money from the thousands of pilgrims who would visit the Tabernacle on the Hebrew holidays of Passover, Feast of Weeks, and the Festival of Booths.

As Barak approached the Tabernacle area, he could see the rectangular enclosure which surrounded the entire structure of the courtyard, the Holy Place, and the Holy of Holies. Approaching even closer with great urgency, his mind reflected on the robbers.

When Barak approached within fifty cubits of the sanctuary, he could see some of the bandits riding off frantically. He decided not to pursue them because he was alone. No doubt, his stratagem of stirring up the dust and blowing the ram's horn had worked. He dismounted from his horse in a stately manner, held his head high, and looked around in all directions searching for any sudden danger. He wondered had they desecrated the Holy of Holies within the veil.

Barak had to press his way slowly through the standing crowd in order to talk to the Levite guards at the entrance to the courtyard of the Tabernacle. A multi-colored curtain of purple, red, blue and white draped the entrance to the Tabernacle. As he pressed forward, he remembered from his previous visits that the tent of the Tabernacle was located in the western half of the court; and the largest area of the court was situated in front of the tent.

When Barak approached the guards at the entrance to the Tabernacle, the anxious crowd demanded to know the details of what happened.

"Some bandits forcibly took some gold shekels and some other coins from the treasury of the sanctuary, and two of them were killed in the foolish act of robbery. The rest of the robbers were scared off by the loud sound of the ram's horn which came from beyond the hills," explained one of the guards.

Then Barak stepped up to the guard and spoke. "My name is Barak, and I came to see Elder Ariel."

"That name sounds familiar. You wouldn't know who blew that ram's horn would you?"

"Yes. It was I."

"You … ? You know, if you hadn't blown that horn, many lives would have been lost. Follow me and I'll take you to the Elder."

The guard led him to one of the private tent chambers near the rectangular enclosure. There he introduced Barak to the eighty-nine year old elder. The elderly man had yellowish skin; and one could discern that he had mixed blood in his ancestry. Barak smiled and bowed to him slightly and said, "Peace be unto you oh honorable one."

"Peace," replied the Elder. "You wouldn't happen to be the General Barak from the tribe of Naphtali, would you?"

Barak nodded his head in agreement and said, "I am he."

While he spoke, the Elder cast his light green eyes down at the ram's horn Barak had stuck in his waist. "No doubt, you must be the same man that blew the horn and scared away the robbers."

"Yes I am," answered Barak modestly.

"Then it is a blessing that you came to our town. Because, when the bandits heard the sound of the ram's horn, they stopped fighting and robbing and made haste out of town. Our people are very grateful to you."

"It was just a small thing that I did."

"That was no small thing! If it hadn't been for you, perhaps some Levites would have died in the fighting. As it stands now, we have only a few flesh wounds."

"Did anyone recognize any of them?"

"No. They all had their faces covered with part of their white headdresses; however, I did hear one of them refer to the other, who seemed to have been the leader, as Reuben and he walked with a slight limp." The Elder paused for a moment and passed by a small vase containing a fern plant, and then he continued. "Oh! What brings you to our town, General Barak?"

"I have an important letter from Deborah Lapidoth, from the City of Bethel. Do you know her?"

"Do I know her? Yes," he answered, pointing to a cushion for Barak to take a seat. "Deborah and I have had many conversations. Especially about a certain court trial that took place in the City of Beer Sheba. She has a very good reputation." After reading the letter, he commented, "There shouldn't be any problem for you to obtain the Certificate of Authority."

"Good," Barak smiled.

"You come very highly recommended. She said that you could catch a thief even if he crawls in a foxhole. Do you agree with her?"

"Your Excellency, I am the youngest son in my father's house, who am I ... to question the Prophetess and the prettiest woman in Canaan."

"I understand. Now all I need is the signature of two more judges. Wait here!"

While Barak waited for Ariel to return, he could smell the aroma of sweet meat roasting on the altar of the inner court. Then he took a deep breath and leaned back with delight.

His appetite was stirred up, and he wished he could saver its delights.

Within a short while, Ariel returned with two judges and a scribe. The Elder told the two other judges about the strategy that Barak used to scare off the bandits, and they thanked him for his ingenuity. Then Ariel dictated the provisions of the Certificate and the scribe wrote them down on papyrus. Ariel placed the seal of the court on the document, and all the judges signed it. The two judges and the scribe departed, and Ariel remained with Barak.

Elder Ariel rolled up the papyrus and gave it to Barak. "Well, it looks like everything is all set."

"Thank you," he nodded. "I am just sorry that I waited so long to see Deborah because I could have had this certificate early."

"That's all right, Barak. Sometimes, if it were not for the last moment, some things would never get done. Moreover, the work that you are undertaking will be a great service to our people. As you probably know, the enemies among us are sometime worse than the ones from without."

"I agree Elder Ariel," said Barak, "That our people, at times, can be their own worst enemy." Finally, Barak understood more fully why Deborah asked him to accept this task.

"Tell me Barak, is the war situation with the troublesome Canaanites getting any worse?"

"It is worsening. Sisera has increased his patrols throughout the Jezreel Valley and other areas. With his control of this Valley, he has managed to divide the Hebrew nation north and south of the Jezreel. Our people are afraid to use the open roads and to travel through the plains. Because of this, I have stepped up our patrols. This situation keeps me very busy, and

I believe all-out war will come. I want to unite more Hebrew tribes against Sisera, but it is difficult."

Ariel placed his thumb and index finger of his right hand on each side of his mouth appearing to be in deep thought. "I see …" Ariel paused. "If this is true, will you have the time to apprehend fugitives and bring them to justice?"

"I'll make the time. I promised Deborah that I would bring them in to stand trial."

"Ummm, I understand," Ariel groaned suspiciously. "You promised? It seems that you might have other interest in her. Is this not so?"

"Well, yes. She has many good qualities, and I like her. Is there anything wrong with that?"

"No. Of course not! However, I would hate to see you overload yourself. You see, it is our custom for a man or woman to perform everything that proceeds out of his or her mouth. Here lately, the law and the other customs of our people have been disregarded and that's the reason there is so much distrust among the tribes of Israel."

"I understand," he said, as he looked up at the two brown impressive cherubim embroidered on the purple curtain. "When Deborah asked for my help, I promised that I would give it. I meant it even if I have to make a great sacrifice."

"Very well, I believe you. But before it is all over, you may have to sacrifice your life. Remember this, Deborah is no ordinary woman! She has her own wick business. She is a spiritual advisor, judge, ruler, prophetess, and a mother in Israel to many people. Now, there is something which I must warn you; some people complain that Deborah takes a man's role, but in these terrible days, good men are hard to find; and it was the need of the hour that pushed her into this position."

"Can you explain to me how she was pushed into this ... this need of the hour as you call it?"

"Yes Barak, but first let us go over to my house and have supper ... then we'll talk further," he offered, as he lifted himself up slowly supporting himself with his staff.

"Let me help you, elder," said Barak, grabbing hold of his arm.

CHAPTER 4

As the evening approached, they both walked down the path about fifty cubits north of the Tabernacle to Ariel's house. "When we are sitting comfortably in my house, I want to tell you Barak, about the details of a court trial in the City of Beer Sheba. At that time, Deborah was in court and her reputation was in question."

"That sounds interesting," said Barak. "I would like to hear more when you are ready."

They passed by the palm and fig trees which lined up along the way. Then Barak picked up a small branch of a fig tree that had fallen to the ground. The branch was comparatively soft and light brown. The leaves were dark green and resembled the shape of a pear. Barak smelled the leaves which emitted the fragrance of the sweet skin of a ripe orange. The sweet smell reminded him of whatever the fragrance Deborah was wearing, when he was with her, and he held the branch close to his heart.

They entered into the gate of the five-cubits-high stone wall and walked to the courtyard in the back. Beautiful pink and purple flowers were growing along the side of the wall. They sat down on soft cushions placed along the side of a low, stone round table. This table was only about one-half cubit from the floor. Then Ariel called his housekeeper and instructed him to prepare an extra serving for Barak. After the introductions, the housekeeper asked Barak. "Would you like something to drink?"

"Just water please, thank you."

"Where were we last?" asked Ariel.

"You were getting ready to explain to me how Deborah was pushed ... ."

"Oh yes. How Deborah was pushed into her social position. The answer to your question is in two parts. First, what qualified her for the public work she does. And second, what were the social conditions that pushed her into her public role," he explained, as the big orange-red sun was setting in the west.

"Yes, this is what I want to know."

"You must understand Barak, Deborah's parents died of an unknown disease when she was four years old; and her Uncle Yoetz helped to raise her. Her uncle taught her about our laws, customs, and history. He was also one of the leaders of his tribe. On many occasions, when he had to go to discuss tribal matters, he would take her with him."

"It sounds as though they were close," said Barak, observing the housekeeper placing the water on the table.

"Yes, they were very close. By the way, Deborah had a great memory. As her uncle grew older, his memory waned; and he would rely on her to help him to remember things he had forgotten. When she went with him, she preferred to sit in an adjacent room and listen to the discussions rather than to go play with the other children. She preferred to be around older people, and often said that she could not learn anything from children her own age. Deborah listened to her uncle's instructions on history, philosophy, and the law—month after month and year after year until she became proficient in legal matters."

"Wonderful." Barak stood up, took one step, held his hands behind his back, and gazed at the setting sun reflecting its red rays on the white clouds.

Now Ariel, the Elder, began to tell Barak about a special event that Deborah had experienced several years ago, while she had visited her brother, Asher, in the City of Beer Sheba. She could not talk to him long because he was the recorder for the local court, and a trial was about to begin. In view of this, Deborah decided to stay around and to listen to the proceedings. Deborah's brother introduced her to Shallum, the head judge. After a short talk, the Judge was so impressed with her demeanor and her knowledge of legal matters; he invited her to participate in the trial against Zadekiyah, who was charged with adultery.

"Who taught you about the law, Deborah?"

She replied, "It was my Uncle Yoetz."

"Hmmm, that name sound familiar. It will be interesting to see how you perform in this trial."

"I have a feeling that she will be found not guilty."

"You do? We'll see."

Usually, the trials were held in the small brick building at the entrance gate of this town; but the crowd was too large so they held the court outside under three large palm trees.

After the preliminary formalities were finished, the head judge among the seven on the panel asked, "Is everyone ready?"

"Yes we are, your honor," answered one of the judges for the prosecution.

"The court of Beer Sheba will now begin its proceedings," said Shallum, the head judge. "Are the witnesses and the defendant present?"

"Yes they are, Judge Shallum," answered the officer of the court. "Zadekiyah, the wife of Abraham, the merchant, is charged with adultery."

"Zadekiyah, what is your answer to this serious charge?" Zadekiyah was a petite, five feet- 4 inch tall young lady with a smooth carmel complexion. "I am absolutely innocent. I … ."

"Hold your peace," interrupted the head judge. "You will get your chance to speak."

Rising to his feet, the prosecutor said, "I call the first witness, Dan Ben Shafat. Dan, do you swear the holy oath to speak the truth?"

"I do."

"Dan, please tell the court what you know about this case."

"Well, it isn't very much. But on the late morning of the 27th day of last month, I saw Zadekiyah holding the hand of a man as I walked by her house looking through the gate."

"Have you ever seen that man before that time?" asked the prosecutor."

"No."

"Are you sure?"

"Yes," I know everyone in this town; and I never saw that man before the 27th of last month."

"Thank you Dan." The prosecutor then turned to Zadekiyah and asked, "Do you swear our holy oath to tell the truth?"

"Yes, I do."

"Was your husband at home on the 27th day of last month?"

"No. He went out of town on business, and he hasn't returned yet."

"Did any man come to your house on that day?"

She answered, "Yes." Then the crowd looked at one another with astonishment.

"What is his name, and how long have you known him?"

"His name is Benjamin—Benjamin Ben Hur—and I have known him for over three years," she answered, as the crowd roared in surprise, gossiping.

"Zadekiyah, why did this man come to your house?"

"He returned some jewelry which I had loaned to my sister."

The prosecutor walked away from her, stopped, and he turned around toward her. "Zadekiyah, why didn't your sister bring the jewelry to you instead of Benjamin?"

"The reason was she gave up the ghost. But before she died, she told her husband Benjamin to bring the jewelry to me."

"Are you claiming that this man Benjamin was married to your sister?"

"Yes."

"What time of day was it when he arrived at your house?"

"It was just before noon."

"Where is this brother-in-law now?"

"I don't know. I sent for him to testify on my behalf, but he hasn't showed up yet."

"You don't expect your lover to show up, do you?"

"He is not my lover!"

"Do you have any maid servants?"

"Yes, I have two."

"Where were your maid servants when your brother-in-law came to your house?"

Zadekiyah looked down and remained silent.

"Answer the question," ordered the head judge.

Zadekiyah raised her head slowly. "I sent them to the market," she said reluctantly.

"How convenient this was for you. Isn't it true that you sent your maid servants away so that you could be alone with your lover?"

"No ... ! It is not true!" she yelled crying.

"Then why was a married woman like you seen holding the hand of another man?"

"I don't know," she answered, looking very confused. "It happened so quickly ... ," she paused. "Furthermore ... he was my brother-in-law."

The prosecutor looked at her suspiciously and said, "Oh I see. This is your excuse."

Then the chief judge interjected, "Deborah, do you have any comments?"

Deborah rose to her feet, raised her head slowly, and spoke softly, "It is clear to me ... that there is more to this case than what meets the eye. If we put to death—on false charges—every innocent young woman, there wouldn't be any women left to marry your sons," responded Deborah, as the crowd smiled and chuckled.

The prosecutor turned to the audience and spoke. "Deborah calls her an innocent woman who would be put to death on false charges. Now, we shall see ... !" He walked three steps towards Zadekiyah and stared in her eyes, "You admitted that your husband was out of town; you admitted that you sent your maid servants away; you admitted that you held the hand of another man on that day. Moreover, everything was made more convenient for you and your lover. Zadekiyah, why don't you confess your guilt and save the court money and time?"

"No! No! No! I'm innocent," she sobbed, dropping her head into the palms of her hands, and her light blue mantilla mixed with pink flower fell from her head exposing her long black curly hair.

As Deborah watched and heard the proceedings, she said to her handmaid Sarah, "This woman is going to need lots of help. Oh Lord, I beseech Thee, please give me the wisdom to help her."

The prosecutor continued, "Were you once a close friend of the man, Benjamin?"

"Yes," answered Zadekiyah, as the audience sighed in surprise.

"Isn't it true that you were once betrothed to marry him?"

She remained silent for a moment, "Yes," she answered hesitantly, as fear enveloped her.

"Isn't it also true … that you have lain with that man, Benjamin?" Zadekiyah lowered her head in silence.

"Well … answer! Isn't it true?" he demanded.

Zadekiyah raised her head slowly and labored to speak. "Yes," she snapped, yelling reluctantly with pain in her voice knowing that she was incriminating herself. "But that was a long time ago before I got married."

The prosecutor pointed his finger at Zadekiyah and then looked at the audience and asked, "Is this who Deborah calls an innocent woman?"

Deborah lowered her head a little and remained silent.

Waving their fists high over their heads, the crowd yelled, "Guilty, Guilty, Guilty!" There was more silence.

"Well Deborah! You have nothing to say?" asked the head judge.

Deborah walked slowly toward her seat appearing to be in deep thought. She stopped and turned towards the head judge and the prosecutor. "People of Beer Sheba, even if she had lain with Benjamin that was before she got married to her present husband. She cannot be guilty of that. Furthermore, our law requires that a matter be established by two or more witnesses … as of now, I have heard from only one."

The prosecutor looked at Deborah and gave an insidious smile. "We have them, two reliable witnesses. The court now calls Ishmael and Katan." These two were well-respected businessmen of long standing in the community. The judges and most people in Beer Sheba knew them, and the word went out that many folks supported the accusations of these men.

Then Deborah whispered to Sarah, "This prosecutor is very shrewd."

"Yes, and he blocks you at every turn."

"But he can't block the Lord."

After the two witnesses came up to the front row, the prosecutor asked them: "Do you swear our holy oath to speak the truth?"

"We do."

"Please give to the court your complete names and your occupations."

"I am Ishmael Ben Jacob."

"And I am Katan Ben Zeef. We are business partners of Joseph Ben Abraham, the husband of Zadekiyah."

"Now Ishmael and Katan, will you please tell the court what you observed," asked one of the judges.

The older man Ishmael spoke up first. "We arrived at the house of our business partner, Joseph Ben Abraham and looked through the opening of the gate and saw Zadekiyah holding and kissing a stranger."

"What was the date that this act took place, and what was the time of day?" asked the prosecutor.

Both men answered simultaneously, "It was the 27th day of last month, around noon time."

Katan continued, "The stranger fondled her all over her backside; then they went under a tree surrounded by some bushes," he reported, as he looked at Zadekiyah.

"That's a lie—lies, lies," shouted Zadekiyah, with grief and anger.

"We must have order! We must have order in the court! One more outburst like that and you'll be fined," warned the head judge. At that time, the prosecutor smiled with delight.

Deborah turned to her handmaid and said, "I don't like the sound of this case; it has all the trimmings of a frame-up. This young lady is going to need help," she said to Sarah in a low tone. At that moment, Deborah said a short prayer again. "Oh Lord, I beseech Thee. Let Thy truth be revealed."

"Have you ever seen that man before," asked the another judge, with his right fist and index finger resting on his chin and jaw.

"No Ephraim—I mean, no your honor." After that slip of the tongue, the head judge looked at Katan and Ishmael suspiciously.

The head judge leaned forward and probed further. "How would you describe this man you claim you saw?"

Ishmael looked upward and thought for a moment. "The man was over six feet tall, heavy built, brown skin, black beard, and about forty years old. Also, he was wearing a light blue tunic."

"Now let's hear from the other witness," requested one of the judges.

"Katan, let's hear your side of the story," said another judge.

"I—I—agree with Ishmael," he stuttered.

"Speak up! Speak up! I can't hear you," the judge commanded.

"Everything that Ishmael told you is exactly what happened, your honor. We both looked through the gate at the same time."

"Did any of you warn the so-called stranger that what he was doing was wrong?"

"No! We were afraid for our lives because he was a huge man"

"Lies, lies, lies," shouted Zadekiyah, once more with tears running down her cheeks.

"Order, order, this is enough. You are fined five shekels," the head judge reprimanded her.

"Guilty, guilty, guilty," shouted many of the people in the courtroom. "Our law says that we only need two witnesses to punish, and we have them."

"Quiet or I'll clear this court. Officers, if there is another outburst like this, you have my permission to remove anyone from this court." Everyone was completely still; there was a dead silence; everyone was afraid to speak.

"Is there anything anyone would like to add before we recess to make our decision?"

Deborah stepped forward three paces graciously and slowly with a commanding appearance. "Your honor, I have some information which I think will be valuable to this court. This information will cast light on this case and help bring out the truth."

"Oh … !" the head judge uttered. "Tell us about this information you have!"

"It is information about the procedure pertaining to the interrogation of witnesses. If it pleases you, your honor, may thy humble servant, Deborah, suggest that each witness be interrogated separately and more in depth."

"This is highly irregular," exclaimed the prosecutor. "We know that she is guilty. Let's not waste the court's time and pronounce sentence at once."

"Not too fast." The head judge raised the palm of his hand at him indicating for him to hold his peace. "Deborah, on what grounds do you support your request?" asked the head judge, sympathetically.

"In the scroll of Deuteronomy, it is written that: 'And the judges shall make diligent inquisition: …' in regards to legal matters and the questioning of witnesses."

"This is a waste of time," shouted an angry man from the audience. "She is guilty." Finally, two officers grabbed the man and removed him from the court.

The head judge spoke to Deborah. "I assume you have training in this area of the law?"

"Yes, I do. My Uncle Yoetz instructed me in these matters."

"I remember that name more vividly now. Did he not sit on the Council of the Seventy Elders at Shiloh?"

"Yes, he was on the Council for many years."

The prosecutor interjected once more: "Judge Shallum, I vehemently object to Deborah's suggestion. We have the testimony of reliable witnesses. Never before have we had procedures like this in our town."

"And in this town, we never had a trial like this before. A woman's reputation and life is at stake. The purpose of this court is to seek out the truth so that justice can triumph. For these reasons, I shall permit her to proceed."

"You may begin, Deborah," the head judge encouraged.

"Your honor, can we have Katan the second witness escorted from the court area so that I may question Ishmael alone?"

"Yes, I shall allow that."

After the usual formalities were complete, Deborah asked Ishmael many questions in the categories of queries, inquiries and cross-examinations. Deborah continued her battery of questions. "Ishmael, how many times would you say you had visited the house of Joseph, the husband of Zadekiyah?"

"Ah ... ah ... about 15 times."

"And when you went there, how many times did you see Zadekiyah?"

"I would say about eight times."

"Did you ever discuss with anyone about the fact that Zadekiyah is a beautiful woman?"

"No ..." answered Ishmael with a surprised look on his face.

"Do you think that she is beautiful?"

"No," he answered sharply.

"Aha!" Deborah turned to a lady that was standing next to her and asked, "Do you think that Zadekiyah is a beautiful woman?"

The woman replied, "Yes, she is very beautiful."

"This is very strange," Deborah remarked. "Ishmael, you are a man and you don't think that she is beautiful; and the lady next to me thinks that she is very beautiful. This is very strange indeed."

The prosecutor then spoke up. "I don't see where Deborah is going with this line of questioning."

"I do, and I will allow it," replied Shallum. "Deborah, you've made your point. Now I must ask you to get to the specifics."

"Ishmael, you claim that Zadekiyah committed adultery. Tell the court where this act took place?" asked Deborah.

"It took place in her courtyard, under a tree surrounded by bushes."

Deborah lowered her head and paused and looked up. "What kind of a tree was it?"

"Ah ... ah ... I believe it was a fig tree," Ishmael stuttered.

"Now, in regards to his clothing, what was the color?"

"Light blue."

"Are you sure?"

"Yes."

"One more question, Ishmael. Did this act take place before sunset or after sunset?"

"It was before sunset."

Next she summoned the officer of the court to bring in Katan for interrogation. "Katan, you said that the defendant was kissing in the courtyard. Exactly, where in the courtyard did this kissing take place?"

"Under a tree," he said wiping the sweat from his forehead, looking nervous.

"What kind of a tree," she asked sternly.

"It was an Olive tree."

"Did this alleged meeting between Zadekiyah and the stranger take place before sunset or after?"

Katan paused and then said, "After sunset. Yes! It was after sunset." Deborah turned around slowly and looked at Ishmael and paused. Ishmael lowered his head and rubbed the upper bridge of his nose.

"Are you finished Deborah?" inquired the head judge.

"Not quite your honor. I have one more question for Katan. What was the color of the clothes the stranger was wearing?"

"Must I be questioned like some common criminal?" he asked, turning to the head judge.

"Answer the question!" ordered Judge Shallum.

There was a silence. Then the head judge reminded him. "If you want your testimony to be accepted, you must answer the questions truthfully."

For the second time, Deborah asked Katan, "What was the color of the clothes the stranger was wearing?"

"His clothes were ... white," he said hesitantly.

Noticing the contradiction in their testimony, Deborah asked, "Are these men who the prosecutor calls reliable witnesses ...? I am finished your honor," she said, as she noticed the judge nodding his head in approval.

The prosecutor glared at Deborah and rose to his feet and called for the defendant Zadekiyah. "Did you commit the crime as alleged by the two witnesses?"

"No! Absolutely not! I love my husband, and I would not do anything like that," she assured him.

"Where were you on that day and at the time stated by these two men?" asked one of the judges.

"I was at home."

"Was there anybody else in your house with you, male, female, or both?"

"No. I was the only one at home your honor."

"Do you have anything to add to cast light on this case?"

There was a period of silence in which Zadekiyah didn't say anything and the judges stared at her waiting. "I shall repeat. Do you have anything to add? We are waiting!" replied the judge.

"No. No," she murmured. "These are evil men."

There was a deep silence and pause as the judges looked at her with wonderment in their eyes. "Are there any more statements that anyone would like to make?" There was a long silence, but no answer. "Now, we shall recess and then bring you our decision. Deborah, would you like to join us in our discussion?"

"I would consider that an honor."

CHAPTER 5

They went to a stone structure about thirty feet from where they were. There was beautiful green shrubbery planted around the sides and front. As they walked along the beige stone walkway toward the building, Deborah could see a replica of the Ten Commandments engraved over the front door. Then she read the ninth commandment in a low voice: "Thou shall not bear false witness against thy neighbor." The rest of the judges heard her reading and looked at her with approval.

After they finished the serious deliberations and reached a decision, they agreed to let Deborah render the summation of the case; and they returned to the court area outside.

The news about Deborah traveled rapidly, and she noticed that the crowd increased in size as she looked around the court area.

"May I please have your attention? The court of Beer Sheba is now back in session," proclaimed one of the officers.

"You may begin Deborah," the head judge urged.

Deborah walked up front and began to speak: "First of all, I call this case, *The Ghost Man*. We have a complete description of the alleged evil man, who is supposed to have committed adultery with Zadekiyah, but we do not know of his whereabouts. It is doubtful that he even exists at all which I shall demonstrate … ."

The chief judge said, "Continue Deborah."

"The facts and truth of this case," Deborah explained, "hangs only on the testimony of the two witnesses, Katan and Ishmael. First of all, Ishmael testified that he saw the defendant kissing under a fig tree; and Katan said that it was under an Olive tree. This answer renders their testimonies void."

"Aha!" gasped the entire crowd.

"Second of all, Ishmael testified that the clothes of the stranger were light blue; and Katan testified that they were white. This is a contradiction that renders their testimonies again void."

Again, the audience shouted, "Aha!"

"Point number three, Ishmael testified that the act took place before sunset; and Katan stated that it happened after sunset. This discrepancy renders their testimonies void again because everyone knows the difference between 'before sunset' and 'after sunset.' In view of this, the prosecutor calls these men reliable witnesses? This case has all of the signs of a frame-up. From all of the evidence presented in this case, we must conclude that the man, who was alleged to have committed adultery with Zadekiyah, does not exist at all."

"Judge Shallum," interrupted Ishmael, "we are men of high standing in this town. Are you going to let this … this woman stand here and humiliate us?"

"The chief judge stared at him. "Pertaining to the truth, our law has no respect for gender. If you feel humiliated, then it is your guilt that has seized you."

"What?" You mean that you are going against us?"

"Your lies and wickedness have blinded and condemned you. This court finds you and Katan guilty of being false witnesses. What you and Katan sought to do to Zadekiyah, so shall it be done to you!"

Then Ishmael stared at the judge with a hateful look. "Curse be the day you were born. You will pay for this."

"No!" Shallum snapped back. "You will pay for your transgressions and lies. You have accused Zadekiyah falsely, and now you have reviled a judge of Israel. Officers of the court seize the false witnesses!"

As the officers escorted the false witnesses away, the crowd stood up in an uproar and shook their fists at the prisoners. Then Shallum rose to his feet and raised his hands above his head. The crowd became quiet and listened attentively, and then he sat back down. "You have heard the evidence in this case; and it is the decision of this court is that no charges be brought against Benjamin Ben Hur. Moreover, the defendant, Zadekiyah Abraham, will be set free. As for Ishmael and Katan, their wickedness and lies have condemned them. Furthermore, let it be proclaimed from here northward to the tribe of Dan, that these two men have been convicted for bearing false witness against a daughter of Israel. This we do in order to remove evil from our people. Also, we want to give thanks to our God for sending us our beloved sister Deborah whose knowledge, wisdom, and fortitude helped to exonerate the innocent and convict the guilty. This court is now dismissed." Then the chief judge stood up with a satisfied look on his face.

Shortly thereafter, Deborah went over to meet with Zadekiyah. As soon as she saw Deborah, she embraced her and smiled. "Thank you! Thank you! Thank you so much, Deborah; you are God sent. Without you, I don't know what I would have done. Oh! Would you like to come over to my house for dinner tonight?"

"Yes! I'd like that."

"During supper, we'll have plenty of time to talk," added Zadekiyah anxiously.

"There's more isn't it," asked Deborah.

"Yes, I'll see you this evening," said Zadekiyah, and walked away.

After a few minutes, Deborah walked over to where the chief judge was standing. Seeing her, he walked in her direction and spoke. "I want to congratulate you on your great performance on interrogating witnesses. You are a credit to our people and our way of life. I wish you much success in all your endeavors. By the way, I will be sending a special report to the Council of the Seventy Elders in Shiloh."

"Thank you, your honor for allowing me to assist in this trial," and Deborah walked away.

Just before supper, Zadekiyah's husband returned home from his business trip, and Zadekiyah introduced Deborah to him. When the meal was finished, Zadekiyah's husband went into his study to review some contracts. While the two ladies were alone, Zadekiyah revealed to Deborah the reason the two men wanted to frame her. After her visit with Zadekiyah and her brother—Deborah returned to her home outside of the City of Bethel.

When Ariel, the senior Elder of the Supreme Court had finished telling this story, he looked at Barak and said, "That court case in Beer Sheba was the starting point that began to push Deborah to national fame among the tribes of Israel. After that, people from many tribes came to her for judgment, knowledge, counsel, spiritual advice, and inspiration. Her audience included men and women, but many women came for special reasons because it was said that they could confide in her concerning intimate issues. In short, the people knew—

that in Deborah—they had an understanding and receptive ear. She was open, accessible, and humble. These were her spiritual qualities as they are written in our sacred scrolls."

Barak lowered his head, scratched his eyebrow, and looked perplexed. "Wait a second, my dear Elder. Let's back up for a moment. There seems to be something missing about that court case in Beer Sheba. Was it ever revealed why those two wicked men brought false charges against Zadekiyah?"

"Yes. I'm glad you asked me about that. When Deborah went to Zadekiyah's house for dinner that night, Deborah asked her did she have any idea why those two men wanted to frame her. This is what was revealed: You must understand; these two men had been coming to her house to discuss business with her husband; this is how they knew Zadekiyah. Zadekiyah was a beautiful woman not quite thirty years old. As time passed, their minds were drawn to her with lust. So, one day, when they knew her husband was not at the house, they came and pleaded with her to lie with them; but she refused. Finally, after she had turned them down many times, they said to her: 'If you don't lie with us, we shall tell the judges that we saw you commit adultery with a stranger.' "

"Those evil men," asserted Barak, as he took a deep breath with disbelief, shaking his head.

At that moment, the servant brought in a water basin with a towel, bread, very warm beans, cut corn simmered in onions and olive oil, vegetable salad, and hot roasted, juicy lamb chops and placed them in front of Barak.

"Wow!" he shouted, as he breathed the aroma through his nose. After the recitation of the blessing of the bread, Barak took a spoon-full of fried, fresh creamy corn and exclaimed, "This is delicious."

During the course of the meal, Barak reflected again on the two accusers of Zadekiyah; and his spirit was troubled. He started to take a bite from the tender lamb chop that was in his hand, but paused. "Why didn't Zadekiyah testify in court that her accusers wanted her to lie with them?"

"Good question," commented Ariel. "Zadekiyah knew that her husband had a very special business deal with two business men, and she didn't want to say anything that would disrupt that arrangement. In view of this, Zadekiyah didn't even tell her own husband that the businessmen wanted to lie with her. Somehow, she had hoped that the men would leave her alone. You see, Zadekiyah knew that the business deal meant a lot to her husband, and that's why she didn't want to reveal anything during the trial that these men wanted to lie with her. She was hoping somehow that the case would be thrown out of court, and the men would be set free."

"Hmm. Well. Wasn't the business deal still in jeopardy during the trial?" asked Barak.

"Not really. The special business deal that her husband had was not with her two accusers, but with two other men. But Zadekiyah didn't learn of this fact until after the trial when her husband came home."

"Oh what an interesting trial that was in Beer Sheba. I wish I had been there. Incidentally Elder Ariel, how did you manage to remember all of the details of this trial?"

"I received a written report from Judge Shallum and some information from Deborah."

Then Barak took a bite from the piece of lamb chop and continued eating the rest of his food sopping the bread in the bowl. "You mentioned earlier that there were other social conditions that contributed to the rise and fame of Deborah. What were they?" he inquired.

"It was the complete breakdown of the political, religious, and social structure of the Israelite nation. You must understand that after the death of Moses, Joshua, and the elders that outlived Joshua, there was no central leadership or king in Israel that had witnessed the miracles and experiences that our ancestors had faced in Egypt and in the wilderness."

"It seems that this was truly a dark time for our people," Barak commented.

"Yes, and during the time that Moses and Joshua led the Hebrews in the wilderness, all the Israelite tribes were encamped around the Tabernacle—the shrine of our central leadership. All the tribes looked to the Tabernacle for leadership and guidance because Moses, Joshua, the high priest, and the Council of the Seventy Elders were there. However, after Joshua had completed the distribution of the land to each tribe in Israel, everything changed. The tribes were no longer encamped around the Tabernacle but were remote from it."

At this time, Barak looked at a pomegranate tree in the courtyard with its bright, green lance-shaped leaves and reddish-orange flowerers, and commented, "Also, my tribe is remote from the Tabernacle," Barak confirmed, "and we have the same problems that you are explaining."

"Many elders, heads of tribes, and judges stubbornly refused to come to the Tabernacle here at Shiloh to seek advice, guidance, and instructions from the Lord, from the high priest, and from the Council of the Seventy Elders. Many of the people did what they thought was right in their own eyes. They should have asked for advice from the elders at the Tabernacle who knew more than them, but they didn't ... ."

When Elder Ariel paused, Barak leaned forward and spoke, "I can recall my father saying to me: 'Remember the days of old, consider the years of many generations, ask thy father, and he will show thee, thy elders and they will tell thee.' "

The Elder placed his hand on Barak's shoulder and praised him, "Barak, you are blessed to have a good father; many children are not as fortunate as you. Good fathers give a head start, in life, to their children. Either we prepare them for a good future, or, by our neglect, we prepare them for failure and a life of crime."

"You are so right."

The Elder leaned toward Barak. "When you are training your young men for war, remember to teach them also how to be good fathers. Above all, be a good example in everything you do because our sons and daughters are watching us. I have reached almost fourscore and ten years; I give less notice to what people say; I just observe what they do."

"Elder Ariel, what is the most important thing to teach our young men and boys in order for them to be good husbands, fathers, and to stay out of trouble?"

"This is digressing from our main subject; nevertheless, I shall answer your question because it is important. The simplest way to develop good husbands and fathers is to teach and prepare the males while they are young. Then when they reach marital age, they will already know how to be good husbands and fathers. Next, we must teach them to honor God, parents, the neighbors and their property. Afterward, we must teach them that marriage and lying down with a female, is a big responsibility because crying babies are the result. In addition, we must prepare our sons to learn a vocation or trade and to acquire property or a business before marriage. Later, they will be in a better position to support a wife and children. When a father has a trade or business, he can teach his sons how to operate it. This fulfills the words of God as it is written in the scroll of Deuteronomy: 'And thou shall teach them diligently unto thy children, as thou sitest in thy house and when thou walkest by the way … .' " Barak looked at him with a satisfied look on his face. Elder Ariel continued. "Now Barak, what was the last part of your question?"

Barak looked at him and smiled. "It was about the things to teach our young men to get them to stay out of trouble."

"Oh yes, we must teach constantly until they learn the difference between right and wrong. Many parents don't take the time to teach their children, because they are too busy with other matters; consequently, the children get neglected and have to raise themselves without guidance. To make sure our sons and daughters stay out of trouble, we must show them a lot of love. Looking after their welfare, considering their interest, having patience with them, involving them in activities that are good for them, the boys and girls will grow up to be good and successful. This is achieved best under the supervision of the parents."

"As you explain these things, I realize that there is a lot of work to be done, and I promise to be a good example to my men and others."

"Yes, Barak" After that comment, the Elder continued with his main topic before Barak interrupted him. "You must understand, Barak that the leadership of the Hebrews became corrupt from top to bottom. They took bribes, committed idolatry, adultery, robbery, convicted the innocent and let the guilty go free. In essence, the people corrupted themselves in every way possible."

"Now I understand—more than before—the reason Deborah sent me here to obtain a Certificate of Authority."

"It is good that you understand. At this time, I shall continue; our people did evil in the sight of the Lord. They saw no unity among themselves, no central leadership, no justice, no righteousness, no mercy, no harmony, no peace, and no moral example of how a decent person should live. Our people emulated the bad practices of the Moabites, the Ammonites, the Philistines, and the Canaanites. For example, the Hebrews cut their flesh and marked up their skin like the Canaanites. Their social structure based on the law completely crumbled. Distrust, jealousy, despair, and hopelessness were the norms of the day. Despising themselves, the Hebrews rejected their history and culture."

At that moment, Barak stood up and shook his head in disgust. "What you are saying, I see this condition everywhere I go. How sad ... how sad it is."

"There is not much that is good in life for the descent people to emulate. The good people look around the country; and they see mostly corruption in government, exploitation of the poor, lewdness, negativity, vulgarity in speech, and dress. I'll give you a parable to illustrate my point: There was once a great ship that was wrecked in a storm on the Great Sea. All the sailors drowned, except two men who managed to survive in a small boat. The storm finally subsided; and for two days, the boat drifted under the hot sun; and the men became very thirsty. Then one sailor scooped up some water from the sea with the palms of his hands and gulped it down. Shortly afterwards, he became sick and said to the other sailor, 'there is plenty of water all around us but none good to drink.' Now Barak, what does the water symbolize?"

Barak stared at him. Later, he looked away in the direction of a tall evergreen tree that stood by the high wall. He thought for a short while and turned toward Elder Ariel. "I think that the salt water represents the evil and misguided people among us."

"You are so right, Barak. The few good people are tempted to follow the bad examples of others because it has become popular. Evilness and crime run rampant in our communities because law-abiding and moral-minded people refuse to take action to stop it. They are afraid to speak up. But speak up they must … or else life will become too unbearable and dangerous."

Barak gritted his teeth and said, "I understand and agree with you. We leaders have a big responsibility. If we want things to change, we must organize, speak out, and take action. I want to change things, but there is a lot of opposition."

"Indeed, you must realize, Barak; it was all of these evil conditions that contributed to the rise and fame of Deborah. The time was ripe for her. She became the welcomed cool breeze that came after a long hot spell of hopelessness."

"Your Excellency, I could listen to you all day and night."

"I am so sorry to disappoint you Barak," he chuckled, "but the days are for you to listen … and the nights … are for me to sleep!"

Barak smiled and continued. "Why didn't more leaders of the various tribes come up to the Tabernacle for instructions?"

Ariel sighed with a deep breath and paused. "The heads of the individual tribes, and the elders of the various towns, became self-centered; they became infatuated and protective of their own petty tribal authority and power."

Barak interrupted and made the following observation, "That is an example of how too much power corrupts."

"You are so right Prince Barak. Now, I shall continue with my thoughts. "Many times the local leaders retained the tithe for themselves and refused to give it to the central leadership. If they had given this tithe, they would have helped to make the government at the Tabernacle much stronger. Instead, it grew weaker, and weaker. In short, the tribal leadership became too haughty. They interpreted the sacred laws according to what they thought was right in their own eyes and for their own personal gain, and it did not benefit the people."

"Elder Ariel, I see that you possess great knowledge."

"Thank you for your words of praise, but I hope I have acquired also a little wisdom."

"You have." Barak assured him without hesitation.

"The high priests and the Supreme Court of the Seventy Judges at the Tabernacle did not intend for the interpretation of our holy scrolls to rest in the hands of the individual tribes. These supreme judges were the men of higher knowledge established by the Great Prophet. The scroll of Deuteronomy instructs us in this regard: 'If there is a matter too hard for thee … then thou shall arise and get thee up into the place which the Lord thy God shall choose (that place is the Tabernacle) …' " said Ariel.

"Now that you mentioned it, that makes sense," Barak admitted. "And, some of the leaders in my tribe also are guilty of not going up to the Tabernacle to seek guidance from the Supreme Court."

"Ah … I am going to put it very simple young man, and I say young man because I am more than twice your age. When the elders of the various tribes rejected the guidance of the learned men of the Tabernacle, they rejected knowledge; and when they rejected knowledge, they rejected God; and when they rejected God, God rejected them. Consequently, He delivered the Hebrews into the hands of their enemies, the Canaanites, to punish them for their transgression—just as a parent punishes their children when they do something wrong. In view of all of these evil conditions, many of our people were ready for a change … ready for something better

… ready for righteous spiritual leadership, and Deborah was right there to give it to them."

"An extraordinary lady," remarked Barak, as he yawned. "I have one last question, Elder Ariel. Some of my soldiers asked me how they can get wealth. Can you give me some advice for them?"

The elder yawned, stretched, placed his hands behind his head and stared into Barak's eyes for a while and then spoke slowly. "I can explain; but wealth is not the important thing; good health, happiness, and helping others are more important. Now, concerning wealth, the answer I give you may not be the answer they want to hear … !" He paused, "the way to get wealth is to give first. Then it will return to you many folds from another source. I'll use a parable to convey my complete answer: First, pursue the lady of knowledge and pursue the lady of wisdom … and use that knowledge and wisdom to help mankind. Afterwards, the lady of wealth will get jealous and pursue you," he said, with a smile on his face.

"My dear elder, I am sure that our young soldiers will be delighted to be pursued by this pretty lady."

"Yes, that would be the natural reaction of your young men. Oh! One last thing, Barak: Tell your soldiers that they aren't truly rich until they have something that gold shekels and silver talents cannot buy. You can't buy good health, happiness, or true love; however, when you have these three things, you are truly wealthy."

"Umm," Barak expressed surprise. "I like that answer; you are a fountain of wisdom."

At that moment, the elder nodded off to sleep, and when he opened his eyes, he stood up and stretched. "Oh, Barak your day time for listening has passed, and the night has come. Now, it is time for me to go to sleep."

Barak rose to his feet, bowed, looked at the elder and smiled: "I thank you very much for giving me so much of your precious time."

After their discussion, Ariel asked Barak to sleep overnight at his house; and the next morning Barak continued on his journey to the City of Kadesh, in Naphtali.

Chapter 6

A month later, on the fifth day of the week, two days before the beginning of the Hebrew Sabbath, Deborah received a letter from Barak. The letter was in the form of a rolled-up piece of parchment which he had deposited in a pouch made from animal hide. As she lay on her bed, Sarah—her handmaid—handed her a pouch. She wondered if anything had happened to Barak. Deborah opened it and read from right to left (as it was the custom of the Hebrews):

> *Peace be unto you, Deborah. I hope you are well. It seems like it has been a year since the last time I saw you. I stopped by the Tabernacle and had a long informative discussion with Ariel, the elder. He gave me the Certificate of Authority, which I requested, thanks to you. Also, I would like to inform you that we had a skirmish with a Canaanite company of soldiers. We lost three men and I was slightly wounded on my right arm. But I am much better now, so much for the unpleasant news. I have*

been thinking about you every week. I
wish I was there with you right now.
I miss your presence, your smile,
your beauty, and your tenderness.
By the way, your name has become
a household word and your fame has
spread all over the northern tribes.
People have nicknamed you Mother
Deborah. In closing, I hope there is
a place in your heart for me. I'll see
you as soon as I can. Peace be with
you.

   Your friend, Barak.

As Deborah lay on her bed, she reflected on Barak's letter with mixed feelings. After her morning prayer and meditation, she finished the breakfast that her handmaid served her.

"My lady is there anything that I can do for you before I leave for the market?" asked Sarah, as she held a pot in her hand.

"No, but wait for me. We will go together."

Nachshon, the gatekeeper, prepared the donkeys for the market. He took several sacks from the storage room and placed them over the backs of the donkeys. In these sacks, they usually put the food and other items they bought. At that moment Nachshon said to Deborah, "When we reach the City of Bethel, I want to stay near you to give you closer protection."

"Why do you say that, Nachshon?"

"Well, the last time I was in Bethel, I heard some men say that they didn't like you poking into men's affairs."

"In that case, stand nearby and stay alert."

The fifth day of the week was the most important shopping day because the next day was the beginning of the Sabbath. Among the Hebrews, the Sabbath began in the evening the day before the actual Sabbath day; and most people had their cleaning and cooking completed by high noon on the sixth day of the week. Sarah and Deborah walked together and Nachshon remained behind five or ten paces to allow the women some privacy for women talk. As they walked, Deborah noticed a flock of black birds eating worms and insects from among the grass. When Deborah's retinue approached, the leading bird flew away and the rest followed. Nachshon then spoke: "Deborah, if you and Sarah are getting tired, I'll be happy to help you on the donkeys."

"Thank you Nachshon, but we need the exercise to help us keep in good shape." They continued on their way to the City of Bethel about a mile and a half down the road that connected Jerusalem with Shechem. It was at Bethel that this road intersected with the east-west road that led from Jericho to the Mediterranean Sea. Bethel was a thriving town long before the arrival of the Hebrews. It had many houses, shops with pavements, and a sanctuary. There was an adjacent mound and several springs where the local inhabitants could get fresh water. Deborah was in deep thought as she walked along the main road to Bethel. For the first half mile of the walk, there was no conversation between the women. Sarah looked at Deborah, but she held her peace for a while. Then as they walked a little further, they could see the City of Bethel off into the distance.

"Deborah, I don't want to appear prying, but is there something troubling my lady?" Sarah asked softly and cautiously.

Deborah held her peace and looked up at the gray clouds. "I have a lot on my mind today," she said, guardedly not intending to reveal too much. She stepped up the pace of her walk leaving Sarah a few steps behind. They passed palm and sycamore trees as they walked. Sarah was a woman at least 15 years passed childbearing age, and she had worked many years for Deborah's late husband. She had a slender built, and she was about 17 years older than Deborah.

"My lady, I have worked for you and your late husband for many years and have tried to be a good servant. Seeing you like this causes me great concern. Please, I beseech you ... tell thy humble servant what troubles thee? It is about that letter you received this morning, isn't it?"

"Yes ..." she said reluctantly.

"Would thy handmaid be wrong in saying that the letter is from the handsome man with the mustache that came to our house on the last full moon?"

"No ... you are not wrong. The letter came from him," answered Deborah, looking at Sarah with amazement.

***

They began to enter into the central section of the City of Bethel. There were many shops, inns, and houses. Some houses had stone steps on the outside that went up to the second floor. Others had courtyards with plants and trees inside. In addition, men, women, and children were walking in the outside market area leading their donkeys, camels, and asses along the way. The Hebrew people were bumping into each other not watching where they were going because they were gazing at the fresh produce, meats, animal hide, rope, pottery, beads, and clothing.

In many parts of Israel, as well as in the City of Bethel, the Hebrew population contained a mixture of colors: dark brown, brown, tan, yellow, and white. This variety of colors resulted from the mixture of whites with brown-skin, Hebrews, and other Semites in Syria, Assyria, Palestine, and Egypt. These whites came from the region around the Caspian and the Black Sea in southern Russia. In the Middle East, these Europeans were known as Hurrians. In Egypt, the Hurrians introduced the chariot and established the 15th and 16th Dynasties. However, the Egyptians didn't call them Hurrians but Hyksos or Shepherd kings. The word Hyksos is a corruption of the Egyptians words, "heka khasewet," which means—rulers of foreign lands. They ruled northern Egypt from (c.1720-1575 B.C.). All over the Near East and Egypt, these Hurrians amalgamated with the Canaanites, Hebrews, and the Semites and adopted some of their culture. In addition, when the Pharaoh, Ahmose I expelled the Hyksos from Egypt, many Hebrews left with them. This fact is confirmed by other scholars and Hebrew records which states that— "And a mix multitude went up also with them." Everyone could see the "mix multitude" in the marketplace of Bethel.

The marketplace, for many, was a good place to come for shopping; but it also served the purpose for gossip. People could meet old friends, talk about their personal concerns, discuss something new—and watch the strangers going and returning from—Egypt, Arabia, Moab, Syria, and Tyre. Moreover, there were Greeks from Europe, and Circassians from southern Russia who were shopping in the marketplace. These travelers were headed to Egypt.

Deborah sensed that Sarah wanted to talk more about the letter she received; but the congestion, the crowd, the conversations, and the greetings of the people kept Deborah busy. She also had her shopping to do, so they didn't have much time to discuss personal matters. Nachshon, the gatekeeper, acted as a bodyguard especially when Deborah was away from the house. He was a very tall man weighing about two hundred and seventy-five pounds and moved closer to Deborah to be ready to protect her against any would-be assailants. Nachshon was an expert fighter; and he had received his training in the army of Shamgar—the last Hebrew judge who fought the Philistines.

Many people who knew Deborah greeted her and smiled. Various people were saying to each other, "that's Deborah, the Prophetess." As Deborah walked in the market, she gazed at the onions, beets, leeks, beans, grapes, nuts, melons, and other produce. After she bought a sack full of vegetables, Nachshon fastened them to the donkey.

"Can I pay you with these shekels and gerahs?" asked Deborah.

"Yes," replied the shopkeeper.

Standing on the opposite side of the market, were two men. The older man, named Melek, spoke to the other: "That lady over there wearing the green shawl is Deborah. Familiarize yourself with her appearance, and keep your ears and eyes open. The Prince Abihu has a secret task for us to do a little later."

"Yes master."

"Also, he wants to know every important person she meets with. Be very careful, and don't let Deborah and her company know that you are watching them."

After Deborah paid for her produce, she turned around and bumped into a shopper. "Oh! Is that you, Ophrah?"

"Yes!" she said with excitement.

"I haven't seen you since mandrakes were ten gerahs (ten cents) a basket," said Deborah, as she embraced her. Ophrah was a sleep-in house servant for Deborah's brother-in-law, Caleb.

"I've been hearing so many good things about you, Deborah."

"How is Caleb? I have not heard—Oh Ophrah, how did you get that bruise on your arm?" she asked, with deep compassion.

"Oh Deborah, you shouldn't ask me," she commented pitifully.

"Has Caleb been mistreating you?"

"He supports me and my children."

"But has he been mistreating you?" Ophrah lowered her head and remained silent. Then Deborah stared at her with empathy. "I understand. You can't talk about it because you are afraid that if Caleb finds out, he will punish you."

She raised her head and eyes slightly and looked at Deborah. "Sometimes you just have to bear it," she mumbled weakly.

Deborah took a deep breath and exhaled as she placed her arm around Ophrah's shoulders. Both of them walked slowly away from the crowd. Then Deborah spoke again. "I am sorry for your sake and mine that this has happened to you."

"You are sorry for your sake? I don't understand."

"It is a long story, but you will understand before the end of many days."

Ophrah turned toward her. "So be it, as you have spoken."

"I think that you will be free of this burden that you have."

"Did the voice of God tell you this?"

"No! It is just a strong feeling that I have, and I am usually right."

"Yes, you usually are."

"Ophrah, we must support one another. What I am saying is that if things become too unbearable with Caleb, you can always come and work for me."

"Thank you, Deborah. You are so kind, and it is good to know that I have another way out."

"Furthermore, I want you to pray daily; and God will answer your prayers." Then both ladies embraced each other and went on their separate ways.

As Sarah and Deborah passed by a beggar sitting on the ground he said, "Alms for the poor? Alms for the poor?"

Noticing him dressed in his dirty torn clothes, Deborah had compassion for the man and walked over to him and commented, "I spent all of my silver coins, but I can give you some produce."

"That is so nice of you," he said with a smile.

"Oh Nachshon, will you bring over some food for this poor man?"

"Yes Deborah, right away." Nachshon went and got the food and set it in front of the beggar.

"I thank you so much for your kindness," he said.

"You are very welcome, and you have a nice smile. What is your name?"

"My name is Azuv. And I thank you not only for the food, but also for the conversation."

At that moment, Deborah, Nachshon, and Sarah departed and continued down the road. Then Sarah looked at Deborah. "My lady, it shows that you are a very compassionate person when you help others."

"Sarah, the sick, the neglected, and the poor don't want to be ignored. They want to know that we care about them, and that we are willing to help."

"It was good that you stopped to talk to him because you have so much knowledge and wisdom to share."

"That may be true Sarah, but people don't care how much we know until they are convinced how much we care. By helping others, by talking less about how bad things are, by doing more to help the sick, the misguided, and the poor, we can build love in the world. When we do this, we show true love."

***

It was now midday and Deborah and her servants were on their way back home. After reflecting on the letter from Barak, which she received that morning, she was now in a better mood to discuss it.

"My lady, before we arrived at the market, you were telling me that the letter you had received came from Barak; and it seemed to have disturbed you. Did it not?"

"Yes, it did … . Barak was wounded in battle."

"Oh no … !" she said, as she walked turning her head toward Deborah. "Was it serious?"

"No. It was just an arm wound."

"My lady … because your countenance fell, I thought it was something more serious than that. Could it be that your heart and eyes are drawn to him like a flower is drawn to the shining sun?"

"I don't know … I like him but my life is uncertain."

All of a sudden, Deborah, Sarah, and Nachshon heard the sound of horses and a chariot racing rapidly behind them; they moved to the side of the road to let them pass. As the horses raced by, they noticed that the driver was an Egyptian; and he had a whip in his brown strong right hand which he cracked at the team of horses. Suddenly, the Egyptian yelled out something in his language. The whip swung around in Deborah's direction and could have struck her in the face, but she ducked down just in time to avoid being hit.

"That was close," she said. "Sarah, what did the Egyptian yell out in his language?"

"He said, 'Get out of the way, you peasants.' "

"Oh Sarah, you are such an asset to me. I am grateful that you are able to speak several languages."

"Thank you, my lady." After that incident, Deborah and Sarah returned to their previous conversation and continued down the road. "My lady, what did you mean when you said that your life is uncertain?"

"I'll reveal it to you when I know more about the problem that is vexing my heart. I promise."

"All right ... . ! But on the other hand, Barak is a handsome man; many women would want him."

"True. He is handsome, he is a prince, he is a general, and he has a large estate. But on the other hand, his spirituality is doubtful," she reminded Sarah. "Because I am spiritual and in tune with my Creator, my mate or husband must also be the same. If he is not, he could make light of my spiritual pursuits and deem them unimportant."

"What did he say that suggested to you that he was not spiritual enough?"

"Barak told me that, 'if he had half the number of men and chariots that General Sisera had, he would attack tomorrow,' this was his boasting. Then I told Barak that he would need more than chariots to beat Sisera. His reply to me was, 'we will see.' You must understand, Sarah, he left God completely out of the picture."

"Did he mention anything personal about how he feels about you?"

"Yes. He said that he 'thinks about me every week, he misses me, misses my smile and my tenderness, and he wants me to hold a place in my heart for him.' "

Sarah listened attentively while studying her countenance. "Will you?"

"I am not sure—he has a lot of the qualities that I admire; but he congers up unpleasant feelings in me."

"Feelings—like what, my lady?"

"Feelings like …" Deborah paused, and then continued, "like sorrow and death."

"My lady, where do those feelings come from?"

"They come from my late husband, Lapidoth. As you know, he was killed by Canaanites. Barak fights Canaanites and was recently wounded by them." Deborah stopped walking and stared at Sarah. "If I hold a place in my heart for Barak and he falls dead in battle, the emotional pain will be too much. Can you understand my position?"

Sarah took a deep breath, stared at Deborah, and nodded her head in consent, "I understand."

They continued to walk along the side of the road passing by other men, women, and children with their animals travelling north and south on the road. Walking further down the road, Deborah saw a bush of beautiful red roses; she picked some to take home; she pricked her finger on a thorn, and a little blood oozed out. "You see, Sarah, we cannot even enjoy the pretty roses without their thorns. Is this the nature of life?"

"It seems that way."

"I would like to get married again to the right man, but right now, I can't commit myself to Barak or to any other man because of the problem that is troubling my soul."

"What problem is that?"

"Sarah, I mentioned to you earlier that I have a problem that troubles my soul and I promised to reveal it to you soon, but not right now. This is one of the reasons why I can't commit myself to anyone."

***

They arrived home late in the afternoon while the sun was still up. Sarah and Nachshon performed their usual duties. In the meantime, Deborah had made inspections of her flax and wick factory. Afterwards, her supervisor, Madreech, reported to her: "The servants did excellent work today, and they accomplished a lot."

"Well, let's reward them and send them home early"

"The servants will like that," he responded, walking away from her to give the good news to the workers.

By now, the sun had set but it was not yet dark. After supper, she reclined on the couch for a few minutes. Not long after, she heard a shout at the front gate but paid it no attention, thinking that it was one of the servants. Then her gatekeeper, Nachshon, called her. "Mother Deborah, you have a visitor; it is your brother-in-law, Caleb. Where shall I take him?"

"Caleb?" She repeated, with surprise. "Give him a seat in the dining room and offer him something to eat. I'll be out in a short while." *Finally, he shows up when I least expect,* she thought. Waiting for his decision for more than two years caused her much anguish. She wondered what would be his decision now. Did he have a selfish reason for coming? This was the final moment that Deborah was expecting. Her heart pounded in anticipation of his decision.

Sarah came to her room. "Can I be of service to you, my lady? Oh! You are perspiring." Sarah pulled out a handkerchief and wiped her forehead. Deborah sat down for a minute; she closed her eyes and thought: I must get control of myself. Whatever happens, it is God's will. He has His purpose in mind, and it is not for me to understand all of His actions at once.

Then she got up with confidence and went into the dining room to meet with Caleb. Caleb was about 15 years older than Deborah, and his height was 5 feet 9 inches. He was bald on the front half of his head and was wearing a brown garment with yellow borders. Also, Deborah had heard reports that Caleb squandered his money on sensual pleasures and gambling. He looked physically and emotionally drained, and he was a bloated physical specimen. When she entered the dining room, Caleb's back was to her, and he was looking up at a painting on the wall. It was a painting of the beautiful Jezreel Valley with Mount Tabor on the north. She labored to speak. "Peace—be unto you, Caleb."

With a smirk on his face, Caleb responded slowly. "Peace, Deborah. I was admiring the picture of the Jezreel Valley ... . It seems so peaceful," explained Caleb, turning to face Deborah.

"And that seems so contradictory in light of the fact that so many wars have been fought there. I was there during my childhood, and sometimes I fee ... feel like I shall return there for some special reason," Deborah added.

"Deborah, I am sorry for not contacting you sooner to give you my decision on levirate marriage. I must fulfill my duty to my deceased brother so he can have an heir. This is our law," he emphasized, as he walked to a shelf and picked up a small scroll of the Five Books of Moses.

"Before we talk about marriage, I want to talk about another matter ... . I was at the market in Bethel today and I met your maidservant, Ophrah."

"Oh!" He almost dropped the scroll and looked up at her with surprise. "I suppose she said some bad things about me."

"No, she didn't. Are there any bad things to say about you?"

He gave a silly grin and looked away. "You know how some women like to gossip and exaggerate."

"She had a bruise on her arm and no telling what's on other parts of her body. Is this an exaggeration? How did she get the bruise, Caleb?"

He stuttered and searched for an answer. "Sh-sh-she fell. Yes, she fell down the stairs."

"Do you expect me to believe that? If Ophrah had fallen down the stairs, she would have told me."

"It is not my concern what you believe."

"But you came here expecting me to agree to levirate marriage. How can I do this knowing that you abused your maidservant? If I marry you, would you abuse me also?"

"I don't intend to abuse you."

"You don't intend to ... . By the way, it has been three years since your brother's death; you could have given me your decision earlier," she pointed out, walking to a large cedar table and took out three nuts from a clay bowl. "I wrote to you three times in three years; all you could say was that you were busy and that you would let me know soon."

Feeling guilty, Caleb bowed his head in shame. "Well, I was busy."

"You could have given me your decision three years ago, or two years ago, or even one year ago," she jeered, placing the three nuts back in the bowl. "Why at this time, Caleb? Why now?" She looked at his potbelly and waited for an answer.

"I … . I … ." he stuttered. "I neglected to give you my decision earlier, but I am here now ready to fulfill the law. You see, our marriage can increase and combine our assets, and I can get out …" Caleb paused, making a slip of the tongue.

"Out of debt you mean, don't you? Hmm. I understand. You came here now to make a proposal of marriage to help you get out of debt," concluded Deborah, staring at him with distrust.

"The fact remains that you do have a legal obligation to marry me regardless of what you imply that my motives are," he rasped, with a cunning smile placing the scroll back on the shelf. "What will it be, Deborah?"

"Give me a little time for meditation. I shall return shortly. Then, I'll give you my answer."

Deborah went into her room, sat on a soft mat, folded her legs with her back erect, took deep breaths, and exhaled slowly. After she had relaxed, she evoked the Lord of Creation and the God of her ancestors. At last, there was a total silence in the depth of the darkness. At that moment, the voice uttered: "Do what you know is right and then let God work out His purpose."

After the meditation and prayer, Deborah returned to the dining room. As soon as she walked in, Caleb stood up. He gazed at Deborah with a long stare as if he had seen a ghost. His hands trembled as Deborah spoke. "I agree to marry you to fulfill our customs, not because I trust or love you."

"He uttered softly, "Who said that levirate marriage had anything to do with love."

"I get your point, but with most women love is foremost. Do you have a date in mind?"

He stood still and reflected for a little while "Will six months from now be fine?"

"I think so."

In a hurry to leave, Caleb said, "I'll contact you to discuss the plans. Peace be with you."

Deborah sat down and thought about the conversation she had with Caleb. It bothered her, and she wanted to talk about it. Then she remembered that she had promised Sarah to reveal to her what was troubling her soul, and there was no better time than now.

Hearing her handmaid in the next room, Deborah called, "Sarah, will you please come here."

As Sarah entered the dining room, she bowed slightly and asked, "What can I bring you, my lady?"

"I don't want you to bring me anything. I want you to give me your ear."

"Oh my lady, I am at your service."

"Let's go outside into the back courtyard," Deborah suggested.

The night was clear, the stars were shining bright, and the moon was full. At last, Deborah was full of things to say. "Sarah, I told you that I would soon reveal to you the things that have been troubling my soul. Now, I am ready to talk. My deceased husband's brother, Caleb, visited me earlier this evening and asked me to marry him. I agreed to do so, but I am not in love with him."

Sarah displayed an earnest desire to help, "Why did you agree then?"

"I am bound to do so under our law of levirate marriage."

"That's right! There is a law that stipulates that you must marry your deceased husband's next of kin."

"Yes! But it is conditional."

"What do you mean by conditional?"

"If a brother dies without a male heir, his brother must marry his wife and the first born male, which she gives birth to, shall succeed in the name of the dead brother, so that his name will not be blotted out of Israel. As it is, I don't have a male child, so it is my duty to marry Caleb."

"Is there any other way out of this marriage?"

"Only if he refuses, and this he has not done. Finally, there is a Divine way out; but that is left up to God to work out His plan."

Deborah felt confused and emotionally torn—torn between disobeying the customs and laws of her people—or on the other hand, marrying a man she did not love. She knew that if she refused, she would be denounced as a fraud and disgraced in the eyesight of her people. In view of this, Deborah poured out her soul unto the Lord: "Oh my Heavenly Father…! Why couldn't there have been another man that I could have loved? Oh Lord, I beseech Thee, hear my cry and deliver me from this awful pain," she murmured, as tears ran down her cheeks.

"That was a very touching prayer, my lady," then she embraced her.

CHAPTER 7

As Barak led his mountain fighters through the hills of Zebulun, a personal conversation developed between him and his next in command, Captain Enoch.

"General, you seem to be deep in thought," observed Captain Enoch, a competent yellow-skin officer with curly black hair.

"Deep in thought?" repeated Barak.

"Yes! I have been watching you for the last three days … your body is here with us … but your mind has flown away like an eagle to some distant land. Would you be willing to confide in your humble servant and reveal to me what weighs heavily on your mind?"

Barak hesitated; he looked at Captain Enoch with a serious glance then smiled. "All right, I might as well bring my mind back from that distant land that you speak of and let you know about my secret thoughts."

"A little discussion," said the Captain, "will no doubt cast some light on a dark problem."

"Well Captain, it was some time ago that I wrote a letter to a friend of mine named Deborah; and I haven't heard from her since."

"I had a hunch that your problem had something to do with a woman … . Women are strange creatures who are sometimes difficult to understand. Do you think that she likes you?"

Barak remained quiet and looked down at the ground. Captain Enoch grabbed his horse's reigns and said to Barak, "Hold your thoughts!"

The General glanced at him suddenly, "What thoughts?"

The Captain looked at him and grinned. "I mean your thoughts about Deborah. Do you need more time?"

"No! I believe she likes me; or should I say, she admires me."

"Give her a little more time," urged the Captain. "You'll probably hear from her soon."

"You have a point. Riding around in these hills, day after day, has made me lonely. I truly miss her."

After the conversation about Deborah, Barak spent the rest of the summer pursuing and capturing Hebrew lawbreakers. The capture of transgressors and criminals became a necessary step to bring about social tranquility, trust, hope, and justice in the communities. On a higher spiritual level, if the Israelites expect God's deliverance from the oppression of the Canaanites, they also had to improve their ways. As Barak hunted the robbers and thieves from Upper and Lower Galilee and from the eastern and western ends of the Jezreel Valley, he noticed the growth of the flowers, trees, grapes, barley, wheat, and other vegetation.

Then the fall came, the season of the blowing of the trumpets, repentance, atonement, and the harvest festival. Some people went to the Tabernacle at Shiloh and others remained at home. The harvest season came to an end with the dwelling in the booths. This festival also commemorated the dwelling in booths when the Israelites came out of Egypt. As

Barak and Captain Enoch road through the hills near Mount Carmel, Barak mentioned his previous visit to the Tabernacle. "General, I miss going to the Tabernacle this year. I can remember when we carried and waved the palm branches."

"Yes, I miss it also. I enjoyed the festival, the meeting of different people from the various tribes, and eating the delicious fruit." During this time, the leaves of the trees turned yellow, red, and brown. The green pine needles of the evergreen trees fell to the ground and turned brown. The rainy season of the fall, which was so vital for this land, came in abundance. Many times, these rains became so unbearable when hunting down lawbreakers that the soldiers had to take refuge in tents and caves.

By the time of the approaching winter, Barak had put under his command one thousand men. He divided these men into four companies and appointed a captain over each one of them. This conscription of men was very essential because of the increased confrontation with the Canaanites and hunting lawbreakers. Until now, Barak had never commanded a thousand-man militia. He thought about how his army was increasing and that all-out war with General Sisera was unavoidable. Because King Jabin and Sisera imposed heavier taxes on the Hebrews, because their soldiers molested some of the Hebrew women, because the Hebrews could not use the open roads for traveling, because the Canaanites put more Hebrews into hard labor camps, Barak concluded that he had enough of Sisera. He knew that this situation could not remain the same for long. He increased the training of his men; he wanted them to be ready when war broke out. But there was a scarcity of spears and swords. In view of this, Barak relied on slings and stones, rocks, and spears without the iron tips.

The Hebrew training camp was located in the Zebulun hills. At this time, the number of new recruits had increased in size, and General Barak designated Captain David to be the training officer. The living quarters for these recruits were tents made from goat's skins. These tents were located inside and outside of the fortress.

One day when Captain David was training his new recruits, General Barak came out of his tent to watch their performance. The soldiers drew images of men on white cloth with burned charcoal and attached this cloth to crude wooden frames to make targets for practice. Then they fastened the targets to various trees and posts. Also, they had moving targets attached to ropes like a clothesline. The rope extended from one tree to another or from one post to the other pulled by a soldier. After the soldiers practiced with their spears and swords for a while, Barak came over to Captain David and remarked, "The men are performing much better today."

"Yes they are, General Barak. I am glad that you see the improvement." Captain David was a tall brown skin man with dark brown eyes.

At that moment, Barak walked away; then he stopped and turned to Captain David. "Oh Captain, remind the men to keep their eyes on the targets and to hold the spears at the place where it is balanced. This will give them more speed, force, and accuracy."

One day as Barak was leading his men through the hills of Zebulun, just north of the Jezreel Valley, a messenger on horseback arrived. "Where is General Barak?" the young man asked. "I have a letter for him."

"Who sent it?" inquired Captain Enoch.

"The letter is from Deborah Lapidoth."

"I am he!" answered Barak anxiously, as he nudged his horse Laban over to the young man to receive the letter. Barak opened the pouch, unrolled the letter and began to read:

Peace be to you Barak. I received your letter and you informed me that you were wounded. I hope that you have fully recovered. Your good health means so much to our nation and us. I was grieved to hear about the loss of three of your men. I realize that war is so terrible, but sometimes it is necessary for the greater good that will result. So much for that and I'll move on. Now, no doubt, you have heard about the Hebrew robbers in your area. They have been raiding and stealing cattle, sheep, and goats and selling them to the Canaanites. Your task is, should you accept it, is for you to catch these transgressors as soon as possible and bring them to justice. Keep your arm strong against all transgressors. It is your mighty arm and soldiers that makes the law legal. Without the enforcement of the law, the law has no weight. Our people will not have trust in one another until we get rid of the crime in our neighborhoods. I have confidence in you that you will succeed. May God bless you and be with you.
Deborah Lapidoth.

After Barak finished reading the letter, he rolled it up and thought about what Deborah had said and what she had not said. He wanted to hear pleasant and intimate things of how she felt about him. But he didn't get them; and his soul became heavy with disappointment. The weather was cloudy and chilly all around him, and he felt gloom overtaking him. Nevertheless, he pressed on trying to find the thieves which Deborah had mentioned. Barak had been looking for these robbers for more than a month without any success.

After searching all day for the thieves, Barak decided to pitch camp for the night. He noticed that his men were showing signs of weariness due to the cold rain. His camp was not far from the City of Shimron near the foot of one of the hills. He stationed guards at strategic points; he ate supper; he had a briefing with his first officer, Captain Enoch. The Captain was about forty-three years of age with green eyes. He had been with Barak about ten years and he was a loving husband and father.

"I think that we should get an early start in the morning," advised Barak, as he placed his hand over his mouth and yawned.

"How early, General?"

"I don't think anything will happen tonight. Just before dawn is when these robbers do their dirt—when most people are asleep."

"I agree, General. By the way—before the messenger departed, he mentioned the name Deborah. Is she Deborah, the judge?"

"Yes, that is her."

"I bet she's beautiful!" asserted Captain Enoch, waiting for a confirmation from Barak.

"What makes you think that?" asked Barak, as he stood up and closed the flap to his tent.

"Well, after spending about ten years with you, I think I know the kind of ladies you like. Besides, you smiled when I mentioned her name, General. I am—" Captain Enoch paused.

"Speak up! Speak up! What's wrong with your tongue, Captain?"

"General, I am confused. After you finished reading the letter from Deborah, you seemed sad; but now, after I made a reference to her name, you smiled … ."

"Yes? Get on with it," Barak encouraged, wanting to hear more.

"Well, I am confused, General. Would it be in good taste for your humble servant to ask you to explain this difference in mannerism?" he asked softly.

"Hmmm," Barak sat back, remained silent, raised his head, and thought deeply: Shall I let this man into my private world? After all, he is just a subordinate; and I am the General. On the other hand, if I tell him about the letter and how I feel, maybe he can be helpful as he has been in the past. Stop being too proud; he reminded himself; just open up as ladies do in conversation. Could it be that I am too close to my problem to have all the answers? "I'll explain."

"Anything you tell me General, I'll keep it between me and you."

"You better or else you'll be demoted to a foot peddler."

"I understand," the Captain assured him.

"All right, this is the situation. I smiled because I was thinking about the first time I met her. She was so beautiful inside and outside, so warm, so tender, and so compassionate. I was sad after I read her letter because she didn't mention anything that suggested that she liked me as a friend. What I am saying is that I was expecting her to have said more than what she did. Since she didn't, I was disappointed. Maybe—I was expecting too much."

"Perhaps, may I see the letter?" he asked softly.

Barak hesitated and then gave him the letter. After reading it, the Captain said, "I understand what you mean. There are a couple of subtle things I see about the letter."

"Oh! I should have known you would pick it to pieces like a shepherd shears the wool from the sheep," commented Barak.

The Captain smiled and continued. "The fact that she wrote to you, I think this indicates that she is interested in you. She didn't have to write you," the Captain said looking very positive.

"Maybe, she wrote me because she wanted to tell me about the cattle robbers."

"Not really. We probably knew about them before she did. Most of these events take place in our territory, and we know about them before the rest of the country."

"You really believe, wholeheartedly, in what you are saying, don't you, Captain?"

"Yes, I do. Secondly, she mentioned that 'your good health means so much to our nation and us.' Deborah could have ended that sentence with 'our nation,' but she chose to conclude with the words, 'and us.' I truly believe that she wanted to say "and me." Other words, the sentence should have read: 'Your good health means so much to our nation and' me."

"Captain, you give a very convincing argument," Barak complimented him as he held his head up high and smiled.

"For some reason, I felt that Deborah was uncomfortable to express her true feelings; and General, when you see her again, this is something you might want to explore with her."

"I think I'll do just that. Well Captain, this discussion has been very revealing. Now, let's go over and join the men at the campfire."

As Barak and the Captain walked closer to the fire, they could feel its warmth because the wind blew the heat in their direction. Approaching the campfire, Barak stepped on a small dried branch, which cracked, and the sound alerted the men that they were coming. When the men turned around and saw Barak and the Captain, they started to stand up; but the Captain stopped them. "As you were men, continue to tell your jokes and riddles."

"We just finished Captain, and we would like to hear one of your stories or one from the General," requested a recruit.

"Yes!" Another soldier agreed.

"Yes! We would like this," echoed someone from the back of the camp.

"Yes!" shouted some of the soldiers who were new volunteers.

"Tell us General, about one of your most important battles," another soldier requested.

"All right, since you insist. It was the battle that we had planned at a meeting in the City of Kadesh over two years ago," he told them. Barak and his officers had met to plan a surprise attack on a company of Canaanite soldiers. Barak had wanted this meeting because the Canaanites were taxing the Hebrews heavily, and those who could not pay, or refused to pay, were forced into hard labor. The Canaanite soldiers executed this policy by the orders of General Sisera. In view of this, Barak wanted to put an end to their actions; or if not totally, he wanted to reduce them by some great measure. At that meeting, Barak asked, "Captain Enoch, would you bring over that map?"

"Yes, General Barak." The Captain attached the map, which was made from cowhide, to the wall. The map showed the area of the Jezreel Valley, the hills of Zebulun to the north, and the tribes of Asher, Issachar, Zebulun and Naphtali which included parts of the Galilee area.

"My fellow officer of the Hebrew nation, I shall make myself brief. We are here today, to discuss ways of how we can attack larger Canaanite patrols. In the past, we attacked only smaller units of thirty to fifty soldiers; however, this is going to change." Barak emphasized looking stern.

"How are we going to do this General Barak? We neither have chariots nor sufficient spears and swords," commented Captain David.

"Good question. We're going to deal with that in a few moments," he said, as he took a sip of water from a goblet. "I have spoken with the elders and I've asked for more men, gold shekels, and supplies; but they informed me that they will not consider any request until we defeat a Canaanite force of more than four hundred men. They want us to destroy more of these Canaanites who are capturing our young men and women to be used in hard labor and some sacrificed to their idol god, Baal."

"That's just about impossible, General considering our predicament," said Captain Enoch looking bewildered.

"I also said the same thing when the elders mentioned it to me. But on the next day, as I was reading: *The Book of the Wars of the Lord*, and *The Book of the Wars of Joshua*, I realized that we could succeed if we set a trap for the enemy. Now, this is what we shall do." Barak then explained to his officers the strategy and all the details of the trap which he had prepared for the enemy.

A week later, Barak brought his soldiers to the place where he had planned to set the trap. The place was in the mountains and hills of Zebulun near the City of Japhia. This city was located on the northern edge of the Jezreel Valley near the hills and only six miles west of Mount Tabor.

Barak led his men going southwest until he first reached the valley, north of Japhia, which is now called Nazareth. He rode past the steep cliffs and hills which were covered with aromatic herbs with pink, purple, and yellow flowers. He continued south and arrived at the section of the valley where it became narrower on the southeast and ended in a winding pass leading to the big Jezreel Valley.

As he entered the winding path, he explained to Captain Enoch, "We shall hide men in the cliffs of the mountains. And when the enemy pursue after us into this pass, we shall rain down rocks and stones upon them like hailstones from heaven."

"But General, how are we going to get the enemy to pursue us?"

"That will be simple. We shall have one of our men to disguise himself as a Canaanite, and when he sees a Canaanite patrol coming, he will tell them that the Hebrews stole his sheep. When that happens, we'll have five or six men not too far from him with some sheep, and when the Canaanites see them, we hope they will pursue the Hebrews into the pass."

"Oh, I get it General. When the Canaanites pursue the Hebrews with the sheep, they will lead them into the winding pass where we will be waiting for them," commented Captain Enoch, with a big smile on his face.

"I knew you would understand it, Captain."

Then Barak ordered Captain Enoch to select a special person to disguise himself as a Canaanite and to select six men to act as sheep thieves. Also, Barak told the Captain to select lookout men and post them on the high cliffs. These watchmen will let the rest of the Hebrews know when the Canaanites will arrive by using the wailing howl of a jackal. The Captain informed all the men of their duties, and all plans were prepared.

The first day passed without any observation of the Canaanites. By the arrival of the third day, the men began to get restless and bored. After a while, the Captain came and reported bad news to Barak.

"General, the men are getting tired of sleeping among the rocks of the cliffs and in caves. They say that the Canaanites are not going to come."

"By the sound of your voice, it seems that you too are getting weary."

"Well … yes. I might as well admit the truth, I am."

"Listen Captain," Barak took two steps to the side looking down and then looked up and reminded him. "Tell the men to be patient. Many times, when men think about giving up, that is the time the tide will turn. Victory is lost many times because men do not hold out to the end. This will be a good lesson in self-discipline for them."

Toward the late afternoon of the fourth day as the soldiers sat around talking, they heard the wailing howl of the lookout man. The Captain ran over to Barak and asked, "Isn't that our signal?" The wailing howl sounded again.

"I believe it is." Moved with ardor, Barak ordered, "Tell your men to take up their positions quickly, and don't attack until you hear the sound of the ram's horn."

After giving the men their instructions, Captain Enoch returned to Barak. "All the officers know their positions on the cliffs and know what is required of them, General."

"Good, the ram's horn will be blown after the last Canaanite soldier enters into the winding pass. Soon after, we shall seal off their exit points so that none will escape."

"General, let me express my joy to you for your upcoming victory. Your fame will now spread all over the land of Canaan from Dan to Beer Sheba."

"I am not seeking after fame," snapped Barak suddenly, as he stomped his foot on the ground. "My task is to annihilate the Canaanite threat so that we can bring peace and order to our people. Is that understood?"

"Yes General!"

At that moment, Barak heard the sound of the hooves of horses. He looked to his right and saw the six Hebrew riders leading the Canaanites unaware into the winding pass. The Canaanites rode into the pass with horsemen pursuing the Hebrews relentlessly. After the last Canaanite horseman rode into the pass, Barak gave the orders to blow the ram's horn, and his five hundred men began the sustained barrage of stones and rocks. At the same time, they sealed off both ends of the pass with large boulders, and with bonfires. The Hebrews were able to subdue the Canaanites quickly, because they surprised them, and they held the high ground.

When the battle was over, Barak and his men went down into the narrow pass to count the dead and wounded and to recover the spoils.

"We have a great victory, General," commented the Captain, as he passed by a huge rock on the cliff.

"Yes, we do. Get me a complete count of the dead and wounded, and collect all the booty," ordered Barak, as he walked by the wounded Canaanites.

After a short while, Captain Enoch returned to Barak with the good news.

"General, we counted five hundred and sixty-four Canaanites. This number includes the dead and the wounded. We have more than exceeded our goal."

"Well done Captain. Is there anything else?"

"Yes there is. We have a double victory," said the Captain, with a smile on his face.

"Captain, my time is valuable. I have no time for playful words. Explain yourself."

"Not only have we defeated this Canaanite regiment, but also we recovered 11 Hebrews who the Canaanites had chained to a cart. No doubt, the Canaanites were going to put these men in hard labor. We found the cart near the entrance of the pass which leads to the Jezreel Valley."

"Well, this is good news. The elders will be pleased to hear this," said Barak, with a happy smile on his face.

"Oh—General Barak, there is one final piece of news; we captured a Canaanite officer."

"You did? Well, bring him to me!"

Captain Enoch turned around quickly to some of his soldiers and ordered, "Bring over the Canaanite officer!"

When the soldiers returned with the captured officer, Barak was talking to Captain Enoch. The General turned around slowly and looked at the officer inspecting him up and down. Then he walked around him scrutinizing the officer's uniform—his leg protections, his coat of mail, his helmet, and his purple epaulet—the symbols of his authority. He was dark brown and about the same height as Barak. Completing his inspection, the General remarked: "Soldiers of the Hebrew tribes. Do you see what we have here? We have a fancy well-dressed officer." With a stern look on his face, Barak stopped in front of the officer and asked, "What is your name and rank?" At that time, the Canaanite officer stared at Barak with defeat and contempt; and he chose to remain silent. The General asked, again, "What is your name, Canaanite?" There was a silence. "I warn you; I am not going to ask you a third time."

The lips of the officer moved slightly; then he managed to speak. "My name is Zaeer, Captain Zaeer of the King's Elite Regiment.

"Did you graduate from a military academy?"

"I did."

"Didn't they teach you that you don't dispatch your soldiers into a narrow pass unless you check it out first?" Zaeer made no attempt to speak. Barak looked down at his feet and raised his head again. "I am waiting," said Barak. Still, there was no answer.

At that moment, Captain Enoch suggested, "Let's tie him down on the ground, with four stakes, on top of an ant hill, and that will loosen his tongue." Barak agreed and told the captain to proceed.

After this, the Canaanite officer spoke up, suddenly. "Wait! I'll talk. Yes, they instructed us at the academy to be careful about bringing our soldiers into a narrow pass."

"So why did you do it?" asked Barak, looking into his eyes curiously.

"Well, you were just—" The Canaanite hesitated and looked up in deep thought.

"Go on," prompted Barak.

"You were just—simple shepherds—living in the mountains."

"I see—you failed to remember that leopards live in these mountains, and you have to watch out for them. You made a stupid mistake, and you have the nerve to call yourselves the Kings Elite Regiment. Captain Enoch, retain this officer for future questioning and assemble the men. We are moving out."

"Yes General."

Now, as Barak sat around the campfire, he finished telling his soldiers about that battle and the strategy he had planned for the defeat of the Canaanites. Moreover, this victory gave the soldiers more confidence in their General.

After Barak finished relating his story, one of the squad leaders named Isaac spoke. "We thank you, General for explaining to us your well-planned attack on the Canaanites. It was very exciting and ingenious."

"You are welcome," said Barak.

"If it is all right with the General, I would like to take the liberty to request that Captain Enoch entertain us with some of his rare jokes," Isaac requested.

"Captain Enoch has my consent, if he feels so pleased to amuse you."

"I agree, General since the men have been board with nothing to do," added the Captain. Now, I want you to be aware that most of you have heard my best jokes so the ones I tell you now may lack that powerful punch."

The squad leader Issac spoke again. "It is my feeling that the men will be pleased to hear anything you have to share with them."

Captain Enoch sat down on a rock near the campfire and he looked very deep in thought. Slowly, he raised his head. "I shall begin with one of our remote ancestors. When Adam was in the Garden of Eden, he asked his wife, 'do you truly love me?' Eve: 'there is nobody else!' " At that time, the soldiers laughed with joy and one of the men fell off his rock laughing.

After Captain Enoch told nine more jokes, General Barak said to him, "We have time for only two more, and make these your best jokes, Captain."

"I'll do my best, General." The Captain then remained silent, looked up at the multitude of stars and thought. He smiled and began. "This joke is a conversation between Abel and Nahor in the City of Gilgal. Abel: 'Wow! Do you see that pretty lady over there?' Nahor: 'Yes, I see her and she has one more thing that will certainly knock your eyes out.' Abel: 'Wow! What is it?' Nahor: 'Her husband!' "

Hearing those words, the men chuckled and one stood up and said, "I would like to meet her twin sister." Then he sat back down laughing.

When the men settled down, Captain Enoch continued. "A grandson wanted to buy a gift for his grandmother as a New Year's present. He decided to purchase a pretty parrot that could whistle special songs for a woman who lived by herself. He paid a lot of money for the parrot and had it delivered to her house in the City of Ramah. Three days later, he stopped by her house: 'Grandma how did you like the gift?' Grandmother: 'Delicious,' she answered."

After hearing the last joke, some soldiers said with surprise: "Oh no, she didn't," and the rest of the soldiers just smiled.

Barak rose to his feet and remarked, "Let's give Captain Enoch a hand. Well done Captain," he said, patting him on the back.

"Thank you, General. It was a pleasure."

"Now, before you go to sleep for the night men, I want to discuss some ideas with you concerning how to be good fathers. Elder Ariel, the chief elder of the Supreme Court in Shiloh asked me to have this discussion with you. I shall talk about sex, love, marriage, and fatherhood.

"First of all, soldiers, I want you to understand that there is a difference between sex and love. Having sex, in most cases, is passion and excitement and it last relatively for a short period of time. Making love in many cases is nothing but having sex. However, true love is not based on sex. It is deeper and it lasts longer in duration. True love is caring, giving, and sharing with your partner even when there is no involvement in sex.

"Another point, you should not get married unless you are in love with your spouse. If you are not in love, you will bring misery to yourself and to your wife and this will affect the behavior of the children. In short, make the right choices in life.

"There are some people who engage in sex before marriage because they think that they are in love and later they find out that there is no love. Then there are some persons who indulge in sex just for the pleasure of the moment and disregard the consequences of their actions. If children come as a result of this situation, the burden of raising and caring for them falls on the mother or the grandparents. Furthermore, in many instances, the children suffer because of the absence of a strong male image in the household. I realize that some of you soldiers are going to have sex before marriage. But when you do, first, I want you to think seriously about the consequences of your action. In view of all this, the ideal state under which, I believe, to raise children is marriage. A good loving relationship in a marriage gives balance, happiness, and security to both partners and children. I saw these excellent qualities between my father and mother.

"Above all, teach your sons a trade so that they will be able to support a wife and children. You must understand; marriage is a big responsibility to your wife, daughters, and sons.

"How many of you have sons who do not live with you?" There was a silence, and Barak waited for an answer. He looked around the crowd and insisted. "There must be someone here who has a son that doesn't live with you." As Barak looked to the right, he saw a soldier raising his right hand very slowly. "What is your name soldier?" Barak asked.

"Jacob Ben—Keter," he said hesitantly. "I have three sons and they live with their mother."

"What are their ages?"

"They are one, three, and five."

"I hope you are giving them some kind of support."

Jacob replied, "I do, General."

Barak spoke again. "Jacob, I want you to get your house in order. Before those boys reach the age of ten, I want you to do your best to make arrangements for the boys to live with you. After a certain age, many boys tend to disobey their mothers but yet, they look for the mother's love. Boys want the discipline and image of a male. They need a father to teach them how to be men. If they don't learn how to be men, they will learn how to be something else, or they will join up with the wrong company and become thieves, robbers, and murderers. If this happens, I shall have to send the army after them; and they will end up in prison or dead."

"Your words mean a lot to me and since I have been with you General, I have learned much."

"Good, I am glad that you see the light. Our children need a lot of teaching, and good role models. My father always taught me that sons and daughters should honor their fathers and mothers. When we honor and obey our parents, it is less likely that we will end up in trouble. If we don't teach our sons and daughters and live by being good examples, how are they going to know right from wrong? We must teach them that the following are wrong: murder, robbery, thief, assault, burglary, adultery, incest, disrespect of parents and other authority figures, deception, lying, forgery, vulgarity in dress and language, cursing parents, sassiness, alcohol and other addictions, prostitution by males or females, slander, rape, physical and mental abuse, bribery, hatred for no good reason, showing favoritism in court because a person is popular or wealthy, neglecting the poor, hostage taking, persecution, slavery, etc.

"One of the main problems in our society today is that many people do what they think is right in their own eyes. There are people who want to be alcoholics, and some fall victim to other addictions, some dress indecent, and others speak vulgar language. And because they want to do these things, this does not make it right. I'll give you an example: a man or woman who wants to steal, rob, murder, or commit any of the wrongs mentioned above eventually become a danger to himself, herself and a bad influence on the general society because people will copy the bad habits of others. When this happens, society gradually falls apart and self-destructs. In short, our only hope is to love our neighbor as thyself and to do to others as you would have them to do to you.

"When the sons see their fathers preforming their duties in the home, the sons can also learn by example. Now I have said enough; it is time for me to retire for the night." Barak yawned and placed his hand over his mouth and departed.

At that moment, Captain Enoch stood up and said, "The General explained that your children need role models; now, I am asking you, who is your role model?" There was a long silence. The Captain looked over the entire audience and no one proffered an answer. The Captain had a look on his face as though he was expecting a reply, but none came.

Then far back in the crowd of soldiers, he heard a soft voice utter a single word, "Barak."

The Captain became overjoyed to hear that excellent answer after a long period of silence. As he left the area, he said, "Good night men, get some sleep."

CHAPTER 8

Just before daybreak on the following morning, Captain Enoch awakened General Barak and informed him of the approach of men, goats, and sheep. Barak immediately jumped to his feet and asked him: "How many are out there?"

"We don't know, General."

"Put all standard orders into action; treat them as the enemy until we know otherwise. I'll be out in a few moments," Barak ordered, as he put on his sandals, vest-like garment, and adjusted his pantaloons and girdle belt.

As he walked outside of his tent, he fastened his sheath to his belt and went over to the five-foot high boulders where the Captain was standing with some of his men.

"General, I think we have found what we have been looking for ... the robbers," declared the Captain, as he gazed over the boulder into the dimness of the dawn.

"Are you sure? There is one way we can find out. Get your men ready to move on a moment's notice and report back to me."

"Yes General!"

After the soldiers were assembled and ready for action, the Captain returned to the General. "Captain, order your men to blow the ram's horn. If the men remain with the flock, this probably means that they are honest men. If they run and leave the flock, this probably means that they are thieves. In that case, assign some of the soldiers to gather up the flock."

When the men blew the ram's horn three times, the suspected thieves ran away on their horses, donkeys, and camels towards the Jezreel Valley. Barak and his soldiers pursued the thieves into the Jezreel plains which separated Lower Galilee from central Israel, called Samaria-Ephraim.

There were about ten men in the group of thieves, and Barak's soldiers first caught up with the three men who were riding on the slow moving donkeys.

"Grab those men on the donkeys and tie them up," yelled the Captain, as he veered his brown horse towards his men.

Because the suspected thieves were escaping, Barak and his soldiers pursued them across the Valley towards the Hill of Moreh. "Hurry up Laban, we don't want to lose those men," he urged his horse, as he leaned over his long white mane. Barak looked back and saw Captain Enoch coming up on his rear. The thieves were no longer in sight; they lost them somewhere around the Hill of Moreh and the adjacent hills. Because his horse was panting hard, Barak slowed his horse down a little to let him rest. Then Captain Enoch and his men caught up with Barak. "Captain, they can't be too far away. They must be hiding in these hills," indicated Barak, as he focused on the landscape.

"Or they might be hiding behind some of the boulders or bushes," suggested the Captain, as Barak heard a noise far in the distance.

"Captain, take your men around to the right of the hill, and I'll go to the left. Let's search every foot of this hill thoroughly. I don't want these villains to get away."

"Yes General!" Both companies of Captain Enoch and Barak searched on and around the Hill of Moreh and the nearby area; and they met at the southeastern spur of this group of hills.

"Captain did your men see anyone?"

"No General, we searched every hill and all through the bushes, and nothing. I don't understand where they could have disappeared," he said, looking at the orange sun rising in the east.

Momentarily, Barak looked disappointed. He wanted these thieves caught to help bring more trust and hope among his people. Also, he had to admit to himself that he had another reason to bring these men to justice. If he apprehends these men, it would make him look good in the eyesight of Deborah. As he sat on his horse, he wondered which direction they could have gone. Reflecting and remaining calm, he knew that he could not waste any more time. If he did, the thieves would get away. Realizing that he had to make a decision right away, he turned to his officers.

"General, you look like you have gotten a revelation," commented one of his junior officers.

"I have," Barak said enthusiastically. "I don't think that the men went southwest toward Megiddo. If they had, we would have seen them. I believe that they fled toward Mount Gilboa and to the southeast. We couldn't see them in their escape because the Hill of Moreh was blocking our view. However, there are two reasons to back up my contention that they went to Gilboa. One, there is plenty of water at the Spring of Harod; and second, they can easily hide among the multitude of trees."

"That makes sense," the Captain remarked.

"Captain, assemble the men; and let's make a fast run to Gilboa."

"General, the men haven't eaten yet."

"Then they'll have to nibble on bread as they ride. We can't afford to lose these scoundrels," Barak said, as he sped away.

The mountain range of Gilboa was about six miles from where they were. They rode their horses at rapid speed in a two-column formation. As they approached the mountain range of Gilboa, they stopped about fifty cubits from the foot of the mountain where the Spring of Harod was located. This spring was situated near the northwest part of the mountain range. Barak took a hard look at the ground near the spring to ascertain if the thieves were drinking there or hiding among the nearby evergreen trees. He quickly concluded what he must do.

"Captain Enoch! Give orders to your soldiers to surround this entire mountain range and then report back to me. We want to cut off all escape routes of these bandits."

"Consider it done, General." After the Captain had cordoned off the entire mountain, he returned to General Barak. "All of the soldiers are in place, General."

"Good Captain. I ..." Barak paused because he was interrupted.

"Excuse me, General. May I suggest that we give water to the men and the horses?" asked the Captain.

"I was going to get to that. But first, send one of your junior officers to the tribe of Zebulun; and get reinforcements because our lines are spread very thin. After that, you can see to it that water is given to the men and horses." Barak goose stepped his horse around the general area of the Spring of Harod and watched the deployment and watering of his soldiers.

While Captain Enoch was talking to one of his officers some distance away, Barak realized that he had not questioned the three captives who were riding on the slow moving donkeys. Then he got the Captain's attention and beckoned him to come.

106 Mary L. Windsor and Dr. Rudolph R. Windsor

"Yes General."

"Do you have the three men who were riding the donkeys?"

"Yes General."

"Bring them to me! I want to question them"

The Captain's soldiers brought over the three men, and they seemed to have a guilty look on their faces. In addition, their hands were tied behind their backs. "What are your names?" asked Barak, looking at them sternly.

The men slowly raised their heads and muttered, "Dan."

"Aaron."

"Benjamin"

"Where are you from?" asked the Captain.

"We are from the tribe of Asher," answered the older looking man.

"Where were you going before we stopped you?" Barak asked.

"To ... to the Valley," uttered one of them.

"Yes! That's right—to graze the sheep in the Valley," answered the second man.

At that moment, Barak sensed that they were just trying to make up lies as they mumbled. "Why did you run off when you heard the sound of the ram's horn?" inquired Barak, watching their every reaction.

Each man looked at one another as if they were searching for an answer, and replied. "We ran because we thought you were murderers."

Checking them over carefully, Barak noticed something hanging on the neck of one of them. "You—come over here!"

"You mean me?" asked one of them.

"No! I mean you—you with the long beard. What's that hanging on your neck?"

"It's nothing ... just a charm," he casually replied.

Barak then leaned over the side of his horse and took a close look at his so-called neck charm. "What do you think I am—a fool? This is an image of the idol god, Baal. You are idol worshipers! Get them out of my sight," Barak commanded. Then the soldiers grabbed them.

"General, the reinforcement should be here shortly," assured the Captain.

"Good, now you can begin the all-out search of Gilboa. If possible, bring all of those scoundrels to me alive for questioning."

They blew the ram's horn, and the search of the entire mountain range began in earnest. Barak was convinced that he was going to catch these bandits this time. It was just a matter of time. After an hour's search, Barak approached the Captain. "Have your men seen anything, Captain?"

"Yes! We saw one dead man. He looked like he was mangled by a wild beast."

"I wouldn't be surprised ... bears and lions have been seen in these parts. Press on with the search, and tell the men to be careful."

"Yes General."

"Oh! By the way, tell the men that if they come upon a cave, don't go in; first, set a fire inside the opening of the cave and smoke out whatever is in there."

"Yes General."

After an hour, the reinforcements of five hundred men arrived under the command of Captain David.

"I came as quickly as I could General. What is the situation here?" he asked.

"We have about seven bandits trapped in these hills. The entire area is surrounded by our soldiers, and they are searching for them right now."

After Barak had finished briefing Captain David, he gave him his orders. "Captain, send half of your men into the mountains to help with the search and keep the other half here at the foot of the mountain as stand-by units. Your stand-by units can help protect and guard the rear of the searching parties, which are in the mountain, just in case any of Sisera's Canaanite patrols come."

As Barak watched the sweeping search operation on the mountain, he thought of what Deborah stressed in regards to capturing criminals. Their capture was necessary to bring more trust, love, and unity among the Hebrew tribes. The army was needed to achieve this objective, because the local law enforcement had broken down; and the Canaanite and Philistine danger was evident everywhere.

Away in the distance, there was a horseman riding rapidly in Barak's direction. As he approached closer, Barak could see that it was Captain Enoch. The Captain came to a sudden halt, and Barak knew that something was wrong. "A Canaanite regiment of soldiers has been spotted, General," he reported, as his horse panted for breath.

"What is its location?" he asked quickly.

"It is coming from the direction of the rising sun; but it is closer to the City of Beth Shean," the Captain informed him anxiously.

"How many are they?" he inquired.

"We believe that there are between seventy-five to one hundred charioteers," he estimated, eagerly waiting for further instructions.

"Hmm … charioteers," he mumbled. Barak thought that this was too large a force for him to deal with. "Give the orders to your men, who are at the foot of the mountain, to kneel down in the high grass, and it will be less likely that they will be seen by the enemy."

"Is there anything else, General?"

"Pray that the enemy will turn north or return to the east. If they continue to come in our direction, we'll have to give up the search; and the chances are that the bandits will escape." Barak nudged his horse toward the mountain. "I am going to keep a close eye on this Canaanite regiment. If you need me, I shall be at the lookout post on top of the mountain. Oh Captain, I see some brown vultures circling around the mountain. This indicates that something is dead up there."

"Yes General. You probably are right."

Within a short time, one of the soldiers at the lookout posts spotted smoke going up from the middle position of the mountain range. Then the soldiers knew that the bandits were in that area, and they closed in on them from every side. There was a fight, and the thieves were subdued and brought to Barak with their hands tied. The soldiers also brought to the General a dead body, which they wrapped in a linen cloth, but Barak was not sure whether the dead man was one of the men he was chasing. Barak then gave an order to bring all the soldiers around to the western side of the mountain so that the Canaanite regiment could not see them; but he left men at the three lookout posts.

Now, he was ready for the questioning of the six bandits which they captured in the mountains. After Barak received their names and the name of their tribes, he continued to question them. "Why did you run?"

"We ran because we thought you were robbers and violent men," one man said hastily.

"It is an old saying that a guilty man flees when no man pursues him," said Barak. "And you fled like wild geese—before we pursued you."

As Barak was questioning the suspects, he was glad that he had good news to report to the Supreme Court in Shiloh and to Deborah. Then he continued his questioning. "How many men were with you?"

"There were 11 of us," said one man who acted as spokesman for the group. He was about forty years old and over six feet tall.

"And, what might your name be?" inquired Barak.

"Rueben"

"Rueben ... ?" asked Barak.

"Do you recognize that name, General?" asked Captain Enoch.

Barak raised his head, closed his eyes, and spoke slowly. "I've heard that name somewhere ... but I can't seem ... to place it."

Captain David interjected, "Can we continue, General?"

"Yes." Barak concurred. "We captured three men before you reached Gilboa," he emphasized, as he stared at Reuben, "and captured six of you after you reached this mountain. That's a total of nine. Where are the other two?"

"They probably ran away."

"Well, one of them didn't run fast enough. Captain Enoch, have your men bring over the dead body!"

The soldiers brought over the body, which was covered with a large white fabric, and then took off the covering. It was obvious that a wild beast mauled the man. His neck had teeth marks on it; and his stomach was torn open.

"Do you recognize this man?" asked Barak, as he rubbed the neck of his horse.

"Yes! I do … cover him up … that's a nasty wound," Reuben snapped, as he turned his head away with a horrified look.

"We'll need to notify his kin folks. What is his name?" inquired Captain Enoch.

"Nathan," answered the spokesman.

"Was he a Hebrew?" inquired Barak.

"Yes! He was from the Asherite tribe."

"Well, that accounts for ten men, but you said there were eleven. What happened to the eleventh man?"

"He reached Gilboa before the rest of us. When we arrived here, we never saw him again. So he must have escaped. Evidently, he had the fastest horse."

"Mm … . What was his nationality?" Barak probed, searching for all the information he could get.

"It is interesting that you asked because that man was a Canaanite."

"Canaanite?" Barak asked with astonishment, as he looked at Captain Enoch.

"I suppose you wouldn't know what city he was from would you?"

"Uh … uh some name that sounds like uh … Hazier or … uh Hazur," he said with uncertainty.

"Could it have been Hazor?" asked Barak.

"Yes! That's it. That's it … Hazor."

Barak became very perturbed when he learned that one of the escapees was a Canaanite and possibly from the City of Hazor, the city of Jabin, king of the Canaanites and his General, Sisera. Barak remembered that after Joshua destroyed the City of Hazor, the survivors fled to the region southeast of Mount Carmel and established a new city called Harosheth-ha-goiim. Shortly thereafter, it acquired the nickname Hazor. Also, the kings of this city called themselves by the name Jabin. It was a known fact that Jabin had his spies among the Hebrews. It was difficult to tell who was a spy and who wasn't because some of the Hebrews lived among the Canaanites, served their gods, intermarried with them, and even looked like them.

Hadn't Jabin prohibited the Hebrews from taking their armies into the Jezreel Valley? In spite of this prohibition, Barak had done just that. No doubt, sooner or later, this news would reach Jabin and Sisera.

"By the way, Reuben, why did you make a fire on the mountain?" inquired Barak.

Anyone could discern from the appearance on Rueben's face that he was reluctant to speak, but he managed to say a few words. "We thought by doing it—the Canaanite army would see it— and also see your soldiers. Then you would have had to withdraw."

"I understand; but the opposite happened ... because of the fire, we were able to find you sooner."

"But we are innocent; you didn't catch us doing anything wrong."

Barak spoke again. "No, we did not catch you in the act; but there are several things that are suspicious about you. One, you ran away; two, you built a fire in order to get the attention of the Canaanite army so that we would have to give up our search for you, and three, your name triggers up suspicion in me—but I can't place it—just yet." Next, Barak fixed his eyes intensely on Reuben with a disturbed look on his face. He turned and glanced at the other robbers. Then turned back and stared at Reuben again. Finally, he said to his soldiers, "Watch them closely, especially that one ..." pointing at Reuben.

"General, since we do not have any solid evidence against them, perhaps we should release them," suggested Captain David. Barak remained silent and in deep thought.

At that moment, Reuben burst out with a comment: "Yes, release us, we are innocent." He then hobbled over to Captain David and extended his arms to be untied.

Barak watched him very closely, and Rueben's limp revealed the unexpected. "Hmm. Wait! Not so fast … . You are not free—just yet."

"Not free," Repeated Reuben, as he turned half way around toward Barak.

"That's what I said. Aha! Now, I know where I heard your name," Barak recalled dismounting from his horse. "One of the Levites and Elder Ariel heard the name Reuben mentioned during the robbery at the Tabernacle."

"That don't prove anything, retorted Reuben. "There are lots of men who have the name Reuben."

"Yes, that is true," Barak reminded him, shaking his finger at him. "The Elder at the Tabernacle said that one of the robbers with the name Reuben walked with a limp; and this description fits you!" Barak emphasized, pointing his finger at him.

"You have no real proof; your words aren't worth cow's dung. What kind of a general are you? " asked Rueben, with perspiration running down the side of his face.

"I am the kind of general that is smart enough to catch a dirty snake like you," Barak smirked and faced Captain Enoch. "These men are under arrest. Hold them to stand trial before the Council of the Seventy Judges at Shiloh."

Suddenly, Rueben turned and swung at Barak with both of his hands tied and shouted, "I'll get you for this you nit wit." Barak saw the punch coming. He immediately blocked it and struck Rueben on the jaw with a powerful blow. This knocked him backwards, and two of his soldiers grabbed him.

Barak gazed at Reuben with an angry look: "That was a stupid mistake you just made. Get him out of my sight!"

Sensing that the situation was under control, Captain David asked, "General, is there any further orders for me?"

"Uh ... yes, I would like you to deliver the dead body to its nearest kin so that it can be buried before sundown."

"Speaking of burials, General, why do we bury before sundown?" asked Captain David.

"I thought you knew," interrupted Captain Enoch. "It is our law to bury as soon as possible to show respect to the dead. Furthermore, I will add ... some of our sages and elders teach that as long as the body is not buried, the soul is not at peace because it yearns to get back into the body."

"Oh . . ! That's interesting," remarked the Captain, as he saluted and departed.

"Captain Enoch, I am going to take a seven-day leave of absence. I'll be two days at my estate and one day visiting Deborah."

On that same day, Barak sent a messenger with a letter to Deborah informing her that he would be arriving in a few days. Barak had exciting news to tell Deborah and something special to give her.

CHAPTER 9

Deborah was walking along the path lined with palm trees when Barak arrived on one of the days of his leave of absence. Ambling along, she wondered why he wanted to see her at this time. Before he arrived, she had given instructions to Sarah her handmaid and another female worker to follow behind her twenty cubits so that no one would question her integrity and conduct. After all, she was obligated—by the customs of her people—to marry Caleb even though she did not love him.

As she waited for Barak to arrive, she thought about the fact that she had to reveal to him her engagement to Caleb. This weighted heavily on her heart. She wondered how she would tell a man who she liked that she was engaged to marry someone else. She knew that it would not be easy, and it drained her energy like a parasite that drains the vital fluids from its victim. After all, she was human.

It was the middle of the winter. The leaves had fallen from the trees; the day was cloudy and a little chilly. She prayed and spoke softly: "Oh Lord, I beseech Thee, give me the strength, the courage, and the wisdom to deal with this pain." She could feel the despair in the air all around her.

As Deborah raised her head, she could see Nachshon, her gatekeeper, escorting Barak to her. When Barak approached three cubits from her, he held out his hands to hold hers; but she decided not to reciprocate. She reasoned that it would not look right, and it would send the wrong message. But in her heart, she wanted to accept his sign of affection.

"Is all well, Deborah?" he inquired, with an expression of worry on his face.

"I'm fine. We've had a very good harvest this year, and the business is thriving," she said, as her blue cotton mantilla fell from her head and shoulders.

Barak then bent down to pick it up, and his muscular thigh accidently touched her well-defined hip. He placed the mantilla over her shoulders and smiled with pleasure. She enjoyed the attention, but she did not encourage him.

"You've talked about your business but haven't said much about yourself. I've missed you, and I am glad to see you," he remarked, waiting for a response.

There was a silence, "I've had … ."

"You've had what?" Barak probed.

"Let's not talk about me right now. Oh Barak, I am so glad you are healing well from that wound you received on your arm." She noticed, with heart-felt sympathy.

Deborah did not want to reveal any news about her marriage to Caleb at this time. She wanted to move slowly. "Have you had any success in catching law-breakers?" she asked, turning her head and looked into his eyes.

He chuckled and Deborah knew that he had good news. "Come with it. Tell me about it," she urged.

"Well, we caught ten men, cattle and sheep thieves." Barak told Deborah all about the capture of the sheep thieves. This included the details of the man killed by a wild beast; the details of the Canaanite who escaped, and all the details about Reuben—the leader of the thieves.

"You were wonderful, just wonderful, the way you organized and executed that search and capture at Mount Gilboa." As she praised him, she looked at him with admiration, respect and gave him a big smile. Now, she knew that she could rely on him to accomplish anything he set his mind to do. At this time, she wanted to hug and kiss him; but she restrained herself for obvious reasons. A moment later, she offered, "I get the feeling that the escaped Canaanite is a spy for Sisera."

"He just might be…. By the way, Deborah, how and when did you first hear about Sisera?"

"Oh, that was many years ago when I was a young woman of 19 years old. That's when I saw him for the first time."

"You saw him?" Barak turned around in surprise, "Where?" he asked anxiously.

Deborah began to tell Barak of the time when she had been living with her Uncle Yoetz in the City of Jezreel. She had been spending a lot of time with her uncle after her parents had died. On a certain day, while Deborah was sitting in front of her uncle's house doing needle work, her friend Malcah and her boyfriend, Dan, stopped by to visit. They were seventeen years of age and holding hands. All three of them talked for a little while.

Shortly afterwards, Sisera was approaching the town with his army. As soon as Deborah learned that the Canaanite army was coming, she ran and told her uncle who was reading a scroll inside his stone house. "Uncle Yoetz, I believe the Canaanite army is approaching."

"Quickly my dear, go … ! Gather up the children and the young ladies and hide them in the stable"

"Yes, yes!" she replied eagerly.

"And don't forget to hide under the straw," he shouted, as she hurried out the door holding her cute white puppy in her arms. The puppy was a Shih Tzu born in the Far East and brought to Palestine by caravan merchants.

After Deborah and her friend Malcah finished hiding the children under the straw, they peeped through a crack in the barn because they wanted to see what the soldiers would do. Deborah watched the soldiers ride up and stopped about twenty cubits away from the stable. The man who was riding ahead of the soldiers appeared to be the leader. Deborah could see that he was dressed in a fancy uniform of red and gold with a black leather girdle around his waist. He took off his gold colored helmet, which was a symbol of his rank, and held it in his left hand. There was no one outside to be seen.

"Lieutenant Sabar, order the people to come out," Sisera commanded, as he wiped the sweat from his baldhead.

"In the name of Jabin, the King of Canaan, and General Sisera, I command all of you to come out at once." There was complete silence, and no one moved. Again, the lieutenant spoke: "We know you are in there. If you are not out by the count of ten, we shall break down your doors and drag you out." He began to count, "One, two, three, four, five, six, seven—"

At the count of seven, an old man appeared at the door of one of the cluster of houses. He stepped out three feet and stopped. Next, the others opened their doors slowly and came out. Sisera put back on his gold colored helmet and nudged his horse forward a few feet. "I am Sisera, the commander of the King's army. Who is the head elder of this place?"

As Deborah peeped through the crack in the stable, she watched her uncle turn to one side and answered, "I am," he said softly.

"Speak up old man! What is your name?"

"Yoetz"

"What is your last name?" Sisera snapped.

"Yoetz Ben Joshua," he answered, stroking his long white woolly beard.

"Uh … Joshua," Sisera sneered with scorn. "Do you have your back taxes for last year?"

Elder Yoetz cleared his throat, hesitated, and then spoke. "No, General Sisera."

"And why not?"

"We've had a famine for the last two years, and we are a very poor village."

"Excuses, excuses, that's all I hear. Now, the King has ordered that if you do not pay your taxes, we will take two of your men to work in the stone quarries. We will also take two of your boys to be sacrifices in the fire to our god, Baal. Now, what will it be?"

"Oh my lord Sisera, I beg of thee. Ask us not to make a choice because we have no choice in this matter," remarked the elder, walking up close to Sisera. "I beg you, give us another year, my lord," he asked pitifully.

"You want another year? You have had an extra year already. Get out of my way old man," ordered Sisera, as he pushed the elder to one side.

As soon as Deborah saw this incident, she started to go out to help her uncle; but Malcah grabbed her arm. "You can't go out there, Deborah. If you do, you will be taken away and you will endanger all of us in here."

"You are right, Malcah."

Looking through the crack, Deborah saw and heard Sisera again.

"Lieutenant, take a squad of men and search the houses. There must be some children and young ladies around somewhere."

After a thorough search of all the adjacent houses, the lieutenant returned to Sisera. "General Sisera, we found only a cripple old man lying on the floor."

Then Deborah heard the lieutenant address Sisera: "Do you want me to search that stable over there?"

"That's a good idea, go right ahead."

As Deborah peeped through the crack, Malcah said, "The soldiers are coming, let's go and hide."

They hid behind a large pile of straw on the opposite side of the stable. As they were kneeling down on the ground, they heard the door open. Deborah held her puppy close to her rubbing his head gently. When the three soldiers passed through the door, they stopped and looked around cautiously. Everything was quiet and still. The lieutenant walked slowly over to an animal's stall and looked in it. No one was there. Afterwards, he walked back to the other side and he stepped on a dried twig and broke it. The puppy that Deborah held in her arms made a growling sound. The lieutenant looked at his men and asked, "What was that?" He put his hand on his sword and began to walk around the pile of straw. Then the lieutenant saw a pitchfork leaning against the wall. Without hesitation, he ordered one of his soldiers: "Take that pitchfork and poke it in the straw. If anyone is in there, he will jump out for sure." The soldier began to poke in the straw.

Deborah could see everything that was happening. Her lips moved in silence and she let the puppy loose. It ran over to the lieutenant and began sniffing around his feet and legs with its black nose. The attention of all the soldiers was now focused on the puppy.

"Oh, it's just a puppy. Ah, you are a cute, friendly little thing; and you have a nice royal look."

Suddenly, the lieutenant heard a shout. It was the voice of Sisera. "Do you see anyone lieutenant?"

The lieutenant rubbed the puppy on his head and remarked, "No General, not a soul, just a cute little puppy," and he walked out of the barn holding the puppy.

"Put that creature down. We have more important matters."

Finally, Sisera turned to Elder Yoetz. "Where are the young ladies? Did you send them off?"

"No, we married them off." He deceived him so that he would not place them in a risky situation.

"Well! Since you don't have the taxes, two of your young men will be taken and placed in hard labor." said Sisera angrily. "Seize them!" Sisera ordered his soldiers.

In the meantime, Deborah and Malcah returned to the front of the barn. Peeping through the crack, they could see and hear everything that was said.

Because the Canaanite soldiers seized the young men, Malcah cried. "They are taking my boyfriend. What am I going to do?" When Malcah hastened to walk toward the door, Deborah grabbed her arm.

"There is nothing you can do, Malcah; it is all in the hands of the Lord."

"But, I'll never see him again," she wept, looking at the door.

"You can't go out there. If you do, they will take you and abuse you. And finally, they will burn you in the fire as a sacrifice to their god, Baal. Do you want this to happen?"

"No," she replied crying on Deborah's shoulder.

Then Deborah heard Sisera once more. "Now, this is the King's order: Next year, your taxes will be twice as much; and if you cannot pay, your property will be confiscated."

"Oh lord Sisera," pleaded the elder. "We cannot pay this year's taxes; how are we going to pay double taxes next year?"

"That's your problem," shouted Sisera, as he grabbed the reins of his horse.

"You are milking us dry," cried the elder looking helpless. "You are like a man who milks the goat of all its milk, and then butchers the goat for its meat."

"I had enough of your whining. If you were as good at paying your taxes as you are with your flowery words, you wouldn't be in this situation."

Sisera turned his horse around and said to the elder, "Get out of my face old man," and then kicked the elder in the chest. The elder fell backward to the ground, and the soldiers galloped away. After the soldiers had gone, Deborah asked Malcah to bring out the children and young ladies. Following that, Deborah ran out to see how her uncle was doing.

"Are you all right, Uncle?"

"Yes, I'm fine I just feel like I was hit in the chest with a thunderbolt. How are the children?"

"They are fine, Uncle."

In the meantime, Malcah came out with the children. "The incident in the barn was a close call; that was a smart thing you did in the stable by letting the puppy loose." Malcah remarked. "It prevented the lieutenant from finding us. If you had not let the puppy loose, the lieutenant would have walked over in our direction and found us. What made you do it?"

"I was praying silently for God to help us, when suddenly, I heard a soft voice in my mind say; let the puppy loose, Deborah. Oh Malcah, I am so sorry that they took away your boyfriend, Dan," and she embraced her.

At that moment, Malcah sobbed, "Thank you, Deborah." She walked away while Deborah remained there listening to her uncle.

"Because you listened to the inner voice, which spoke to you in the stable," explained her uncle, "you saved yourself and everyone else. How did you feel when you heard the voice?" he asked, as both of them strolled over to a stone bench and sat down.

"At first, I hesitated because I didn't want to part with my dear puppy," she said, as the puppy played at her feet. Suddenly, he jumped on her lap. Then she picked him up and continued. "The voice was direct. It was as though God was inside me," she explained, caressing the white hair on the back of her puppy.

Her uncle turned to her. "You know, as time pass, I believe that you will become even more spiritual and possess a keener sense. You will become something like a prophetess, or seeress."

"How do you know this, Uncle?"

He turned towards her: "The passing years teach my dear child, and I've watched you grow up. You have a sharp mind and an unexplained good inner sense to know things. Now, I think it is time for me to teach you the steps of how to fast, to relax, to meditate and to purify your body and mind. We'll start tomorrow!"

Deborah turned around and looked down past several houses from where she was sitting. Seeing several women crying, she concluded that they were crying because Sisera took their sons captive. She got up and went over to them to express her sympathy for their loss.

After the terrible event of this day, Deborah never forgot the cruelties of General Sisera. Moreover, she knew that this would not be the last time that the Canaanite soldiers would affect her life.

Now, here was Deborah, almost 19 years later siting in her courtyard. She just finished telling Barak when she first had seen Sisera and had learned of his cruel ways.

Barak looked directly at her. "From your account of the story, I've learned a lot about you and Sisera. Deborah, I admire you for the way you handled yourself."

Chapter 10

It was in the late afternoon that Deborah escorted Barak to the factory which she had inherited from her late husband. The building was large; her workers made linen garments, fishnets, twine, shrouds, sails, and wicks. All these products were made from the flax plant that grew in the land of Israel.

"Deborah, a while ago, I mentioned to you that you have not said much about yourself. I mean—how do you feel about me?"

"Isn't it a little bit early for that," she reminded him gently.

"Did not Jacob fall in love with Rachel first sight … and did he not kiss her?" he asked, as he bent down to pick up a dried flax plant.

"Well, that was a different situation. Rachel was single living in her father's house. I've been married before … and now, I have the responsibility of my business and my communal duties to perform."

"Are you saying this because you are too busy and don't have time for me?"

She stopped walking, turned around, and remarked, "Yes and No! Let's think about it, Barak. You have your own estate; you are a prince of your tribe; moreover, you are the general of the northern militia. This makes you a very busy man." As they passed by a worker peeling stalks from the fibers of the flax plants, she asked, "Do we have time for each other?"

"Well, you do make a good argument; but it will not always be this way?"

"No. It probably won't. But there are other things."

"Other things?" he inquired, looking at her confused.

"Yes, other things. For example: permanency and spirituality in a relationship."

"Please explain Deborah," he asked, gently and sincerely.

"You see, Barak, if two people are going to have harmony in a relationship, they must be as one spiritually. You are a good man, but you believe in the might of your army, and I believe in spiritual things. This is the difference between us. It is not by might nor by power, but by the spirit of the Lord. Barak, if you can learn this, you will be more successful in your everyday struggles."

Barak listened carefully and took in every word without interruption. "I understand what you mean, Deborah. You are truly a spiritual woman."

"Barak, there is another thing that keeps me from thinking about you in a serious way. It is your dedicated fight with the Canaanites. My late husband died by the hands of the Canaanites, and if I open my heart to you, I would have to live in constant fear thinking that the same thing might happen to you. Can you understand the situation that I am in, Barak?" Deborah couldn't resist asking, with trembling in her voice.

Barak answered reluctantly. "Yes, I do."

"I am only trying to help you to understand that the greatest might and enlightenment comes from heaven. If you can't understand and accept this ... now ... I am sure that you will in the near future." Both of them walked by several stone buildings and noticed flax lying on the roofs to dry in the open air and sun which had been previously soaked in water. They saw and passed by another group of workers separating the fiber from the stalks. The last process was the hackling. Finally, they came to her supervisor, Madreech, who was giving instructions to a worker on how to weave the fiber into wicks to be used for lamps and torches.

The name of Deborah's late husband was Lapidoth which means torches. He first started his business by making wicks and torches. In the passing of time, they became known as the man and woman of torches.

As they were walking back to the house, a group of six year old boys and girls were frolicking on the grass in a playful manner; they were the children of the servants who worked on Deborah's estate. Also, two other boys played catch with a pomegranate. When Deborah and Barak passed by the boys, one of them threw the pomegranate over Barak's head and Barak reached up and caught it with one hand.

The boy responded, "That was a good catch …"

"Thank you, young fellow. Also, I use to play this game when I was young. By the way, what is your name?"

The boy who threw the pomegranate responded, "Ben." Ben was a light brown skin boy, small frame with curly brown hair.

"My name is Prince Barak. It is nice to meet you."

"Ben lives here with his mother," said Deborah. "His father died from a bad accident when he was two year old."

"I am so sorry to hear this," commented Barak. "How old are you now, Ben?"

"Six, when I grow up, I want to be tall and strong like you."

"Well, you will have to eat good food and work hard to build up flesh on your bones. Also, you need to increase your knowledge to help you in other areas of your life."

"I would like to know something about camels, can you teach me?" pleaded Ben, "can you?"

Barak looked at him with sympathy, and said, "All right, I'll tell you a few things then I will have to leave. First of all, there are two kinds of camels—the two-hump camels, and the one-hump camels. The two-hump camels are found mostly in colder countries north of here. This is why you don't see them around here. But the one-hump camels, you see them around here and countries to the South."

Ben looked down and then looked up eagerly. "Where do you sit on the two-hump camel?"

"You sit between the humps. Now I have to go Ben. Perhaps I'll see you again at another time."

"Thanks, Prince Barak." Then Ben ran off joyfully to the other boys and girls repeating: "Ha, ha, ha, I know something you don't know."

After hearing the entire conversation between Ben and Barak, Deborah added, "That boy likes you; you made him feel so good. You must understand Barak, that boy needs a good man to guide him through life and you are the man!" At that moment, Barak gazed at her attentively and nodded his head in agreement.

Passing yet further, they had about another one hundred cubits to go. Then Barak decided that he would ask Deborah about the two women who were walking about twenty-five cubits behind them.

"Deborah, I am curious … those ladies behind us have been following us for some time. Something is wrong! You sent me a letter a short time ago; and you didn't mention anything about the fact that you find me pleasing in your eyesight, or that you missed me. Something is wrong! When I first arrived to meet you today, I held out my hands to hold yours; and you refused my offer of affection. Something is wrong! Now, tell me … I beg thee; what's troubling you?"

"All right, Barak. I'll tell you. I was going to tell you anyway before you departed ... so this is as good a time as any," she revealed, being somewhat relieved.

"Thank you." Barak remarked, looking a little pacified.

"This is not going to be easy, Barak, and it has left me with a lot of emotional pain. You must understand. I am not really single."

His eyes expressed shock and disbelief. "What in the heck are you talking about?" he asked, with surprise and confusion. "Deborah, relieve me of this pain; and tell me that this is a joke!"

"Joke? Barak, I am serious. This is no joke. You've heard of levirate marriage, haven't you?"

"Yess ... Oh no ... !" exclaimed Barak, realizing the point she was making. He shook his head from side to side. "Are you saying that you are committed to marry your deceased husband's brother?" he asked, expressing complete shock. He moved closer toward her and threw his hands down and stared at her.

"I am saying that."

"What is his name ... and why did he wait so long to decide to fulfill his obligation?"

"His name is ... Caleb. I—I don't know ... I mean I am not sure why he waited so long. I wrote him three times and asked him to marry me or subject himself to halitza. The only reply he sent me was that he was busy, and he would contact me soon. But he didn't until a month ago."

"Deborah, what is halitza?"

"Halitza is a ceremony in which the husband's brother must perform when he refuses to marry his deceased brother's wife. The elders and judges can send for him and speak unto him concerning his obligation. If he still refuses, the deceased husband's wife can come unto him in the presence of the elders. Then she loses his shoe and removes it from his foot and spits before him and say so shall it be to the man who refuses to build up his brother's house. 'And his name shall be called in Israel, the house of him that has his shoe loose.' "

"Do you love this man?"

"Not in an emotional sense—but it is not—a question of love, Barak. It is a question of loyalty to the law and the love of family."

"Well, since you don't love him, why don't you ask him to refuse and let him subject himself to halitza?" he added.

"That would be contrary to everything I believe, contrary to what I teach, and contrary to my position as a judge. It would be like asking me to disregard the law of God which I am duty bound to obey. I couldn't do that. If I did, I would become a mockery to my people."

Barak took a deep breath and shook his head in dismay and anger. "Why in the heck did Caleb wait so long to give you a definite answer? Why now?" he sneered, as he walked between the palm trees. "Why now Deborah," he repeated, as he gestured with his hands.

"This is what I asked also. There was something that slipped out in my conversation with Caleb," Deborah remembered.

"And what was that?" Barak asked, as he turned around to face her.

"When Caleb admitted to me that he neglected earlier to give me his definite decision, he also said, 'But I am here now, ready to fulfill the law. You see, our marriage can also increase and combine our assets and I can get out ...' he paused. "I said to Caleb, out of debt, you mean, don't you? I understand, so you came here to make a proposal of marriage to help you get out of debt. "

"What was his response to that?"

"He said to me: 'The fact remains that you do have a legal obligation to marry me in spite of what you say my motive is.' I want you to understand, Barak that I agreed to marry him not because I love him ... not because I respect him ... not even because I trust him ... but only because it is my duty according to our custom and laws."

"Has a date been set for this so-called wedding?"

Deborah shook her head up and down in confirmation, and said: "You don't have to be sarcastic! The marriage will take place five months from now."

They approached close to the walkway that led to the back gate of the house. The stone walkway was lined with pretty green plants on both sides. The plants looked like green cactus. Barak stopped on the walkway; he looked defeated; he lowered his head; he scratched his eyebrow; he commented sorrowfully. "There must be something we can do ... something," he growled, as he clinched up his fist and hit the palm of his left hand. "Oh, we can hand this matter over to the judges in Shiloh," he added.

"Barak, I want to thank you for giving your attention to my problem and wanting to help me, but there is nothing else you can do at this time. Even if I handed this matter over to the judges, and they ruled in my favor by nullifying the marriage with Caleb, the turmoil from this action would cause a major uproar among my enemies."

"Before any more hair on my head turns gray, please explain to me how this action would cause a major uproar, Deborah."

"If the court ruled in my favor, sooner or later, the bad news would leak out that I bribed the court in order to free myself from marrying my deceased husband's brother who I didn't love.

"Mm," Barak gasped.

"If this happens, my critics and enemies would say, when God's law is beneficial to her—she upholds it, and when it is not, she skirts around it—so that she won't have to perform it. If this occurs, the court and I will lose the trust of the people; and there will be a further breakdown of justice. I can't let this happen, Barak. The importance and righteousness of our laws are greater than I am. I must do the Lord's will first; and then I believe He will work out His purpose even though we may not understand His purpose at first. Let's be patient Barak. Be patient my brother and place your hope in the Lord. Can you understand what I am saying?" she asked gently with compassion.

"Yes, I can understand. But it is hard for me to accept defeat and to accept the fact that you are engaged to a scoundrel you don't love."

"Barak, if this is hard for you, it is harder for me because I have to think about living with this man. At least, you don't have to live with him. Barak, I think you should just forget about me. Go! Find yourself another woman who is not anchored by levirate marriage."

He turned around and faced her. "I don't want another woman. I want you!" he pleaded, gesturing with both hands.

"Well, I am spoken for ... so just go, and leave me be!" she said, turning her back to him with her arms folded.

He approached close behind her and held her by her upper arm. She squirmed and shook herself loose from him. He pleaded. "Please, please Deborah, ask me to do some foolish thing like ... to jump off a pyramid in Egypt ... but ask me not ... to stop from wanting you, or to stop from pursuing after thee because my heart cleaves to you."

"You may want to give me your heart, but I cannot give you mine."

"I feel like you are treating me like a leper. Please Deborah, don't do this to me. When I am away from you … I think of you morning … noon … and night."

"There are plenty of beautiful women in Galilee, discover them Barak … and they will help you to forget about me."

Barak moved quickly in front of her and continued to press her. "I told you that I want only you … ! Can't you understand this? Even if you had a twin sister, I would still want only you!"

She looked up at him with her arms still folded in front of her. "I understand Barak, but you are the one that don't understand. You forget that by our law and customs, I am obligated to Caleb. This … I cannot change!"

Barak stood there speechless and frozen as if he had been struck by a snowstorm.

Then Deborah approached him softly and touched him gently on his muscular arm. "You seem deeply hurt by this, Barak." she observed.

"Yes," he snapped, with his eyes fluttering. "I haven't felt like this since the death … and the loss of my dear mother."

There was a silence then she struggled to speak. "I am sorry Barak, but there is nothing … nothing … I can do. I am so sorry."

Barak turned around with a little consolation on his face. He reached his hand into his inner garment and pulled out a leather pouch. "I bought something for you." He untied the thin leather cord and took out a necklace made from pure gold and diamonds.

Deborah opened her mouth and eyes wide with disbelief and surprise. "Ohhhh … Barak it is beautiful, so beautiful," she said, as she looked down at the necklace.

He pushed the necklace toward her. "Take it … ! It's yours. Take it … !" he urged her.

She took hold of it. "It is so thoughtful of you Barak," she said smiling. Then her countenance changed quickly, and her facial expression became serious. "Oh Barak, I can't accept this." She shoved the necklace back into his hand, turned around, and broke down in tears, dropping her face into the palms of her hands.

Barak took several steps toward her. Stung with hurt and disappointment, he continued. "Why?" he asked. "Why can't you accept it? I had this made with deep love!"

"But … I can't give you my love. Give it to someone else who can return your love."

"How can you expect me to give this necklace to someone else when I had it made especially for you … and only for you?"

Deborah seemed confused, and she felt fluttery inside. Then she squirmed and labored to speak. "Well …" she said hesitantly and slowly. "I'll accept it under one condition … that you expect nothing from me, understood?"

Barak nodded his head in acquiescence. "Yes."

"I want you to understand that I promise you nothing: no intimacy, no marriage, and no special favors."

Barak relaxed a little and explained. "I went through great sacrifice and effort to get this made for you … and I want you to have something of mine."

"I understand," she said.

"Well … the day is getting late," he said, showing exhaustion in his voice. "I must leave now."

She became silent again, and after a few moments, she spoke concerning their earlier conversation. "Oh Barak, previously you mentioned that one of the thieves you were searching for was a Canaanite who escaped. I just want to warn you that when Jabin and Sisera hear that you took your soldiers into the Jezreel, expect some reprisals."

"I think you are right, Deborah. I had thought about that also. Your warning confirms my thoughts, and I shall reinforce my security."

"I want to encourage you, Barak to continue to do good for humanity and this will multiply unto you the best in life. The good that you do will be written and remembered in the heavenly book of life … and when you are in dire straits, your Creator will come to your assistance," she explained compassionately.

"Thank you, Deborah. Your words are very encouraging."

Deborah stood there and watched him walk away slowly. She knew she could not tell him that she loved him. She knew that she could not let him kiss her or embrace her because she was duty bound to the levirate law. She could not even let herself be obsessed with him because that would certainly be a violation of her spirituality.

Deborah turned slowly and faced Barak. As she opened her mouth to speak, her words weighted heavily on her lips. When she spoke, her lips quivered and tears ran down her cheeks. She said, "Be careful Barak. I'll pray for you and for the safety of your soldiers, and keep me informed about the military situation. Go in peace and may God be with you."

Barak departed with a disappointed look on his face—he lowered his head—then raised it and said slowly, "Peace be with you Deborah."

Chapter 11

In the fortress City of Harosheth-ha-goiim, the high officials of this Canaanite stronghold began to gather for a very important meeting summoned by King Jabin. After all of the officials of state had assembled, King Jabin marched to his polished copper throne with his escort and soldiers.

The name Jabin was a title used by various kings of the City of Hazor. After Joshua, the successor of Moses, burned the City of Hazor, some of its people escaped from Hazor in Upper Galilee and fled westward to the southern area of the Carmel Mountain range not far from the Kishon River.

It was here that the Canaanite expert builders constructed a city fortress in the forest and named it Harosheth-ha-goiim. The kings of this city retained the title Jabin and the name Hazor, no doubt, for prestigious reasons because Hazor was the head or capitol of many Canaanite cities before Joshua destroyed it.

The king's throne was located at the far end of the Grand Hall of the Canaanites which was shaped like a rectangle. In back of the throne stood a huge bronze statue of the god, Baal with his brass helmet.

Courtiers and nobles stood along both sides of the hall. As the king walked briskly in, the eyes of everyone were fixed on him. The king passed by the columns that supported the edifice. Torches extended out from the walls every 15 feet to supply heat and light when needed.

"Attention in the name of the King," proclaimed the crier. King Jabin sat down on his throne wearing a purple toga with a golden border draped around his shoulders. He was already past seventy years of age, had the complexion of a coffee bean, a broad nose, thick lips, and was short and stocky. Then he turned to his ministers of state.

"Some of you are aware of why we are here today and some of you may not be. Therefore, I shall have my commander-in-chief of the army give you a complete report. To my left is General Sisera."

General Sisera stepped forward three cubits and began. "I shall set aside the formalities and get right to the point." The General was past sixty-five years old. Then he spoke. "We are here today to discuss the Hebrew problem. The situation has reached a new critical level," he said, as he removed his helmet and rubbed his baldhead.

"Keep it short as you can," the King reminded him.

"Yes, my king. The Hebrews are increasing in alarming numbers, and they are penetrating into the Valley. Our patrols are having more and more skirmishes with them. Recently, one of our spies reported that this ... Barak—a mountain fighter—brought his soldiers into the Jezreel Valley against the King's orders. Finally, Oh King, there are reports that a new leader is rising among the Hebrews," Sisera said reluctantly.

"And what is his name?" the Vizier asked, holding a map of Canaan in his hand.

The General was hesitant to mention the name. Because of fear that he would be ridiculed, he mumbled the name, "Deborah."

"What's wrong with you General? I cannot hear you. Speak up!" the King ordered, sitting up straight on his throne.

"Deborah," he repeated louder.

"That's a woman's name!" the Vizier commented. "Are you sure?" The ministers chuckled.

Sisera replied, "I am as sure as Mount Carmel overlooks the Great Sea."

The King said, "The name Deborah means bumblebee. Be careful … less she buzzes around and inflicts her sting on you … and on the entire Canaanite nation."

The Vizier took three steps to the right and returned. "Tell us something about this woman, Deborah!" he requested, as he struck the rolled up map into his left hand.

"She is supposed to be some kind of a judge," Sisera explained, "and a teacher of the laws and customs of her people."

The Vizier looked down with his dark brown eyes towards the floor then looked up and asked, "Is there anything else?"

"There is. I hear that she is a prophetess," Sisera added.

"Prophets and prophetesses are dangerous folks. Have you heard anything concerning what she prophesizes?"

"The only thing that I have heard is that she tells her people to repent, to return to the laws of their God, to give to the poor, to help the widows, to assist the fatherless, and to treat the strangers with kindness. Also, she teaches that our practice of marrying our daughters and sisters is an abomination before God. Furthermore, she says that our god and goddess, Baal and Ashtaroth, are idols; and the Hebrews should stop worshiping them; or they will face the wrath of their God."

"Blasphemy, blasphemy," yelled the High Priest who wore a large green miter on his head. "We can't let these Hebrews get away with this."

"That's right!" responded all of the ministers of state, looking at each other. "That's right"

The King stood up quickly with his golden turban-like crown sparkling. "I see that we have complete agreement in the Grand Hall," he said, as he sat down pulling aside part of his toga behind him.

"General Sisera, are you finished?"

"Not quite my lord. I have one more things to add."

"Let's hear it."

"Our spies inform me that this woman, Deborah, tells her people that if they obey their God, He will send them a deliverer. This deliverer, she said will crack the jaws of Jabin and his army."

"Did you hear that?" inquired the King, looking infuriated. "Her words are pregnant with the seeds of rebellion."

"I agree, my lord."

"Thank you, Sisera. I heard your report, and I listened to you carefully. We must use cunning in dealing with the Hebrew problem that is growing larger and larger every day. In view of this, this is what I propose. I want you to form yourselves into three committees and do a thorough study of the best way we can deal with these Hebrews. Come up with a good plan and use the best tactics you can. My Vizier will head the first committee; the High Priest will head the second committee; you, General Sisera, will head the third. Are there any questions?" There was no response and the King continued. "If not, report back to me in three weeks."

***

Now, at this time, the season was moving towards middle of the winter, and as usual, the winter manifested itself by providing plenty of rain in Israel. It had been raining for seven days without stop. When Deborah woke up this morning, she felt emotionally drained, and she wondered what kind of day it was going to be. Her instincts were telling her that an exciting unexpected event was going to happen. Therefore, she prepared herself for any eventuality. She usually would meet three times a week with visitors to discuss their various problems and give her decisions. This morning was one of those days. The people would be coming, so she quickly got dressed.

After she finished breakfast, she walked toward the study room and bumped into the side of the door. "My lady, you appear a little tired today," commented Sarah. "Maybe it would be better to have public meetings just twice a week instead of three times, and that would give you more time to rest."

"Thank you, Sarah. I'll be all right. It is a mental thing … you know … mind over matter. You see Sarah; when we came into this world, we came to experience ups and downs, to learn our lessons in life, to grow spiritually, and to help others."

"Well, you are surely doing just that; I must say," she agreed, as she tightened her white apron around her waist.

"Sarah, before I go to prepare for this morning's meeting, I would like to make a point. When my soul separates from my body and is greeted by my departed ancestors and finally passes over to God, then the body that I leave here on earth will have plenty of time to rest."

"My lady," Sarah said, as she walked away looking thoughtful, "you are as deep as a well of water."

Whenever Deborah had a meeting scheduled, she would place a piece of papyrus on the table. As the people came into the sitting area, they would write down their names; and Sarah would call up the attendees on a first-come, first-served basis. The only deviation from this procedure was in the case of an emergency.

After a while, the people started coming—men, women, and young adults. Deborah came in later with two of her handmaids, two male servants—and one was Nachshon. These men helped keep order; and they could handle themselves very well because they received their training in the army of Shamgar, the last judge.

When Deborah entered, she greeted everyone with the word peace and a big smile. "It is so nice to see more young men and ladies here today, and because you came, I want to take this opportunity to speak to you about being good fathers and mothers. Before you have children or get married, it is very important that you make the right decisions because the decisions you make are going to affect your life, your children, and your relatives for many years to come. A short time of pleasure, if there is any, can disrupt your life and cause you many headaches if your decision is not well thought out and planned. Bringing children into this world is a great responsibility. If both of you are not ready for parenthood, don't rush into it. When you want children, you should not only think about what makes you happy but also what will make the children happy emotionally. Most boys who have emotional problems are from families where the father is not in the home for one reason or another ... ." Deborah paused for a moment.

"Mother Deborah, can you tell me what are some of these emotional problems?" asked a young lady.

"Many boys who grow up without the guidance of their fathers during the early years of their lives tend to be shy, distant, fearful, resentful, dependent, girlish, and immature. So be careful about raising boys without fathers."

Another lady far back in the courtyard raised her hand and spoke. "My name is Huldah Bat Navi and I live at home with my grandmother, my mother, my three sisters, and my eight year old brother. He has some of the same emotional problems you just mentioned. Is there anything that can be done for him?"

"Yes, where is your father?"

"He died six years ago."

"From what you are telling me, your brother is being raised around all females. When there is no father in the home, find a substitute father for the boys. I am referring to a good role model. She continued, "This substitute can be a step-father, an older brother, an uncle, a grandfather, an older cousin, or just a decent man in the neighborhood who is willing to guide a young boy in becoming a good man. Ladies, we can provide a boy with food, clothing, shelter, money and schooling, but we cannot be an example to boys because we are females. Boys need good males to be their examples. On the same token, a father cannot be an example and cannot teach his daughter how to be a woman. Only another woman can do that by teaching and being an example day by day."

After Deborah completed her talk about being good fathers and mothers, she proceeded to deal with the matters at hand. Sarah read the first name on the list. After Deborah had finished answering the questions of the first two names on the list, Sarah read the third name. This was part of Sarah's duties because she could read and write in three languages.

"The third name on this list is Shemurah of the tribe of Judah," Sarah called out, as she looked around the crowd for her to answer.

"I am Shemurah. Excuse me my dear sister for not responding right away. First of all, I want to thank Deborah for having these important hearings. These meetings permit us to get our questions answered by someone who knows our holy writings. I live near the City of Jebus, where the Jebusites dwell, and my son met a Canaanite girl he wants to marry. Since she is not Hebrew, can my son marry her?"

"Is that the young lady and your son sitting next to you?" Deborah inquired.

"Yes, this is my son Adam, and over here is his friend, Tamar." Tamar had smooth skin. She reflected the radiance of the full moon and the purity of the springtime. Also, she had a tender loveliness that mesmerized.

"She is very beautiful, and I get a very good feeling about her. Tell me … where are your parents?"

"They are in the City of Jebus."

"Do they know that you are here?"

"No! My parents put me out two months ago, and I now live with Mrs. Shemurah."

"In one sense," said Deborah, "You are fortunate; your father could have given you up to be sacrificed for a price," she pointed out softly. "I want you to forgive your father. When you forgive, you relieve yourself of a heavy burden and you grow spiritually."

"That's hard," Mother Deborah … but I'll try."

"Why did they put you out, my dear?"

"My family is very poor, and there are 13 brothers and sisters. My father said to me, many times, that he would put me out as soon as I reach childbearing age," she cried, as tears ran down her brown cheeks.

Deborah paused a moment so that Tamar could get herself together. Tamar wore a beige color shawl over her head which drooped over her shoulders. "Tamar, how did you meet Adam and Mrs. Shemurah?"

"I first met Adam at the marketplace where I went to buy food for my mother. Here, we use to meet from time to time and talk. On the day that my father put me out, he said to me, 'You are a woman now, you can earn a living for yourself. I cannot afford to take care of you any longer, but here are a few coins to help you get started.' As I left the house, my mother stood at the door and watched me leave without saying a word."

Mrs. Shemurah felt her sorrow. "It is so sad when a daughter is put out of the house, and a mother has nothing to say."

"I wandered around the marketplace until almost sunset; and then I started down the road not knowing where I was going. That's when I met Mrs. Shemurah. She saw me crying and asked what was troubling me. I told her my situation, and she invited me to stay with her," Tamar said, as she wiped the tears from her eyes.

Deborah took a deep breath and sighed. Tamar's story was so touching that it struck at the core of her humanity. She knew that she had to answer Mrs. Shemurah's question—could her Hebrew son marry a Canaanite girl? Deborah knew that there is an answer to the question, but it was not an easy one. The answer should be given in a compassionate and prudent manner. If not, she thought, it would be heaping more hurt on the top of an existing hurt. "We all are stricken with grief from the rejection, which this young lady has received from her father, and we feel her pain. Will you please come up here?"

"Are you speaking to me?" asked Tamar.

"Yes," Deborah said, holding out her hand and drew her close. "Are you feeling better now?"

"Yes!" Tamar answered, looking shy as she cast her head down.

"You see Tamar, every nation and people have their laws and customs; and they are different from one another. Now, the Hebrew laws are very different from most nations." Deborah then took her hand and placed it around Tamar's shoulders. "Tamar, my dear, the Hebrew law is very clear on the point of marriage. It states that we shall not give our daughters to other nations to marry, nor shall we take their daughters for our sons," she said to her softly and gently, as she pulled Tamar closer to her.

With her head lowered, Tamar lifted her head and eyes slightly and said, "I love Adam! Is there something I can, at least ... do?" Adam was a strong, handsome looking young man with dark brown eyes, black hair, and stood six feet tall.

"Well ... there is one thing ... but you would have to make a sacrifice," Deborah assured her.

Tamar looked puzzled. "Mother Deborah, what do you mean by that?"

"You would have to give up something in order for a marriage to take place. By that, I mean you would have to study about our laws and customers for at least one year. Second, if you find that our God and laws are acceptable, you would be asked to give up the graven images of Baal, Ashtaroth, and the other gods with which you were raised."

"Would there be some kind of ceremony after the one year training period?"

"You would have to stand before our priest and elders, and they would ask you questions about our laws and customs. After that, you would be required to take an oath testifying to the fact that you believe in the invisible God of the universe, and the laws that He gave unto his servant Moses, the prophet.

Finally, you would have to undergo purification. This includes the taking a ritual bath and then rinsing or immersing the entire body under pure rainwater collected in a pool. When all of this is completed, you will be accepted as one of us, just as Zipporah, the Midianite wife of Moses, was accepted among us. Does this seem like something you would want to do?"

Without hesitation, Tamar answered, "Yes!"

"Now, you don't have to make a quick decision today." Deborah explained, "You can take your time … and think about it, my dear child."

"Mother Deborah, I thank you; but in all due respect, I don't need to think about it, because I have lived with Mrs. Shemurah for the last two months, and she lives a very righteous life. If it is all right with you and Mrs. Shemurah, I stand ready to begin my studies now."

"All right … it is your decision, my dear."

At that climatic moment, Mrs. Shemurah and her teenage son, Adam, ran up and embraced Tamar and Deborah. Mrs. Shemurah and her son thanked her for all her help.

"Deborah, you were just remarkable. You handled yourself well," Shemurah said, as her husband, Eli walked up.

He confirmed the words of his wife. "Now, I can understand why you find favor in the eyesight of so many people. I had to see for myself; and I am astonished at your knowledge, compassion, and wisdom. Truly, the spirit of the Lord abides within you. The training I give my son in masonry and carpentry will increase since he will be getting married in a little over a year. This trade will help him to support his wife and family."

"I commend you for your interest you are taking with your son. More fathers should follow in your same footsteps," Deborah commented smiling.

"In addition," he added, "I have been thinking about inviting other boys in our neighborhood to take training along with my son."

"I am glad you have become not only a person of success but also a man of value to our community," Deborah intimated.

"Well, thank you, Deborah."

Deborah looked down then glanced quickly at Tamar. "Hundreds of years ago, there was a righteous king who ruled over your City of Jebus and the name of Jebus at that time was Salem. The name of that king was Melchizedek, and he was also a priest of the Most High God. Our ancestor, Abraham, received his earthly learning from him; this included the secret teaching of the ages. When Abraham received the teachings and a blessing from Melchizedek, his spiritual force increased to a higher degree. Abraham paid him tithes to show his thanks. You must understand, Tamar, that many of your ancestors learned about the Most High God from Melchizedek but as time passed, many of these teaching disappeared."

"How do you know all of this?"

Deborah touched her gently on the arm and continued, "There are old records in the Tabernacle at Shiloh which mention this, my dear child."

Before Mrs. Shemruah and her family departed, Deborah made arrangements for Tamar to meet with her once a month to review her studies. Moreover, Deborah informed Mrs. Shemurah that if Tamar needed a job, she could come and work at her estate.

***

Not too far away in the City of Hebron, the elders and princes of the southern Hebrew tribes of Simeon, Benjamin,

Dan, and Judah held an important meeting. The subject of the meeting was to discuss the rising star of Deborah which they considered a threat to their authority.

The meeting with the princes took place in the rear courtyard of Prince Abihu's estate. Within the center of the white walls of the courtyard, grew a large terebinth oak tree spreading its broad branches in all directions. The elders and princes sat on stone benches covered with cushions along the side of the walls.

Prince Abihu of the tribe of Judah had just completed the welcoming ceremony for the meeting. "All of you have been informed of why we are here," said the thirty-five-year old Prince, wearing a dark blue toga. "Now, feel free to voice your opinions," he said, rubbing his big belly."

"This woman—Deborah—as they call her—is taking away from us the loyalty of our people. Something should be done about it," stressed the Prince from the tribe of Dan.

"Yes, more and more of our people are ignoring us," shouted several others.

Then the Prince of the tribe of Simeon came forward. "There are some people who call her a prophetess. Where is it written in our holy books that a woman can be a prophetess? This kind of behavior is insulting to us. Are we going to let a mere woman take the leadership of the princes?"

"No! No!" they shouted.

"The leadership of the tribes belongs to the tribe of Judah. Is it not written that the scepter shall not depart from Judah?" Prince Abihu reminded them. He continued, "After the death of Joshua, the children of Israel asked the Lord saying, 'who shall go up first against the Canaanites to fight against them? And the Lord said Judah shall go up.' You understand ... the leadership belongs to the tribe of Judah and we cannot let a woman humiliate us," intimated the shrewd prince with piercing eyes.

Then the Prince of the tribe of Benjamin turned to the crowd. "If we let her get away with this, we will lose control of our women; and they will follow in her footsteps."

"Well, what can we do?" Another prince asked.

"I will get to that in a moment," answered Prince Abihu. "Our spies have reported to us that Barak has been seen at least twice at Deborah's estate. They must have some kind of an alliance or a romantic interest or both."

"But, what can we do?" asked the twenty-five-year old prince from the tribe of Benjamin.

Abihu then looked down; he thought; then he raised his head. "I can think of two things: One, we can send a letter to Deborah expressing our dissatisfaction with the way she is placing herself in a man's role. Two, we can send a letter to Barak asking him to come and answer certain questions. After that, we shall know whether or not we can support his war efforts."

"Yes ... that sounds good to all of us," they shouted in confirmation.

"Good!" Then Abihu said, "I will have my scribe to write the letter tonight."

CHAPTER 12

Three weeks later in the fortress City of Harosheth-ha-goiim, which was nicknamed Hazor, the high officials of King Jabin began to assemble for the second important meeting. It was three weeks earlier that King Jabin had appointed three committees to come up with the recommendations to deal with the Hebrew situation. Now, these committees were ready.

King Jabin was a huge muscular man who sat on his throne made of polished copper. The throne was covered with animal skins dyed in purple and scarlet. Guards with spears and swords stood on both sides of the throne. The King had a dark brown complexion with bulging cheeks.

The first order of business on this day was the receiving of the ambassador of Ethiopia. After this had been finished, the King summoned his advisors and the three committees to approach the throne. Before he opened the meeting, he asked the High Priest to render a short prayer: "Oh Baal, our god, praise be thy great name. May thy might and power continue to possess the entire earth; and give us the strength and the wisdom to overcome our enemies, the Hebrews."

"We all know why we are here today, so without further delay, we shall hear from my Vizier, Mashchit."

"My lord, the King, I recommend that we impose more taxes on the Hebrews; and if they falter, we can confiscate their property and put them into hard labor. Point number two: Let the King send out a decree that states that, if any Hebrew brings any of their flocks into the Jezreel Valley, the flocks will be confiscated. Point number three: I recommend that the King offer ten talents of gold for information leading to the capture of Barak. Point number four: And pertaining to this woman called Deborah, I recommend that we send out additional spies to keep a close watch on this queen bee. A queen bee like her could be dangerous, oh King."

"I'll give that some consideration," the King added. "Now, I want to hear from General Sisera."

The General stepped forward in full uniform with his sword on his side, saluted the King, and removed his gold helmet. "My lord, I am in favor of a complete declaration of war against the Hebrews that are north of the Jezreel Valley."

"Why do you recommend war at this time?" inquired the King, as he leaned forward.

"It would be easier to destroy them while they are weak. Every day that we delay, they will increase in numbers and skill."

"Why haven't Barak and his men been caught?"

"There are two reasons, my lord. For one thing, he is as fast as lightening, and that's what his name means. Two, he manages to avoid our larger units on level ground where our chariots are most effective. Instead, he fights mostly in the mountains, hills, in gullies, and ravines where it is very difficult for us to use our horses and chariots against him."

"If that is the case, we must set a trap for him and lure him out into the opening," commented the King, as he placed his elbow on his armrest.

"Another thing my lord, recently, my spies informed me that there has been contact between Deborah and Barak."

"Mm, interesting," the King muttered. "How was this contact made?"

"A horseman was seen receiving something from Barak and he went to the house of Deborah."

After listening to Sisera's words, the King commented, "Have your men continue to watch these two hungry scorpions."

"It is done, my lord."

"Now, I want to hear from our High Priest, Eved-Baal, who is the servant of Baal, our god. He wore a green miter on his head decked with silver and precious stones.

The entire hall of officials gave him a big applause as he walked in the direction of the King. "My priests and I have studied the records of the nations that had contact with these Hebrews. These nations are the Egyptians, the Midianites, the Moabites, the Babylonians, and the Assyrians. We have checked their records and oral reports to see how these nations dealt with the Hebrews. Our search led us to a very interesting conclusion, oh King."

"And what might that be?" inquired the King, as he leaned forward from his reclining posture.

"We found out that they can be conquered easier if we can get them to sin against their God."

"How do you know this?" the King asked.

"Well … we have learned this from the records of Balaam, the prophet of Mesopotamia; from the records of Balak, the king of Moab; and from the scrolls of the Hebrews, called Numbers and Deuteronomy. In some of these scrolls, it is written that if the Hebrews don't keep the commandments of their God, He will curse them."

"In which way would their God curse them?"

"He will curse them with famine, disease, destruction, slavery, oppression, captivity, mental suffering, etc."

"You mentioned that you had searched out the histories of such nations as the Midianites and the Moabites. What did your historical research uncover?" the King asked eagerly.

"After reading the histories of these nations, we read that Balak, the King of Moab, summoned the leader of the Midianites to discuss how they could deal with the Hebrews because they were afraid of them. Finally, they decided to call Balaam of northern Mesopotamia to put a curse on the Hebrews. After Balaam arrived, he told Balak that he could not curse Israel because they were blessed."

"Why were they blessed?"

"They were blessed for the very reason that their God didn't find any iniquity among them nor had He seen any corruption in Israel. In other words, my lord, they were living according to the ways of their God; and they could not be cursed. However, soon thereafter, everything changed. Finally, Balaam explained to the Midianites and the Moabites how they could get Israel to sin."

"Go on ... continue."

"The Moabites did according to the words of Balaam," explained the High Priest. "They brought out the most beautiful seductive Moabite and Midianite women, and the Hebrew men were seduced by them. After that, these women called the Hebrew men to the service of their god; and the Hebrews bowed down to them and corrupted themselves in the eyesight of their God. According to the Hebrew and Midianite scrolls, the God of the Hebrews became angry; and He inflicted a plague on them that killed over twenty thousand Hebrews for their iniquities."

"Very interesting," said the King. "I want to thank you and your associates for the fine work you have done. Is there anything else?"

"Yes my lord. These Hebrews came into our country over one hundred and fifty years ago under the leadership of a man called Joshua, and they have been taking our land ever since. They are like the ox that licks up the grass. They must be stopped or else they will take all our land and destroy our culture including our gods," continued the High Priest.

"What do you suggest we do to get the Hebrews to commit iniquity?" asked the Vizier.

"We can put on festivals in various cities and invite the Hebrews to come. Then get our women to lure them into dancing, drinking, and you know what will follow next. The ladies will seduce them to drink and to eat creeping things. After that, the Hebrews will worship our gods," remarked the High Priest.

"What else can we do to weaken and destroy the Hebrews?" asked General Sisera.

"We can use an old plan called divide and conquer by sowing the seeds of jealousy and hatred among the various princes and heads of the Hebrew tribes. By taxing one leader and not taxing another, we can create discord and distrust among the tribes and families. This can be achieved by giving gifts to those families who worship our gods, Baal and Ashtaroth. Making one family feel that it is better off than another, we will weaken the families and communities and produce more disunity," stated the High Priest with confidence.

"Excellent!" exclaimed the King.

"Ah! My lord, there is one more thing. This ... this woman, Deborah, I think that something should be done about her."

"Are you afraid of a mere woman?" inquired the King.

"Yes! Somewhat! I am fearful of what she can do to our nation, to our people, and to our gods. Her rapid rise in a man's world is a dangerous omen in itself," the High Priest said, looking disturbed.

"Do you think that this mere woman can rise to be a leader over the Hebrews?" asked the King.

"Yes!" answered the High Priest. "We remember the rise of Queen Hapshesut in Egypt. She became the supreme ruler of the land because the gods favored her. It is very possible that Deborah can rise also."

"I shall have my spies keep a close eye on her if this will please you," Sisera volunteered.

The King stood up on his feet. After that, he walked back and forward three times in front of his throne looking down in deep thought with his hands behind his back. He stopped in front of his throne and faced toward his ministers and spoke. "Our plan will be to weaken and to destroy the Hebrews. We shall put into action various methods to get the Hebrews to sin against their God, and I will leave those methods up to you to implement. Are there any further comments or questions? If there aren't, you are now free to proceed with the implementation of our plans."

After the meeting, the three committees went to work right away, discussing, reviewing, and putting the finishing touches on their plan to corrupt and destroy the Hebrews. According to the King, this was a matter of urgency and was to be put into action in a few days. First, they decided to carry out their plan against the Hebrew village near the City of Nahalol.

***

In the meantime, far in the Zebulun hills, Barak was relaxing in his tent. Then Barak heard the approach of a fast running horse. He quickly stood up and looked through the opening. There he could see a young man riding through his camp. The rider said, "I have a letter for General Barak. Where is he?"

"You are looking at him. Who sent the letter?"

"It is from my lord, Prince Abihu," answered the young man, as he dismounted his ebony colored horse.

"Oh yes, Prince Abihu … I've been waiting to hear from him. Finally, he has written to me." Barak took the letter and began to read:

> *To my fellow Prince Barak, Shalom lha (peace be unto you). I hope you are well these days. I shall not trouble thee with the small talk and get right to the heart of the matter. I have met with the elders and princes of the southern Hebrew tribes to consider your request for our soldiers. I would like for you to come to Hebron to meet with me so that I can be able to make a final decision. I do expect to see you soon.*
> *Abihu Ben Abinadab.*

After Barak finished reading the letter, he lowered the letter to his waist, raised his head, and smiled. He thought—could it be that Prince Abihu was now ready to supply Judean soldiers to help him fight the Canaanites. This was the very moment he was waiting for, and he was optimistic. He could not wait to return to the City of Hebron to meet with Abihu, the Prince of the largest tribe among the Hebrews.

CHAPTER 13

The cool rainy winter season passed and the warm bright spring came bringing in the first great Hebrew festival of the civil New Year called the Passover. It commemorates the liberation of the Hebrews from the Egyptian bondage. Deborah is expected to attend this event in the City of Shiloh, and she is planning to give a speech. A month earlier, she sent letters to all the tribes informing them that she has a special message for them. As a result of sending out the letters, she heard that some adversaries had planned to attend and challenge her knowledge and authority; the details of this unknown made her feel uneasy. At the festivals, it was mandatory for all males to make annual pilgrimages to the Tabernacle on Passover, the Feast of Weeks, and on the Feast of Booths. God commanded all males to attend, but it was optional for females. At Deborah's estate, Sarah approached and asked, "My lady, when shall we leave to go to Shiloh for the Passover?"

While Sarah asked her question, Deborah was running back and forward making last minute preparations for the journey. "We shall be leaving ..." she paused, gulped down some water, took a deep breath, and panting she uttered, "in a short while, Sarah."

This is one of the busiest festivals of the year. The roads are crowded with thousands of pilgrims going up to the Tabernacle. There are pack animals loaded down with food and drinks to last them for seven days. Furthermore, the people will slaughter sheep and goats at the Tabernacle, the priest will burn the fat on the altar, and he will sprinkle the blood at its base. Each head of the household will take the lamb or goat to his quarters and roast it.

Meanwhile, here in the City of Shiloh, the people are gathering for the main event. "Where is Deborah? Has anyone seen her?" many people asked. There was no positive answer, and many people shook their heads in disappointment and concern.

"Deborah said that she would be here, but she is not," explained a middle-aged woman. Some people shook their heads again then went on their way. This was a great time for the celebration of freedom from oppression in Egypt. The priests and the Levites blessed God and sang psalms of praises to the Lord, and the people responded in the proper manner. After this, the voices of the people broke out in joyful singing of Hebrew spirituals and clapping hands.

During this season of the Passover—also known as the Feast of Unleavened Bread—Deborah is expected to speak at the plaza just outside of the Tabernacle. This feast would give an opportunity for Deborah and Barak to speak to many people from every tribe at once. The both of them knew that the Hebrew-Canaanite crisis was getting worse. It was getting worse at a time when the Hebrew people were celebrating their freedom from slavery in Egypt. It was just three weeks ago, that King Jabin and his advisors devised a sinister plan to corrupt and destroy the Hebrews.

Finally, Deborah arrived with her bodyguard and handmaid. As she walked through the crowd going up front, the people greeted her with kind words and warm smiles. "We are so happy to see you mother Deborah; we were concerned about you," said a young woman.

"Thank you," she said. "I was in prayer and meditation."

After the priests had completed the morning ritual and sacrifices on the second day of the Unleavened Bread, the people gathered in the plaza to listen to the speeches of Deborah, Barak, and the elders. A representative of the high priest spoke then Barak and a few elders. Deborah was the last person to speak. She felt a little nervous being among all the men such as the representative of the high priest and the Levite officials. But then she eased her mind when she realized that God's presence, Barak and Elder Ariel stood there with her. She knew that she had to be strong like Sarah, Abraham's wife and Miriam, the sister of Moses. She also knew that the Lord was using her for a special purpose.

"Peace, be unto you brothers and sisters of the various tribes. First, I want to give thanks and praise to the Lord our Creator for giving us life and strength. Moreover, it is pleasing in my heart to give thanks to all the priests, Levites, and elders for their untiring service they have given to our people. I would like to say that my Uncle Yoetz, who sat on the Supreme Court of the Council of the Seventy Elders, wanted to be here, but he is now past one hundred and five years old and very weak."

"Yes, we know him," said several of the elders respectfully.

"As many of you know," she continued, "we are here to celebrate the Feast of the Unleavened Bread. It was at this time several hundred years ago that the Lord our God brought out our ancestors from the Egyptian bondage. However, our people today, especially the northern tribes, are suffering under a new oppression of Jabin, the king of the Canaanites. As of this month, it has been twenty years since Jabin and his General Sisera imposed their persecution upon us."

"Um!" Many of the people sighed looking at one another.

"Within the last two weeks," she explained further with eloquence, "we have seen the tension intensify between the Canaanites and us. They have increased their patrols in the Hebrew territory. They have imposed higher taxes on top of existing taxes; and those who cannot pay, they place in hard labor. Furthermore, they are doing everything that they can to get our people to convert to their pagan customs and to worship their idols. I want to encourage all of you to resist the efforts of the Canaanites. I have talked to the elders about this; and we want you to fast, to pray, to cry out, and to pour out your souls in sincerity to God; and He will save us. I feel that war is coming, and I want you to be prepared. I feel this very strongly. If we do this, our deliverance will come soon. I promise you this in the name of our God and in the name of our ancestors. In closing, I want all of you to pray every day; and I shall pray for you and for all of our people. However, remember—that the enemy from among us is far worse than the external one. This means that sometimes we can be our own worst enemy."

When she finished her speech, the people gave a great applause and shouted hallelujah. Many people crowded around and waived to her. In addition, Barak and Elder Ariel continued to stand next to her leaning on his wooden stick. He was eighty-nine years old. At that moment, the people began to ask questions.

"Will God send us a deliverer like Joshua, Ehud, or Othniel?" asked an elderly woman.

"Yes. I believe that He will when our people become more spiritual and righteous."

Another short woman rose up on her tiptoes and asked, "We have been waiting for our deliverance for almost twenty years, and it has not come. Why?"

"We are not ready yet. The sins of our people have caused God to hide His face from the tribes of Israel. The Lord wants sincerity of heart—not talk. What benefit is there to be freed from one bondage and then go into another! This is like being saved on one day from the tiger; and on the next day, you fall into the claws of the lion. When we don't treat each other right, we become our own worst enemies."

"What can we do, Deborah?"

Deborah thought deeply. "Put away the idols, jealousy, lying, adultery, greed, selfishness, hatred, and serve the Lord. Learn self-control and patience. Let every man and woman speak the truth to his neighbor. Act with justice in all your dealings. Give to the widows, the fatherless, and the poor. Behave kindly to the strangers and walk humbly before God and your fellowman."

"These words, which you speak, I have been doing for many years," a middle-aged man pointed out. "Is there more for us to do? Is there more, Mother Deborah?"

"Yes, much more. The Lord wants more of you to give more. I am talking about, not only shekels of gold and talents of silver, but also about non-material things, such as giving a smile, giving conversation, giving a listening ear, giving a helping hand, and giving a kind word. In short … with your willingness to give what you seek for yourself—you keep the abundance of the divine universe flowing in your lives because the energies of the universe flow in powerful exchange. This means, that you will be blessed in wealth, good health, and happiness."

"Talk on Deborah," yelled a woman from the rear of the crowd, "hallelujah."

"When a rich man sees people starving and needing medical help and refuse to give it, this is cruelty. On the other hand, if a man or woman see a rich person in a bad accident and refuse to help him or her, this is also cruelty. You will be expressing true love to all of Adam's descendants, when you give in these ways to humanity, and goodness and success will return to you. This is what the Lord meant when He commanded, 'Love thy neighbor as thyself.'"

A young person about twenty cubits back in the crowd yelled. "Is this what our first great prophet taught?"

"Yes! Our prophet, Moses, taught that if you would keep all of the Lord's commandments and follow His instructions, all the blessings of the universe would come unto you. Because what goes around comes back around, whether it is for evil or good. If you perpetrate evil, evilness will return to you. If you show goodness, goodness will return to you. This is the universal law of God."

As Barak looked over the crowd, he saw a man with a potbelly pressing his way forward through the crowd. Because the man looked suspicious, Barak moved closer to Deborah to be of help if she needed it.

At that moment, the man shouted. "I never heard of you. Who are you?"

Deborah took a deep breath, remained calm, and then spoke. "I am Deborah Lapidoth, a servant of God, and a daughter of Israel."

"I know that!" he yelled.

Barak interrupted him, "If you knew that, why did you ask?"

Then the people roared out in laughter at the man. Finally, the crowd became quiet, and the potbelly man spoke up again. "Shouldn't you be at home cooking and washing dishes?"

Deborah knew that the man had insinuated that she was out of her place. Nevertheless, she remained confident and spoke calmly. "At one time, I did these things as my everyday duties. Now, since the Lord has blessed me, I have servants and workers to assist with these chores. I can now dedicate my life to helping others to attain higher spiritual heights."

The potbelly man looked defeated and spoke again. "One more question."

Barak aggressively intervened, "Are you looking for trouble?"

"No! I am looking for an answer. I am here to have a good time. Isn't that what this festival is all about?" he asked, looking around the crowd for support. A few people nodded their heads in consent, but most remained silent.

"You may speak," Deborah permitted.

The potbelly man continued. "You said for us to give more. My wife and I give tithes to the priest. We have 15 sons and daughters to feed, and she gives to the poor. As it is, I do not get enough to eat. What shall I do?"

"Well, you don't look any thinner to me!" Barak snapped, as the crowd roared again in laughter.

Deborah smiled at Barak's response, and then she asked the man a question. "Do you have any sheep or goats?"

"Yes. I have 15."

"Keep giving, and next year you will have more than twenty-five."

"What's going to happen then?"

Deborah looked at him with surprise. "I thought you knew! There will be a mating of your sheep … and God will bless you."

Moments later, a young man raised his hand and remarked, "We are now in this land, we speak the Hebrew language, we have our princes and elders, and lastly, we have our customs, rituals, nationality, and the history of our ancestors. I feel that we have everything. What do you think?"

"You shouldn't live on just the laurels of your past ancestors. If you do, you are like a potato: the only good thing belonging to you would be underground." The people received her words hard and shook their heads up and down in agreement. "There are more important things then just having and knowing your history, language, culture, and nationality. Our main purpose here on earth is to serve humanity and not just be religious, but above all, to be spiritual."

"Spiritual? What is the difference between being religious and being spiritual?" asked the young man.

Deborah took a deep breath and relaxed her shoulders. "A religious person is one who keeps the beliefs and practices the ceremonies of his religion in the home or the house of worship remaining faithful to God. However, a spiritual man or woman has a pure heart. They are in tune with God every day, and they do not hold feelings of jealousy, anger, resentment, grudges, negativity, nor hatred in their heart against any person. The spiritual person loves humanity in a pure way, without conditions. This is what Our Creator meant when He said—to be a 'holy people.' "

"Mother Deborah, when I am nice to some people, they treat me mean; and when I help certain groups of people, they don't give me credit. What shall I do?" the young man asked.

"Continue to love them ... no matter how long it takes. Your good conduct will eventually break the cycle of hate ... and win them over to your side."

"This seems so hard to do with hateful people."

"Well, sometimes the best things in life come with difficulty. Remember, true love is caring and sharing. Furthermore, I want to remind all of you that our wise men such as: Enoch, Melshizedek, Abraham, and Moses taught that you should strive to be a holy people, and love thy neighbor as thyself. Now, to express love in the true sense is to give something to another without expecting anything in return. When you perform acts of random kindness for mankind, God knows your thoughts, your good deeds, and He will send you a blessing and help you when you most need it. Therefore, you don't have to worry about receiving credit from anyone."

At that moment, Elder Ariel turned to Deborah. "I am inviting you, Barak, and your company to come to my house for lunch."

"Thank you Elder, but before I go, I want to say a few last words to the people. People of the tribes of Israel," she said. "I am going to be leaving you soon; but before I go, I want to encourage you to pour out your soul to God in prayer, meditation, and fasting. Remember, we can have better neighborhoods if we as citizens are willing to give up some of our personal ambitions and work for the betterment of our communities. This is how we can rise as a collective people rather than as individuals. If we do this, we shall win; if not, we shall fail ourselves and our children."

When Deborah finished her talk, the crowd went wild; they clapped their hands; they stomped their feet; they made the yodel cries with their tongues. As she descended the platform, there were thousands of people in the plaza. Her bodyguard,

Nachshon, and Sarah, her handmaid were waiting for her as she stepped down, with Elder Ariel and Barak at her side. "Congratulations! Deborah," said Barak. "You were just wonderful."

"Thank you Barak for your support." She was very grateful for that and gave him a big smile. Many people crowded around and greeted her.

Then Deborah and her retinue walked slowly away from the clapping crowd who smiled with approval. As Barak walked with her to Ariel's house, he said to her, "You spoke very well today. By the way, do you think that young man back there will accept your advice?"

"I think he will … and he got it for free."

"Well, there is one thing about free advice … it is usually worth it."

She turned around, smiled and hit at him in a playful manner. "I see that you can be very witty and amusing."

"Sometimes," he said.

As they walked toward Ariel's house, Deborah thought and remarked, "Oh Barak … I want to thank you again for your support, back at the Tabernacle."

"I am glad I came … I would not have missed that for all the gold in Ethiopia."

Finally, Deborah looked up at Barak with admiration, but her countenance changed when she realized her commitment to another man.

***

It was several days later at the City of Nahalol that the officials began to implement the diabolical plan of King Jabin and Sisera. They designed this plan to corrupt and destroy the Hebrews who lived in the village nearby. Then a small Canaanite delegation came to the Hebrew village to implement their insidious scheme. The head nobleman named Nahash spoke to the Hebrew elders: "There have been harsh feelings between our people for many years … and we want to change this."

"Change this? How and when do you propose to make this change?" asked Elder Tamim.

The head nobleman pointed to five large baskets. "We brought these victuals and gifts as a token of our sincerity and friendship," he said, as he folded his arms in front of him.

"We do place value on your gifts," he said, looking down and scratching his head. "But with us, true friendship is determined by the actions of the heart and not by valuables," the Elder pointed out, looking up.

"I agree, but we must start somewhere—and we have made the first step."

"Yes, you have," confirmed Elder Tamim.

The nobleman then walked over to the Elder and touched him on the shoulder. "We have made the first move by coming to your village. We want you and your people to return the visit by coming to a special festival at our city at noon two days from now. This will give both of our people a chance to get to know each other and build a better relationship."

Rolling his eyes and looking at his people, the Elder answered, "I will have to think about this, and talk it over with our villagers."

"Yes, we want you to talk it over, and we hope that your decision will be that you will come to the festival. We will see you then," said the nobleman, as they bowed and departed.

After the noblemen left, the Hebrews considered carefully the invitation of the Canaanites. They discussed the question for almost a half a day, and they decided to go to the feast. Then Elder Tamim commented, "Even though they come bringing offerings, I suspect them." In spite of this, the Elder and those who dissented decided to go reluctantly.

On the fourth day of the week, the small Hebrew community of one hundred and fifty people came to the City of Nahalol. The Canaanites gave them a great welcome. After the mingling and chatting with the Canaanites, everyone began to eat and drink in the open plaza. There were all kinds of victuals—vegetables, fruit, nuts, meat, wine, and strong drinks available; the wine came from the finest grapes grown in the rich Jezreel Valley.

Shortly after, Elder Nahash approached the pavilion and began to speak. "Citizens of our beloved City of Nahalol, our King is not able to be here today—but he has sent his greetings. He wants me to welcome you and our Hebrew neighbors to our city and feast. We hope that you will learn more about our customs, laws, and become a part of us in friendship. Now, without further delay, let everybody have an enjoyable time, and give the Hebrews plenty of wine and strong drinks."

The music began to play in a louder and snappy tone. Then about twenty young females dressed in skimpy apparels came out to dance. These females danced with intense, sexy gyrations, and began to pull some of the Hebrew men into the dance. "Come on handsome," said one female.

Another said, "Let's see what you can do." Then she grabbed the Hebrew by the hand. Before the Hebrews realized it, they were dancing before the idols of the Canaanites, Baal and Ashtaroth.

After a while, the dancing stopped. At last, a trumpet blew to signal an announcement. Kahan, the High Priest, dressed in a white tunic trimmed in silver around the sleeves, neck, and borders, stepped forward to speak: "I welcome all of you here in the name of the King … Canaanites and Hebrews alike … . I hope all of you have had plenty of food and wine, and there is no end to our hospitality. At this time, I want to inform our Hebrew neighbors that you can have anything—anything— you want—for the satisfaction of your pleasures. Just feel free to indulge."

The head Hebrew, Elder Tamim, turned and spoke to his associate, "I am getting a chilly feeling about what I am hearing and seeing, and I don't like the looks of it. We must remember the words of Deborah," he reminded him, while stroking his gray mustache.

"I agree," said another elder.

Elder Tamim tightened the black sash around his red tunic and advised his associate, "Spread the word around to our people to be on their guard."

"Consider it done, Elder."

As the people ate and drank, the High Priest continued to speak. "Now, while all of you have been standing here drinking and eating to the fullest, our god, Baal, has been neglected … . Is this right? Doesn't his hunger need satisfying?"

"Yes, yes," the crowd roared.

"Let a boy and girl be brought out and be sacrificed to our god, Baal." The statue of Baal sat on a large stone foundation at the highest place in the city. On his head rested the helmet of a warrior with bull's horns projecting out on both sides. The attendees escorted a blindfolded boy and girl up the stone steps to the god, Baal. As the boy and girl walked up the steps, they shed tears and sadness appeared on their faces. Their lips were moving but no one could hear them because of the loud sounds of the drums and the flutes.

After the boy and the girl reached the top of the steps, the escorts laid the girl on a large flat stone in preparation for the slaughter. The High Priest walked slowly to the flat stone and took a sharp-pointed knife from a silver tray where a red embroidered velvet cloth covered it. He raised his left hand high above his head and proclaimed. "We dedicate these sacrifices to our god, Baal and for the glory of the Canaanite people." Then he brought down the knife and stabbed the girl in the heart. She died instantly, and they did the same to the boy.

The facial expression of the Hebrews revealed that they could not tolerate to see the children killed and burned. As a result, they averted their eyes. The Hebrews watched almost everything with disgust and contempt. Someone said, "This is an abomination before God."

Elder Tamim spoke again to one of his associates. "We are going to get the heck out of this place as soon as possible. Deborah warned us about this at Shiloh."

"This will not be easy. We are surrounded by Canaanites, and their ceremony is still in progress," said one of the elders. "If we leave now, they might consider it disrespectful."

As the two Hebrew men were talking in the crowd, the High Priest spoke to his assistant. "Take the girl to our god, Baal." The god, Baal, had a large opening in his stomach with a hot fire burning. The assistant lifted up the girl and placed her in the fire and repeated the same procedure for the boy.

A few moments later, one of the noblemen shouted, "Let our neighbors, the Hebrew people, bring forth a boy and a girl to be sacrificed."

"Yes, yes, yes … let the Hebrew leaders bring forth a sacrifice for our god, Baal," yelled some of the Canaanites in the crowd.

The High Priest held up his hand for the crowd to be silent and looked down at the Hebrews. "Who among you will volunteer a son or a daughter for a sacrifice to Baal?"

Elder Tamim stepped up and spoke. "We accepted the invitation to come here in order to bring friendship among us … not to bring about the death of our sons and daughters."

The High Priest leaned forward and pointed his finger with an outstretched arm. "Do you think that you are better than us … that you can withhold your sons and daughters from our god, Baal?"

"Tell me," asked Elder Tamim, "Is the flesh of the Canaanite children not good enough that you must also have the flesh of the Hebrew children?"

"Our god, Baal, likes a change in his diet every once in a while. He would consider the Hebrew flesh … a delicacy."

Elder Tamim took a deep breath and spoke, "Our God would consider it murder … . It is an abomination for us to worship another god and to sacrifice innocent children. We serve only the Lord, our God."

"Abomination?" asked the High Priest. "Your God will not save you … Deborah and Barak will not save you … but our god might if … ."

"Furthermore," interrupted Elder Tamim, "we have been tricked into coming here. Now, it is time for us to leave."

"Wait! We invited you here with good intentions. We opened the gates of our city to you; we showed you great hospitality; we offered you everything that your souls could desire," emphasized the High Priest. "And this is how you repay us?"

"I have stated my position—and I see no need to repeat it, your Excellency. Now, if you will excuse us," emphasized the Elder, turning half way around.

"Wait! I am not finished." The High Priest walked half way down the stone stairs and stopped. "Do you think that you can come here and show contempt for our god and our way of life—and get away with it—? Well, I had enough of you and your people. My patience is wearing out. Leave, leave! Go back to the sticks from whence you came," he shouted, with intense anger. Elder Tamim stared at the High Priest with a stern look, then turned around and departed with his people. As the Hebrews left, the Canaanites gazed at them with anger and vengeance.

Many Canaanites shook their fists at the Hebrews and others remarked, "You will regret this! You will regret this!"

***

It was late at night when everyone was asleep that Sisera and his army marched into the Hebrew village near the City of Nahalol. The soldiers of Sisera approached the camp silently and lit their torches. They began throwing their torches into the tents. When the Hebrews ran out of the tents frantically, the soldiers shot them with their spears and arrow.

"Burn everything … kill everybody," yelled Sisera, as he pranced his horse through the camp. Leave no one alive. This is our revenge against the Hebrews for showing contempt for our gods."

A woman named Marah and her family was in a tent at the opposite end of the camp. "Quickly Marah, take the children and hide in the woods!" ordered her husband. At that moment, a spear struck him in his side.

"Oh! My dear, you are hurt; I can't leave you."

"Go Marah! Leave me be, save the children."

As she was running into the bushes with the children, an arrow pierced the back of her son; and the second arrow pieced the chest of her daughter. When they fell down, she managed to pull them inside the bushes. She looked up and saw the entire camp in flames, clothing and blankets burning everywhere.

As she breathed in the air mixed with the heavy smoke that blew in her direction, she looked down at her children. They were failing fast. Then she murmured in anguish, "Oh my Lord, my children are dying, and there is nothing I can do."

Then she heard a voice from Sisera. "Is everyone dead?"

"I believe so, General Sisera," said one of his officers.

CHAPTER 14

It was in the spring of the year one week and a half after Passover that Deborah awoke early just before dawn. She decided to say her prayers and do her meditation in the courtyard at the back of her house. On other occasions, she would do these metaphysical routines inside the house in a special room.

She sat down on a hamlet-like seat connected between two palm trees. As she breathed in the pure air of the morning mixed with the aroma of the palm and cypress trees, she had a strange feeling that this was going to be an unusual morning. She felt that she was not alone—that something or someone was watching her.

Then she began her prayers; but she did not pray for herself—but for her people. She prayed that they would turn from their sins, and she asked God to forgive them.

When it was time for her meditation, she closed her eyes and began inhaling and exhaling methodically with rhythm and pauses between breaths. She cleared her psyche of everything around her until her mind became blank. Deborah sank deeper and deeper into a trans-like state until she felt light as a feather—as though she had no physical body—only an eternal soul—a soul tuned in with the Eternal Father. The Lord spoke to her. "Deborah, Deborah, Deborah, I am the God of Adam, Noah, Abraham, and all the families of the earth. Send for Barak and tell him all the words I shall speak unto thee … . "

After Deborah had heard all the words of the Lord, she came out of her trans-like state. She sat there for a moment and reflected on everything that the Lord had told her. Daybreak came, and she could hear the birds chirruping. Her heart was heavy because of the words which God had spoken to her; but she knew that she had to carry out the command. Then she heard Sarah and Nachshon talking, and she went over to them. "Peace Deborah, I see you are up early this morning. Because Deborah looked as if she was not really present, Sarah asked, "Are you all right?"

"Yes Sarah, I am well. I just came out of a deep meditation. Oh Nachshon, make ready the fastest horse we have and send one of the workers to tell Barak, the son of Abinoam, that I want to see him as soon as possible."

"I'll do it right away," he said, walking toward the gate.

"Uh … Nachshon, tell the rider not to take the main road but use the roundabout way and watch out for the Canaanite patrols. Also, tell him to look for Barak at the Zebulun garrison."

The horse rider departed early that morning. Because he had sixty miles to travel to the garrison, it would likely take him an entire day on a fast ride. He would probably rest overnight and get on the road with Barak the following morning, providing that Barak did not have any pressing business to implement. This is what Deborah thought as she observed the rider glancing at the yellow rising sun.

During the course of the day, as Deborah was going about her business, she thought about Caleb, the man she was duty bound to marry but did not love. Then she also thought about

Barak, the prince who had deep feelings for her. However, when he came around her, she tried not to encourage him—not even in the smallest way. Now, she was having internal conflict. The Lord had asked her to send for the very man she was trying to avoid. With Barak in her presence, this would only stir up internal emotions that she would rather keep suppressed.

A few months passed since she had talked to Caleb. Any day now, she was expecting to hear from him regarding their wedding plans. All day and part of the night, her mind reflected on and off about Caleb and Barak. She must tell Barak what the Lord revealed to her, and this would bring on a crisis for some of the northern Hebrew tribes. What she had to tell Barak, she wondered whether he would accept it coming from a woman. Life was presenting to her many challenges: The idea of the marriage to a man she did not love, and what she had to tell Barak, both weighed heavily on her mind. The Lord spoke, and there was no turning back.

In the meantime, Seth arrived at the Zebulun garrison. At that time, he told Barak that Deborah wanted to see him as soon as possible. He slept at the garrison during the night, and the following morning they got up to travel south with a ten-man escort.

***

The next morning Barak thought about the letter he had received earlier from Prince Abihu of the tribe of Judah requesting him to come to his estate. In light of all of this, Barak decided that he would visit with Abihu first and then visit Deborah afterwards. When he arrived outside the City of Bethel, he said to Seth, "I am going to Hebron to meet with

Prince Abihu. Tell Deborah that I will visit with her after my meeting with the prince."

"I will deliver the message to Deborah as you requested, Prince Barak."

Barak continued south to Bethlehem and slept there for the night. Little did he know that the future King David would be born here. He did not know that Bethlehem would be the birthplace of the future messiah of the Hebrew sects of the Ebonites, Essenes, Nazarenes, and the early Christians. He arrived on the outskirts of the City of Hebron about twenty miles south of Jerusalem. Barak came here at the request of Prince Abihu because he wanted to discuss with him the details of supplying soldiers for Barak's army.

Now, Barak was at the northern entrance of the Valley of Eshcol which led to the City of Hebron. He could see the city located on top of one of the mountains. As Barak rode southward, he had great anticipation of a favorable meeting with Prince Abihu.

It was still springtime, and the entire valley was a remarkable sight with the mountains covered with green vegetation. After a long hot dusty ride, Barak and his men road past the western slopes of the mountains. They stopped to take a drink of water, with the palms of their hands, from the Brook of Eshcol. At that time, one of the soldiers took a deep breath and remarked, "Ahhh! This is the best water I ever drank."

"Yes," Barak added. "The last time I drank water like this was from the well in my home town."

They could see that the northern entrance to the valley was very broad with many green vineyards, pomegranates, figs trees, and olive gardens. The shape of the valley ran from north to southeast. As Barak rode deeper into the valley going south, it became narrower and the peaks of the mountains got higher. Then one of Barak's men asked, "General, can we visit the cave of Machpelah while we are here in Hebron?"

"Yes, I suppose so ... I believe ... it is on the east side of the valley," answered Barak hesitating. "Yes! My memory is coming back to me; it is on the east side." Later, Barak remembered that the cave of Machpelah was the place where Abraham, Isaac, Jacob, and their wives were buried. Not too far away from this place, the Hebrews buried Joseph. This cave was located on the side of a hill which Abraham purchased from Ephron, the Hitite, for a burial place for his wife, Sarah. After more than a thousand years, a church and a mosque were constructed over this cave. In later years, this cave became a holy shrine to Hebrews, Christians, and Muslims. When Barak and his men arrived at the eastern slope, they saw the cave.

"Beware," said one of the soldiers, "lest the ghosts of Abraham, Isaac, and Jacob come out of the cave and haunt you."

Because of those ironic words, another soldier chuckled and remarked, "Don't be ridiculous." Dismounting from their horses, walking slowly to the entrance of the cave, gazing at the entrance, the soldiers bowed down to the ground and prayed. Everyone standing nearby could hear them praying in a low tone. After the visit and the prayer, they arose and rode off to the west side of the valley. Prince Abihu's mansion stood on one of the slopes. The workers made the mansion out of hewn stone, and it had a second story.

Barak got down from his horse leaving his men behind and knocked on the front gate of the courtyard. Barak could see a palm tree in the center of the courtyard surrounded by purple lilies. A servant answered the knock. Barak greeted, "Peace be unto you. I came to see Prince Abihu."

"And who might you be?" asked the servant, looking at Barak from head to toe.

"Barak … Prince Barak!" he couldn't resist saying with authority.

"My master is busy at the moment, but you can wait for him on the terrace." The servant escorted Barak up the outside stairs that led to the second floor and to the terrace. When Barak walked up the steps, he noticed that the courtyard walls were white washed with a full coat of lime.

As Barak stood on the terrace waiting for Prince Abihu, he overheard a conversation coming from one of the adjacent rooms. The conversation was between Abihu and one of his tax collectors named Jonathan. This tax collector had an oval-shaped sepia face, and he wore a white headdress with a black band around his forehead. "My master, there are transgressors who commit robbery and murder in one town and flee to another—something must be done about this."

"In what city did this take place?" asked Abihu, glaring at him.

"In the City of Arad just south of here, I recommend that you send soldiers to capture them."

Prince Abihu rubbed his forehead below his white headdress which had an embroidered dark blue band around it. "At the present time, I am busy with the Philistine threat and trying to retaliate against these murderers."

"You always condemn the Philistines who murder Hebrews," Jonathan pointed out, as he leaned forward gesturing. "But you say nothing when a Hebrew murders another Hebrew. Why?"

Prince Abihu looked surprised; however, he managed to utter a few words: "The Philistines are our old enemies … and even the warrior Shamgar had trouble with them." Abihu moved one step closer to Jonathan and touched him on his upper right arm. "You must understand—my tax collector—that I must deal with the Philistine problem."

Jonathan turned away from him walking and talking. "No ... I don't understand." Meanwhile, Jonathan turned around and looked him in the eyes. "Is not the death of the Hebrews, murdered by other Hebrews, just as serious as the death of the Hebrews murder by the Philistines?"

"Yes! But ..."

"Then why don't you do something to help stop the crime in our cities?"

"This should be the concern of the local elders," said Abihu bluntly.

"Local elders ... ? I think that you should be concerned also. These murderers flee from one city to another. This puts them out of the reach of the elders. You are the prince of our tribe, and you have the influence and jurisdiction of the entire tribe of Judah. If you act now, the people will follow you."

"Jonathan, I am taking action on behalf of the people. I am saving them from the hands of the Philistines whenever I can," argued Abihu. He turned his back to Jonathan and faced the picture of a lion which hung on the wall.

"That may be true," admitted Jonathan, "but while you are saving us from the Philistines, who is going to save us from ourselves?"

There was a pause, and Prince Abihu seemed horrified at the question. Finally, he hesitated and spoke softly, "I can't answer that."

Jonathan shrugged his shoulders and commented, "It seems that you don't have either the will or the compassion to help save our people from themselves."

"What makes you say that?"

"I have watched you: when a Hebrew is murdered by a Philistine, you go and visit the family of the slain; but when a Hebrew murders another Hebrew, you pay no attention to the grieving family even though the murder takes place right here in Hebron."

Prince Abihu turned around with intense anger. "I am offended by your remarks ... and I have had enough of it. Now, you may leave," he said, with a stern look on his ebony face.

Jonathan turned half way around to leave but stopped. "I am not finished ... just yet! I think I understand your motives. Yes, it is becoming very clear to me ... . You get most of your fame and money from our people for fighting a few Philistines. Consequently, catching Hebrew murderers have no interest to you. In the meantime, our cities sink into the mire of crime and hopelessness while you fill your coffers with shekels of gold and silver. Is not this the truth, Abihu?"

The Prince looked at him with disdain. "Leave now, or I'll have you put out!" he commanded.

"Why don't you be man enough to admit it ...?" There was a pause. "I am waiting for an answer."

"All right, you want an answer? What prince wouldn't want fame and shekels of gold?"

"That may be true, but I would hope that a good leader would also want justice and order with peace and harmony for his people. To me, this is a sign of excellent leadership."

Abihu stomped his foot on the floor like a mad man, raised his finger, and pointed at Jonathan. "I don't need you to stand here and judge me. I made you what you are ... . I have paid you very well ... and I will not tolerate any further rudeness from you ... or anybody else. Now, leave before I ... ."

As Jonathan walked towards the door, he commented, "I hope you will come to your senses before it is too late."

There was a silence, and then Abihu spoke. "Wait!" Jonathan stopped then turned around slowly. "Why are you so hot about a few dead Hebrews? You never questioned me before!"

"I didn't because I was afraid that I would lose my position. However, I speak up now because a criminal murdered my brother in the City of Arad. A Hebrew murdered him. His wife is a widow, and his children are fatherless. As it stands now, I must support them and do my best to be a father to his children," Jonathan said, as he left the room quickly.

After Jonathan departed, Prince Abihu sat on a stone bench with a soft cushion. He remained preoccupied and still. As Abihu sat in his room, his servant approached and spoke. "Prince Abihu, there is someone here to see you." Abihu remained silent, and the servant spoke again. "My master, there is someone …"

"Oh—oh it's you—I was in deep thought. What is it?"

The servant bowed to the prince and repeated. "There is someone here to see you."

"He has a name, doesn't he?" asked Abihu.

"Yes. The man said that his name is Barak, and said that he is a prince."

"Well—honor him as a prince and show him in," shouted Abihu, as he raised his head suddenly.

The servant stood there in a state of shock. After a moment, he replied, "As you say, my master." Then he bowed and departed.

When Abihu heard Barak approaching, he stood up. "Oh Barak, Barak … it has been months since I saw you. How have you been?" he asked, as he embraced Barak and patted him on the back. After the small talk and the smiles, Abihu led Barak back to the terrace. The prince had the floor of the terrace made from granite stone. As Barak walked onto the terrace, he noticed the green plants, and assorted purple and red lilies growing in the various large stone flowerpots. Barak walked over to the stone banister and stood under the fronds of a palm tree that grew near the side of the terrace. Then he looked over the entire green valley. "Oh how beautiful this country is," he exclaimed. Barak turned around and smiled at Abihu. "This is truly God's country."

"Yes Barak. This country, which our ancestors inherited, is indeed a land of milk and honey."

"And also a land of mountains, hills, and valleys," Barak chuckled, "and dens and caves for thieves and holy men."

"You know, Barak, this can be the beginning of a long friendship between us," Abihu stated, as he ambled up and down with a smile on his face. However, Barak frowned because he was not pleased with the conversation he overheard between Abihu and Jonathan.

Then Abihu clapped his hands signaling to the servants to bring in some refreshments. The servants brought in figs, olives, dates, pomegranates, milk, curd, bread, wine, and honey. After they said the blessings, they dipped the bread in the honey. Next, they poured some wine in their silver vessels. Prince Abihu held up his goblet in a toast fashion, said the blessings, and commented—"To our long friendship."

At that moment, Barak responded with, "Yes, and to our success and happiness."

Abihu walked over to Barak and said, "Barak, now I think that we should get down to business and talk about why I sent for you. The last time you were here, you asked me to consider your request to supply soldiers and weapons for your army.

My decision is pending on two conditions." Abihu took Barak by the arm and guided him to the other side of the terrace. "You see Barak, I need your help!" Abihu pointed to Barak with his arm extended.

Barak looked confused, "My help! How can I help the most powerful man in …?"

"Well, you see—the situation is like this. Judah is the largest tribe; and I believe that Judah should have the leadership over all the tribes … and I need you to help me to persuade the other northern Hebrew tribes to accept my leadership."

"Are you talking about kingship?"

"Yes! Kingship, you see, there is no king in Israel; and we need a king like the other nations."

"Why do you think that Judah should have the leadership?"

"After the death of Joshua, the Israelites asked the Lord saying, 'Who shall go up for us against the Canaanites first to fight against them? And the Lord said, 'Judah shall go up … .' " Barak hesitated and remained silent. "Now, if you can agree to my proposal, we stand ready to supply you with all the soldiers and weapons you will need."

"Why choose me? Can't you select someone else for this task?"

"There is nobody else … Barak. You are the best man for the job! You are respected and well known … the people look up to you … as if you are some king … a deliverer or savior as they looked up to Othniel, Ehud, and Joshua."

Barak took one step forward, he turned to one side, and he scratched his head. "I am flattered; you give a very persuasive argument. Suppose that I am not able to persuade them … then what?"

"Well, I'll have to do a little arm twisting."

"Arm twisting? I see," said Barak softly, looking at him suspiciously. "Are there any other conditions?"

"Yes, I am glad that you asked that question. In fact, there is. Do you know the woman, Deborah?"

Barak raised his head quickly. He opened his eyes wider and answered anxiously. "Yes ... I know her!" Barak stood there and wondered what was on his mind.

"There is something you must understand. This woman, Deborah ... ."

"What about Deborah!" Barak repeated loudly. "You speak of her with contempt ... as if she is some kind of low life." He retorted angrily.

"Well ... you probably wouldn't use those words; however, she is taking away the loyalty of the people from the elders and the princes. Furthermore, she is moving into a man's domain; and your connection with her contributes to her rise in prestige. In view of all this, I must ask you to disassociate yourself from her."

"Disassociate myself? You have the ... ." Barak held back his anger for a moment and continued. "A little while ago, I asked you, suppose I cannot get the elders to accept your leadership; and at that time, you said that you would 'do a little arm twisting.' What did you mean by that?"

"I simply meant that if they give you any opposition to my leadership, let me know their names; and I will surely have them eliminated."

"What? You are talking about tyranny and murder ... and it would only lead to civil war among the tribes."

"You call it tyranny and murder. I call it unity and order among the tribes," retorted Abihu, gesturing with his right hand. "And furthermore, Barak, I am prepared to offer you five thousand shekels of gold for your cooperation."

"You propose to eliminate the Hebrew leaders who oppose your kingship ambition; you bribe me with gold shekels; and you have the gall to ask me to disassociate myself from a very respectful woman. I am disappointed with you Abihu, and you have wasted my time. I will not surrender my moral principles to further your ambitions, nor will I be an accomplice to your diabolical scheme," Barak roared, showing contempt.

"I warn you, Barak. If you stand in my way … ."

Barak gritted his teeth with boiling anger. "No … I warn you, Prince Abihu! If you interfere in the affairs of the northern tribes, I will fight you with everything I can muster," he shouted, pointing his finger at him. "I have had enough of this. I am leaving."

Abihu watched Barak walk toward the stairs and said, "Shamgar and Jael did not complete the total deliverance of Israel. What makes you think that you can … ? Without my help, what are you going to do, Barak?"

"I'll look to another source," snapped Barak, as he turned and eyed Abihu with contempt.

"Without my help, Barak, Sisera will grind you into the dust like corn is ground in a millstone. Furthermore, if you set foot in the province of Judah again, your life will be in great danger."

"I hunt murderers and fight Canaanites every day. My life is always in danger," Barak retorted, as he left. Then Abihu walked over and slammed the door behind him.

When Barak departed from the house of Abihu, it began to get cloudy. He had come to Hebron with great hope of getting help from Prince Abihu; instead, he got no assistance, but became an enemy of the man who he thought would assist him. Moreover, this unpleasant experience weighted very heavily on his heart.

Barak and his men rode away from Hebron with rapid speed because he wanted to leave that sour experience behind him as quickly as possible. As he rode north, he thought about Deborah and why she sent for him. He hoped that his visit with her would be better than the one he had with Abihu.

CHAPTER 15

Barak arrived at Deborah's estate in the late afternoon of the same day he left Prince Abihu. Deborah was inspecting plants and flowers in her courtyard. Seth, one of her young workers entered. "Mother Deborah, Barak has finally arrived with his soldiers."

"Oh! Show him in. He must be tired," she said, pulling the ends of her reddish purple shawl around her neck.

A few moments later, Barak entered. He walked with an authoritative gait. "Peace Deborah," he smiled and then asked, "Is all well?" She took a few steps toward him and wanted to embrace him, but she caught herself and just returned a smile, not wanting to give the wrong impression.

"All is well. You must be tired after your long trip from Hebron."

"I'm just a little dusty from the long trip," he said, as he looked her up and down, smiling with admiration. "What happened to that beautiful bracelet you had on your wrist?"

"I gave it away."

"But I liked it," he remarked smiling.

"Well … I'm sorry that I gave it away." At that moment, Seth passed through the other side of the courtyard. "Seth, would you show Barak and his soldiers to the guest quarters so that they may freshen up." As the soldiers passed by Deborah and Barak on their way to their quarters, Deborah smiled and greeted them. "I want to thank you for the great work you are doing for the safety of our people."

And the soldiers responded in unison. "Thank you, Deborah, for your kind words."

"Barak, we will have supper; afterwards, I'll tell you the important reason why I sent for you."

"I am anxious to hear this mountain-size news," he exaggerated.

Soon after, Deborah went into her meditation room to review everything that the Lord had told her. After she had been in her room for a while, she heard someone calling. It was Sarah, her handmaid. "Yes, Sarah."

"A messenger brought a letter for you. It is from Caleb's estate." Deborah took the letter and put it in her pocket intending to read it later, thinking that it was about their wedding plans. She continued to reflect on what she was going to tell Barak because this was a more pressing matter.

When they finished their supper, it was still daylight; and they walked outside and sat under a palm tree. But before they could begin their conversation, Deborah heard the voice of the little boy, Ben calling from the other side of the gate, "Mother Deborah, Mother Deborah, I heard that Barak is here. I want to talk with him."

"We are busy right now; we have important matters to deal with," she said, with a low voice. Then she walked over to the gate. Seeing that Ben had lowered his head, seeing he was sulking in rejection, noticing that he had turned around to walk away, Deborah changed her mind, "Wait Ben." Deborah turned towards Barak and gave him a silent request with her eyes.

Barak rose to his feet, opened the gate, smiled, and said, "Come in Ben. It is so good to see you. Is all well with you?"

"I am fine. I have been waiting for you to return and now you have come." Without request, Deborah walked to the other side of the courtyard so that they could be alone.

"Deborah sent for me and we have a lot of business to discuss."

"Oh I had a birthday last week, now, I am seven years old."

"Happy birthday, Ben. Here is a silver coin for you."

Ben's eyes lit up like two bright stars. "Thank you Prince Barak, thank you!"

"You said you wanted to talk to me. What would you like to talk about?"

As Ben sat on a stone bench, he placed his elbow on his right knee and the palm of his right hand on his right chin and thought. "I want to talk about things," he said in a cute and innocent way.

"What things, Ben?"

"You know things. My mother and sisters talk about girly things. I am not interested in those things. Barak, where do babies come from?"

"Barak smiled and said, "They come out of the mother's stomach."

"How do they get there?"

Barak thought for a few moments and said, "I can't tell you this right now but I promise you that by the time you reach twelve years old, and if you don't know the answer by then, I will tell you. All I can tell you now is that God helps in the making of the babies. Ben, is there anything else you would like to know?"

"Yes. Tell me more about camels."

"I see that you like camels." Ben looked at Barak and shook his head up and down in consent. Barak began to explain; "It is easier to get on the camel when he is sitting down. If there is a saddle on him, you hold one hand on the reins and the other hand outstretched on the front of the saddle."

"What do you do if there is no saddle?"

"Good question. Then you hold on to the hump."

Ben looked curious, and then asked, "What is in the hump?"

"It's nothing but pure fat, my boy."

"How do you get him to move forward?"

"You kick him lightly with your foot and make a clicking sound by pressing air between your tongue and the roof of the mouth."

"You mean like this?" Ben made the sound.

"That's right Ben. You learn very fast."

"Thank you so much, Barak, for taking the time to talk with me. I shall never forget you." At that moment, they embraced each other warmly.

There was a silence. Ben looked at Barak. Moments later, he looked away. Then he looked at Barak again. "Could you be like a ... .? I don't know how to say this, but could you be like a father to me?"

Barak took a deep breath. "Ben, I am a soldier and I am fighting against the enemies of our people. I don't know how I'm going to get the time to be a good father. I like you and I want to help you, but tomorrow I shall be returning to my soldiers far away from here. The only thing that I can promise you is that if I am alive, I shall return. Is this understood?"

"Yes, Prince Barak." They embraced once more.

"Now run along home, Ben, and be a good boy."

Ben smiled and said, "I'll be good," and he departed.

After Barak finished his conversation with Ben, Deborah returned to Barak and commented. "I see that you are building a good relationship with Ben."

"Yes, he wants me to be like a father to him."

"That seems like a good idea. Now, we can talk about things relating to the war. Barak, I heard that you went down to the City of Hebron."

"Yes, I went there to see if Prince Abihu would supply soldiers and weapons to help me fight Sisera's army."

"And what happened?"

"I carry disappointing news. There will be no help coming from Abihu."

"This does not surprise me."

"He placed certain conditions on his offer that I could not accept. He said that Judah—his tribe—should be the ruling one over all the tribes. Furthermore, he wanted me to persuade the northern tribes to accept his leadership; and if they refuse, he requested their names so that he could eliminate them. Lastly, he tried to bribe me with five thousand shekels of gold to support his ambition."

"Everything has its place," said Deborah, "and every man has his time. This is your time for national leadership, Barak, not Abihu's. Prince Abihu will not be king in his days!"

"I hope not!" said Barak. "If he rose to power among us, he wouldn't be a good ruler; he would be only a butcher."

"Nevertheless, Barak … after many years, great kings will spring forth from his tribe; and the messiah will arise out of Israel; and he will be a light and hope for many nations. Did Abihu say any more?"

"Yes! Somehow, he found out that I had visited you on several occasions. He accused you of pulling away the loyalty of the people from the princes and the elders. Moreover, he wanted me to disassociate myself from you and ..."

She interrupted him. "You don't have to repeat anymore, Barak. He sent me a detailed letter stating his views. But I would be interested in knowing what your reply was to him."

"I told him that he had wasted my time, and that I would have no part of his diabolical scheme. Also, I told him that you were a good person; and that he had no right to talk about you in a degrading manner."

"I am so proud of you, Barak because you stood up to him." She lifted her hands up to embrace him, but she restrained herself thinking that it would be in bad taste. Barak was ready to respond with his hands extended, but she sat down.

She sat quiet for a while looking down, and she looked away. Finally, she looked up at him. Barak's facial expression showed that he was getting anxious, and he broke the silence. "Did you send for me to talk about us?"

"The reason I sent for you is to talk about the war. I was very open with you about my marriage to Caleb; and as far as I know, nothing has changed," she said emphatically. "Barak, have you ever thought about when all-out war will occur? And what would be your geographical position and the position of your enemy?"

"I've thought about it, but war plans change according to the situation. Tell me Deborah, I beseech thee. Why do you talk about war matters?"

"So that you can give deeper thought to what I am going to tell you ... ."

"Go on," he said.

"As you know Barak, Sisera's control of the Jezreel Valley—with his nine hundred chariots—divides our people."

"Yes, that is true."

"This situation cannot remain the way it is for long. His control of this valley affects our unity, commerce, and our pilgrimages to the sacred site at the Tabernacle." She inhaled deeply and exhaled slowly. "The Lord appeared unto me, and told me to send for you. These are His words: 'go and draw to Mount Tabor, and take with thee ten thousand men of the children of Naphtali and the children of Zebulun. And I will draw unto thee to the River Kishon, Sisera, the captain of Jabin's army with his chariots and his multitude; and I will deliver him into thy hand.' "

"Deborah, do I understand you to be saying that you want me to put ten thousand men into the field against Sisera's nine hundred chariots, the rest of his horsemen, and his multitude?"

"I am not saying it; the Lord has said it! Barak, before you came out of your mother's womb, God appointed you to be the deliverer of the Hebrews."

"Listen Deborah, my forces are poorly armed. We do not have any chariots. We do not have enough horses, camels— not even six hundred swords and shields for ten thousand men. Sisera arrested all the blacksmiths years ago. How can my men stand up against his great multitude?" he wailed, with an unhappy look on his face.

"If you become more spiritual, you will be able to understand what the Lord has said. It is the Lord who will defeat Sisera. It is the Lord who will deliver Sisera into your hands."

"To ask me to go up against Sisera," he argued, "is like asking me to put a chicken up against a hungry lion."

"Barak, it is written in our holy books that if you trust in the word of the Lord, 'five of you shall chase an hundred, and an hundred of you shall put ten thousands to flight: and our enemies shall fall before you by the sword.' "

Barak listened carefully and stared at her with a long pause. "Deborah, 'if thou will go with me, then I will go:' " he said, as he gestured with his hands. " 'but if thou will not go with me, then I will not go.' "

As Deborah sat there under the palm tree, she closed her eyes, she became silent, she thought. He probably has a secret reason for asking me to go with him. At that moment, the spirit said to her, "Go with him Deborah … Go!"

"Well, Deborah, I am waiting. Are you going to keep me waiting until the cock crows at dawn?"

"Oh Barak, I understand from your words that the authority that God has given to you … some of it, you want to give to me. 'I will surely go with thee: notwithstanding the journey that thou takest shall not be for thine honor; for the Lord shall sell (give) Sisera into the hands of a woman.' "

"Into the hands of a woman?" he smiled, with a look of uncertainty. "I understand," he declared. However, by the look on his face, the words went in one ear and came out the other.

"Do you agree?" she asked, watching his facial expression.

"Yes, I agree to all the words that went forth out of your mouth," he uttered, with a pensive look on his face.

"Would it be all right if we leave out early in the morning?" she asked.

"The morning will be fine, and this will give me time to get a good night's rest. Finally, the time has come that we can confront Sisera and his army. I can't believe that this is true, and God has revealed it to you."

***

The next morning, they arose early; and Deborah decided to take Nachshon and Sarah with her. She gave final instructions to her overseer, Madreech, and informed him that she would be gone for several weeks.

Nachshon prepared one horse for himself and a donkey for each of the women, and a camel to carry food, water, clothing, and other personal items. As Deborah brought out a heavy clothing sack and a small chest, she said, "Barak, will you help me?"

"My pleasure," he commented, as he lifted the sack up on the camel's back.

"Thank you," she said. "I have everything in it but the kitchen shelf."

"Well, at least you won't go hungry," he said smiling. "Oh Deborah, I will need a lot of rope for the army. Can you spare some?"

"Yes, Nachshon, get all of the rope you can find in the storehouse and give it to Barak"

After a short while, Nachshon returned, "here is the rope Barak"

"Thank you, give me one bundle and give the rest to Captain Enoch." Finally, they took to the road and travelled the usual north-south mountain road that ran from Jebus (Jerusalem) to Shechem and northward. Deborah rode in the front beside Barak, and Sarah rode beside Nachshon about fifteen cubits in the rear while the ten soldiers rode behind them.

It was not too long before they passed through the center of the City of Bethel. They passed over the east-west road that intersected with the road that they were traveling. It was already warm, and there was every indication that it was going to be warmer. Then Nachshon spoke up, "Deborah, do you think we should water the animals at one of the springs in this area?"

"Yes, that's a very good idea … that way, we can save our own water," she remarked pleasantly. They turned aside not too far from where Jacob had built his alter, and he called it Bethel which means House of God. Deborah then made a movement to get down off her donkey.

"Let me help you," Barak volunteered. He extended his hand to her.

"That's so nice of you." Getting down from the donkey, she felt the gentleness and strength of his arms. Then she moved quickly away from him.

After all the animals finished drinking water at the spring, they continued on the road again. Deborah thought about Caleb but mostly about the impending war. She asked herself, did she partly agree to go with Barak so that she would not be around if Caleb came? Then she remembered that the Lord told her to go with Barak. Another point, she hadn't even read the letter she received from Caleb's estate. She was clearly avoiding those matters. Then there was a silence, and Barak didn't say anything.

"You look deep in thought. What is heavy on your heart, Barak?"

"Deborah, I've just been thinking about my wife who died in child birth."

"What about her?"

"Well—there are several things about you that remind me of her things like dedication, loyalty, and compassion." At that moment, his horse stepped on a rock and jolted him for a few seconds, "I think a lot of you, Deborah."

"I am promised to Caleb; and I believe there are many beautiful ladies who would like to have you … in the way that you are thinking—forget about me, Barak."

"That's very difficult."

"Even if I wasn't betrothed to Caleb, there are other stumbling blocks that stand in the way."

"There you go again, Deborah, building a three hundred cubit wall between us. Now, what are the stumbling blocks?"

"They are the responsibilities that I have for my business, my commitment to public service, and my spiritual interest. These things can stand in the way of a good marriage."

"I also have my business, my livestock, and I am committed to the liberation of our people. Nevertheless, I take time out to write and visit you!"

Deborah stopped her donkey and turned to him and explained, "You are a good man, Barak. You are a prince of your tribe; and no doubt, you have a nice size estate. Furthermore, you are risking your life for our people. I admire these things in you ... any woman would. However, there is one thing that I need in my life that will make me happy; and that is a man who will grow spiritually with me. With all your good points, Barak, you are not at this level yet. Maybe you will get there two weeks from now, or a month from now, or six months."

"What can I say, Deborah. I am only a soldier fighting for our people."

"Let me say this, Barak, the things I tell you are in the great tradition of our ancestors. Our great ancestors were soldiers and spiritual men of God at the same time. Try to be more like Joshua; and if you try hard and pray, you will get there," she emphasized, as they continued on their journey.

Finally, they arrived at the City of Shiloh where the Tabernacle stood. Deborah and Barak informed the elders of the Supreme Court and the High Priest about the fact that the Lord told Deborah to call for Barak to go to war against Sisera. Then the High Priest said, "You have our blessings and prayers. From what you have told us, it is evident that God has spoken to you."

"We know that your Uncle Yoetz prepared and trained you well," Ariel, the Elder, reminded her. "He sat on this court for many years ... and we see that the spirit of knowledge, wisdom, humility, righteousness, and prophecy abide in you. May God be with you always," said Ariel, as he waved good-by.

After Deborah departed, one of the elders, who was a military officer in the tribe of Ephraim, said to Elder Ariel, "I think it is best that we mobilize an army on our northern frontier in case Sisera makes an incursion into our territory."

"As usual, your military expertise has been valuable," replied Elder Ariel. "Do what you think is best."

"Thank you, Elder," replied the officer.

Continuing northward for twelve miles, they came to the City of Shechem. This place was an ancient city of the Canaanites and located forty-one miles north of Jerusalem in the pass between Mount Gerizim and Mount Ebal. This city controlled the important trade routes. They saw the beautiful gorges, and traveled through the mountain passes while observing the lush green fertile valley with its yellow and purple wild flowers. It was just to the East that Jacob's sons shepherded their sheep. In this place, Shechem, the son of Hamor, violated Dinah, the daughter of Jacob.

Deborah and her party stopped in Shechem to get water and to eat, and then they continued. As Barak rode along the road, he continued his conversation with Deborah. "When I first came to your house, I found you to be a likable person; and I didn't know you were obligated under the levirate law to marry Caleb. When I came to your house the second time, I got the shock of my life. A ghost appeared, and he was Caleb."

"Are you saying that I misled you?" she inquired, as she looked at him with Mount Ebal in the background.

"No! I am just making a statement. It seems that I expected too much without knowing all the facts."

"Perhaps you are right ... but don't blame yourself too much. You were only being a man. And I had not been sure what Caleb's final decision was going to be."

CHAPTER 16

They continued on the main road veering slightly to the northeast, and came to the City of Tirzah which was about seven miles from Shechem. When they entered the city, they noticed the beautiful scenery of the mountains. It was here that they planned to sleep for the night. After they registered for their quarters, they sat down to eat. There was not enough space at one table for all to sit together, so they had to split up into two parties at the tables on the opposite sides of the dining room. Sarah and Nachshon sat at one table, and Barak and Deborah sat together at another table. The ten soldiers ate and slept outside in tents.

While Deborah and Barak ate supper, they discussed the details of how they were going to present to the leaders of the tribes what the Lord revealed to her. The discussion included the logistics of the army; and they gave special attention to the areas of supplies—water, food, camping equipment, and the mobilization of the troops. "Well, I think that this covers most everything, for any additional matter, we can discuss them with the elders of the tribes," commented Barak.

"Yes, I agree."

When Deborah and Barak had finished eating supper, a group of strangers came into the inn. The headman of the group fixed his eyes on Barak who was wearing a headdress with a gold band around it. Then Barak returned the glance with a nod of his head. The head stranger registered at the desk, and Barak heard him speak in the Hebrew-Canaanite language. After that, a servant took their personal items to their rooms.

The stranger looked at Barak again and noticed that the vest he was wearing had a golden strip around the borders with a fancy designs embroidered on it. He walked by Barak's table to go to his room. Barak stood up and watched the tall handsome gentlemen that approached and introduced himself. "Peace be to you sir. My name is Barak, Prince Barak, of the Hebrew tribe of Naphtali. And you sir?"

"Lysimacus, Demetrius Lysimacus." He was a man in his middle forties with black wavy hair. His dark brown tunic covered his tannish-white skin.

"Where did you learn the Hebrew-Canaanite language," Barak asked, in amazement.

Demetrius smiled in his charming way, "I learned it from several Canaanite classmates in Egypt."

"Are you from the region of the Caucasus Mountains?"

"No, I am from the Greek Islands."

"Oh! What brings you here to this part of the world?"

"I just completed my studies in Egypt, and I am returning home to set up my medical practice."

"Oh … I see … . Then you are a physician," stated Barak, with interest.

"Yesss," answered the Greek slowly.

"Sit down, have a seat sir! I would like to talk with you further," Barak urged him, with a slight smile.

"Thank you. I would be glad to."

"By the way, this is my associate, Deborah."

Deborah smiled and nodded her head in recognition. At that time, Demetrius introduced his three associate doctors, his daughter, and his brown-skinned wife, Isis, who he married after his Greek wife died in childbirth. His twenty-one year old daughter, Hatshepsut, is the result of that childbirth. He kissed his wife, Isis, and daughter and told them that he would join them in their quarters shortly. The medical associates also went to their quarters.

At that moment, Deborah spoke up, "Excuse me—Barak and Demetrius, I am going to my room; and this will give the two of you a chance to get to know one another. Call me when you have finished your conversation with Demetrius." Barak nodded his head in agreement.

Then the both of them sat down at opposite sides of the table. "Oh Demetrius, is your wife Egyptian or Ethiopian?"

"Egyptian. She is one of the daughters of the head of the medical college in the City of Memphis."

"In what area of medicine do you work?"

"My area is surgery."

"Umm! Surgery! How wonderful," said Barak smiling.

Demetrius stared at him with his blue eyes. "You said that you are a prince. Are you anything else?"

"Yes, why do you ask?"

"You dress somewhat like a soldier, and you have the air of an officer."

Barak smiled and looked him straight in the eyes. "Did you serve in the army?"

"Yes! I was the assistant to the chief surgeon in the army of Egypt; and I served in the Ethiopian war, on Egypt's southern border."

As Barak looked down, he raised the palm of his hands and covered his face and eyes. After a few moments, he lowered his hands to the table and turned to Demetrius. "Then you have had a lot of experience treating the wounded, isn't that so?"

"Yes. Barak, I want you to tell me the truth. Are you a soldier?"

Barak stared at him for a short while, shook his head up and down slowly, and smiled at him. Finally, Barak opened his mouth and spoke softly. "I am ... the commander of the Hebrew army in the North."

Demetrius took a deep breath, sat back erect, rubbed his brown beard, and asked, "Are you expecting war ... commander?"

Barak lifted his eyes slowly. "We are at war ... and have been for the last twenty years. Now, we are approaching the final battle."

"Barak, are you thinking of asking me to serve in your army to treat the wounded?"

"Oh Demetrius," Barak said softly and diplomatically. "I would be remiss and lacking as a commander if I did not seize this opportunity to request your expert knowledge and service. Therefore, I am asking you to remain with us for two or three weeks; and I will make it worth your while."

"But ... I have other plans. I am supposed to be at the Aegean Sea in two or three weeks. If I had not missed my turn at the City of Shechem, which would have taken me westward to the Great Sea and then northward, I would not have been here tonight."

"You see!" said Barak. "It was destiny that led you here."

"Destiny?"

"Yes, destiny!" said Barak. "Some unforeseen force guided your steps here."

"Why do you choose me? Someone that is so different from you and your people. There are other good doctors—as the Egyptians, the Libyans, and even the Ethiopians. I know … . I've met them."

"My dear brother, Demetrius, you are also a son of Adam … just as I am. When I crack open a brown egg or a white one, they are all the same inside. When I am hungry, I am not going to deprive myself of the good eating of an egg just because its shell is white. In view of this, I'm asking you to remain with us."

"You are a very wise commander. By the way, who are you fighting?" asked Demetrius.

"Have you heard of Sisera, the Canaanite?"

"General Sisera? Yes, I have heard of him. He has almost one thousand chariots … . Do you have such a number?"

"No," Barak looked embarrassed and lowered his head."

"How many men do you have, Barak?"

Barak hesitated for a moment and then spoke, "Two … two thousand," mumbled Barak, in a low tone.

"That's all?" Demetrius asked emphatically.

"We shall have another eight thousand soon."

Demetrius shook his head from side to side. "You have only ten thousand men … against Sisera's chariots and his entire multitude. This is suicide!" declared Demetrius, raising his voice. "Only ten thousand men … . Surely you don't expect to win?"

Barak hesitated. "We do expect to win," he said, staring at Demetrius. "The Canaanites are not unconquerable. It was King Thutmose III of Egypt who crushed the Canaanites and the soldiers of the Mitanni Empire at Megiddo, not far from here, about three hundred and fifty years ago."

"That is true ... however, in all respects to you ... you are not Thutmose III of Egypt, Barak," he said softly. "Furthermore, did you know that Egypt was a powerful nation—an empire—and the most advanced nation in the world?"

"Yes, but there is something else—I haven't told you. The lady Deborah, who you met earlier, is a prophetess, and she has said that we will win."

"Did she look into her crystal ball?"

Barak appeared offended and replied, "I don't know of any darn crystal ball?"

After noticing that Barak's facial expression had changed, Demetrius backed down. "Excuse me, Barak for being abrupt. I am not going to get involved in your business. However, I did detect a spiritual quality in her eyes. Whatever she told you, that is between you and her. I have said enough."

"Well, I'll just change the subject. By the way, Demetrius, a few moments ago, I mentioned King Thutmos III of Egypt. He is a man that I admire greatly."

"This is understandable," concluded Demetrius, pulling his brown tunic up on his shoulders. "Thutmos III was a good king and a great military leader. It is only natural that you would admire him."

Barak leaned forward and looked at Demetrius with inquisitive eyes. "Demetrius, tell me, what did he look like?"

"He was ... tall and had a robust built."

"Continue!" prompted Barak, looking anxious.

"In addition, he was pure Hamite. He had thick lips and a broad nose and wooly hair, like the sheep that graze in the valley."

Barak asked again. "Was he very dark?"

"Of course," he said. "Darker than you ... ! He had a bold and commanding appearance. You should travel to Egypt, see the world and broaden your knowledge!"

Barak looked contemplative. Finally, he spoke in gratitude. "Demetrius, I do thank you for your sincere advice and concern. However, I do wish you would reconsider my offer to stay and take care of our wounded."

"If Sisera wins, you will not need my help. He will just slaughter everyone. Furthermore, it would just be too risky for my group to remain in a war zone. We would just be too conspicuous if your enemy wins."

"I understand. Well, I guess that's it."

"It's getting late." Demetrius stood up. "I am sorry Barak! I like you, but I cannot give you a yes answer at this time. If circumstances were different ... I probably would." He made a slight bow and then began to depart.

"Oh Demetrius, if you should change your mind, you will be able to find us west of the Sea of Galilee. Just ask anybody and they will tell you."

Demetrius shook his head up and down with consent and stared at Barak with sympathy. Taking a deep breath, exhaling slowly, he mumbled in a low voice, "Sisera." Then Barak watched him walk away to his quarters.

It was now a little after midnight, and Barak sent for Deborah to join him at the table in the dining room. Deborah came and listened attentively to Barak and to everything he told her about the Greek. Deborah raised her head. "When Demetrius told you that he was a physician, I had the suspicion that you were going to ask him to remain and help take care of the wounded."

"You did?"

"Yes! But it is understandable that he would refuse you because of his prior duties and because of your fight with General Sisera's overwhelming odds."

"Do you think that he will change his mind?"

"I really don't know. We shall just have to let the Lord take care of that. But there is one thing that you have in your favor."

"What's that?"

"He likes you!" she said smiling.

After Deborah's last words, there was a silence; and her mind turned back to the letter she had received from Caleb's estate. She had avoided reading it because she did not want to face up to the reality of the marriage to a man she did not love, or trust. However, as she sat there, she decided that she might as well read it, freeing her mind of the contents. Therefore, she could concentrate more deeply on the impending war effort. She took out the pouch from her garment and opened it. At that moment, she unrolled the parchment and read the letter slowly. While reading the letter, she opened her eyes and mouth wide in surprise. She took a deep breath, and tears ran down her cheeks. "The Lord has answered my request," she said crying.

"What is the matter, Deborah? What is it?" He asked eagerly, leaning forward.

"I … received this letter from … Caleb's estate … ."

"What did he say to hurt you?"

"It isn't what he said … it is what he can't say!"

"Explain that, Deborah, don't keep me hanging," he demanded.

"This letter is from his sister," she said, "He gave up the ghost on the ninth day of this month."

"What? How?' asked Barak in shock.

"He was found dead in his bed, and the cause of his death is unknown." Then Deborah wept.

"Why do you weep, Deborah? You admitted that you didn't love him or trust him," asked Barak, with roughness in his voice.

"I weep because his soul didn't use the chance it had on earth to correct itself while it was in his body. If we pray and wait on the Lord—He will always work out His purpose for us; even though we may not understand it in the beginning."

"Where is the soul of Caleb at this moment?"

"It is in heaven."

"Does the soul have any kind of physical form?"

"No it does not. Not in the sense that we are familiar." She looked up and leaned towards him. "You must understand Barak, that when our souls go to heaven, we are neither tall nor short, pretty nor ugly, thin nor fat, Greek nor Hebrew; it is an eternal soul abiding in the eternity of time learning and preparing itself for the next mission and journey on earth."

"As I listen to you talk Deborah, it seems that you are on a different or should I say on a higher level."

"Maybe you are trying to say spiritual level," commented Deborah, as Barak shook his head up and down in consent.

Deborah continued to read the letter. Then she noticed that there was a document under the letter. Caleb's sister, named Emeth, went out of her way to obtain a court document that stated the following:

THE COURT OF GILGAL

After a complete investigation, the court has determined that there are no surviving eligible males of the deceased Caleb Ben Lapidoth, to

> *fulfill the duty of levirate marriage with Deborah Lapidoth. The court hereby grants Deborah the freedom and the right to marry anyone else if she so desire.*
>
> *Elam Ben Eber, judge*
> *Lud Ben Aram, judge*
> *Salah Ben Mash, judge*

The three elders of the court of Gilgal signed the letter. After reading this document, Deborah told Barak about the details. Then she commented, "Bless be the name of the Lord ... and bless be those who wait on His great mercy," she sobbed softly, with trembling in her voice.

"My dear Deborah, the heavy burden has been lifted from your shoulders. Caleb, may he rest in peace, is no more. Now, where do we stand, Deborah?"

Deborah looked up at Barak with surprise: "Caleb's body is not even cold yet, and you are asking me, 'where do we stand?'"

"Yes, I am asking you, Deborah, where do we stand?"

"We stand where we are."

"What does that mean?" he inquired, as he unfolded his hands in front of him.

"You have a duty. God has chosen you. Yet, you never talk about God. I am not sure that you understand the spiritual importance of your mission," she reminded him bluntly.

"I've never dealt with spiritual things before—you have—and in that sense, you have more experience."

"You can become more spiritual, if you let the Lord use you in this way. Then you and I will have more in common."

Barak appeared to be in deep thought, looked away, and said, "I see."

She continued, "The Lord chose you, Barak to lead Israel in battle; and He chose me to help His people, to comfort them, to guide them, to assure them, and to encourage you so that you will rise to a higher spiritual level. But do not reject it. If you reject the idea of trusting in God, then God will reject you at the very time you need Him."

"What you are saying sound good Deborah, but it is hard. It is hard to change over to an idea that you are not use to," he remarked, turning his head from side to side and took a deep breath.

"But you must try and try again and again and again. Finally, you will be victorious. If you can do this, there is a greater chance that we can make it together," she assured him, as she took hold of his hand and comforted him.

"You are a tough likable woman."

"Well Barak, it is time for us to retire for the night. I'll see you at dawn."

He escorted her to her room, and then gently said, "Good night, Deborah."

Deborah really liked Barak. She wanted him; but she wanted him to grow spiritually, without coercion. She believed that he must see the light and truth from within himself and not just because she said it.

She hoped in her heart that that moment would come. Until it came, she decided to hold herself back from him. She concluded that she would not even let him kiss her.

Before Deborah went to sleep, she told Sarah all of the details of the letter that she received from Caleb's estate and about his death. Moreover, she informed Sarah that Ophrah, the servant of Caleb, had decided to remain with Emeth since she inherited her brother's property.

CHAPTER 17

The night passed swiftly and Deborah and her retinue got up very early the next morning and went on their way. Before going to the tribes of Zebulun and Naphtali, Deborah and Barak decided that they would stop at one of the towns of the tribe of Issachar and speak with the elders and princes. This she thought would be proper in view of the fact that the Lord told Deborah to tell Barak to take the Hebrew army to Mount Tabor which belongs to the tribe of Issachar.

As Deborah and Barak continued northwards, they came to Mount Gilboa. They stayed close to this mountain so they would have a place to hide, in the event that they encounter a Canaanite patrol. While they rode around the west side of the mountain, they heard the prancing of the hooves of horses. Then Barak took Deborah and led her behind the ridges and boulders along the edge of the mountain, and gave his instructions to his soldiers to hide.

"Nachshon, quickly take your horse and Sarah's donkey and hide behind that ridge over there." Hearing the galloping of the approaching horses, Barak's horse became skittish and gave a whinnying sound. Then Barak urged, Nachshon to keep the animals quiet.

"Quickly, Sarah, go over there!" Nachshon exhorted her.

Barak and Deborah were pressed tight between a narrow passageway of the mountain. He stood close to her looking occasionally to see when the horses would pass. She looked up at his handsome face and admired his well-trimmed black mustache and beard. He looked down at her and smiled with joy in his eyes. She smiled shyly and thought how wonderful it was to be close to this handsome muscular man. They heard the hooves of the horses get louder and louder. Barak took his arms and put them around her shoulders in a protective manner. As he breathed hard in anticipation of the coming horsemen, his muscular chest rose up against her well-developed figure. She felt a sensation shoot through her, and she looked up at him. Next, they heard the crack of the whips from the charioteers; the chariots careened by at great speed. Then the horses passed. At that moment, he moved his lips slowly toward her; and she wanted him to kiss her, but she turned away. She was not ready for that yet. Barak was not spiritual enough, she thought, but a lot better than Caleb. Moreover, there was much more to concern her in the preparation for the war.

"Why did you turn away from me?" he asked, looking at her reactions.

"You were … you were hurting me."

"Hurting you?" he chuckled.

"Yes! You were squeezing me too tight."

Then Nachshon led the animals from behind the ridge. "I think it is safe to come out now."

"I'll check," Barak said. At that moment, he went out from the ridge and looked to the left and right cautiously. All was clear, and they came out and continued on their way. As they went on their journey, they passed by the many wild sweet-smelling blue flowers that carpeted the near-by mountain area.

The Iris flower grew abundantly in this region. Riding slowly through the Jezreel Valley, Barak began to speak again. "We have known each other for about a year now, and I have been thinking about several difficulties that we had in the past."

"Like what Barak?"

"I first got the impression that you were too independent, and you didn't want to spend too much time with me."

"Oh…! And what are your thoughts now?"

"Now, my thoughts are that you were just taking charge of your life and taking care of the business which your husband left you. When the people came to you for guidance and legal advice, I believe that you were performing a public service for them."

"I, too, had doubts about our relationship from the beginning. I did not want to become seriously involved with you because you were fighting the Canaanites, and they murdered my husband. Worrying about the possibility of your death would have caused me more pain. Now, I have new insight into this problem. The Lord has promised that He would deliver Sisera into your hands. You see, I don't have to worry about you being killed anymore."

"We both have suffered loss and pain in marriage. Many years ago, my wife died in childbirth. Therefore, when I first met you, I expressed doubt in ever getting married again because I feared the same thing would happen to you."

"Well, what are your feelings now, Barak?"

"I have outgrown that fear … and have accepted the fact that my next wife doesn't have to die in childbirth."

"It is good that you have overcome that fear."

"Would you like to have children, Deborah?"

"Yes, a boy and a girl. How about you?" she asked.

"I would like ten sons."

"Not by me," she replied. I don't have that many childbearing years left."

"Well, then two will do just fine," commented Barak.

***

As Deborah and Barak traveled on the road past Mount Moreh, they saw a group of people burying one of their dead. The group was standing about twenty cubits away from the main road. The body of a man was lying near the grave wrapped in a white shroud. Then the elder spoke his last words ... "his spirit returns to God who gave it. May he rest in peace."

A woman kneeled down and leaned over the body. "Joseph, don't leave me," she cried aloud. "Please don't leave me ... don't leave ..." she said, grabbing hold of his body. A few moments later, two women came over and led the woman gently away from the body; and four men took hold of the body, laid it on the ropes and lowered the corpse down into the grave. Then the elder repeated the requiem chant and recited the traditional Hebrew axiom: "Then shall the dust return to the earth as it was, and the spirit shall return to God who gave it."

While Deborah listened and watched what was happening, she knew that the soul-spirit of the dead man was hovering over the grave. She turned to Barak, "I can hear his voice," she mumbled.

"Voice...? Whose voice?" asked Barak.

"I can hear the spirit-voice of the dead man."

Barak looked at her as if she had lost her mind. "What is the voice saying?"

Deborah knew that he did not take her serious, but she continued to speak. "The voice said to his crying wife: 'My

soul is hovering from above and looking down at you. The body that I once had is not my true self, my dear wife. It is nothing but disposable matter—made from fruits, vegetables, nuts, water and bread—which will rot and the worms will eat.'
" Again, Deborah said to Barak. "His wife didn't hear a word he was saying, because she was not in tune with his spirit, and she was in much emotional pain."

"Deborah, the words you just said are very deep and have great meaning … . Are you going to tell … his wife what you heard?"

"No," she answered, looking like she was in a trance. "She is not ready to receive this … just yet."

"She is not ready yet, my lady?" Sarah probed.

"The widow is in no condition to listen. Perhaps, she will in the future when she is in a better state of mind. If she seeks answers, she will find them when she has an open mind. Now, let us continue on our journey."

Finally, they came to the City of Daberath which is located on the northwest side of Mount Tabor. As they rode through the village and the town, the people asked one another, "Isn't that Deborah and Barak?" The news traveled fast and soon there was a crowd following them. Some of the women were singing and beating their tambourines. Then a chant began with cadence, "Deborah, Deborah, Barak, Barak." The people gathered on both sides of them. They could hardly get through.

Barak asked one of the men, "Where is the meetinghouse of the elders and princes?"

"It is the pretty stone building on the right," said the man.

The crowd even got larger—and some of the spectators began to circle Deborah and Barak—singing, dancing, and beating the tambourines. As the women sang, some of them gave Barak a flirting eye and big smiles.

"I see that you are well thought of," commented Deborah.

"Oh, a little bit," he replied modestly.

Finally, they came to the meetinghouse of the elders. Deborah and Barak turned around and faced the crowd, "We thank you for your reception and love."

"What news do you bring to us," shouted a man from the crowd.

"Yes! Tell us Barak ... what brings you here?" asked a woman.

"We can't tell you now, but we will in due time. We must first consult with the elders and princes," Deborah assured them.

"The only thing that we can tell you now is that we are on an important mission," Barak informed them.

"Are you on a war mission Barak?" asked another man. "Because Deborah, the prophetess, came here with our top military officer, we think that you are here on war business. Tell us Barak, are you going to take our sons to war?"

"No comment," he said, as he took Deborah by her arm and escorted her inside.

Deborah and Barak sat down with the local elders of the City of Daberath. Daberath was in the territory of the tribe of Issachar, and this tribe gave the City of Daberath to the Gershonite Levites. Deborah and Barak did not have to introduce themselves because the crowd had already announced their coming.

After Deborah and Barak ate a light snack, the elders asked them why they had come to Daberath.

"The Lord God of our fathers revealed himself to Deborah; and she has a message for you and she will tell you the rest," Barak assured them.

"I greet you in peace honorable elders of this ancient city. It is true that our God appeared to me and commanded me to send for Barak. One part of his mission is to take ten thousand men to Mount Tabor. It is from this mountain that God, Barak, and his men will wage war with Sisera," she informed them looking serious.

Most of the elders had white beards, they looked solemn, and they turned and looked at one another. Then one of them asked, "Is the battle set for a certain day?"

"No. But I'll know that when our army arrives at Mount Tabor."

"I am sure you know what the outcome of the war will be?" inquired another elder.

"Yes ... there is no doubt that we shall be victorious because God will intervene on our behalf," she assured them.

At this point, Barak interrupted. "We don't have much time, and we have a lot of miles to cover so I'm going to get right to the point. One, we would like all the elders, princes, and heads of the tribes of Naphtali, Issachar, and Zebulun to meet together in the City of Kedesh of Naphtali in three days to discuss the details about the war and make preparation. Two, we would like you to help us in sending letters and messengers to the towns and cities in Zebulun and Issachar, inviting the leaders to come to Kedesh of Naphtali. Three, as you travel to Kedesh, we would like you to recruit at least five thousand men and bring supplies including—food, sheep, horses, donkeys, camels, swords, spears, slings and stones, tents—and any kind of farming tools that can be used for weapons. We also would be grateful if you could send a fast horse rider to Kedesh to inform the leaders that Deborah and I shall be arriving in Kedesh within three days with about eight thousand men. Now, if there are any questions, we'll be glad to answer them."

One of the elders spoke. "General Barak, you mentioned that we shall be taking about eight thousand soldiers to the City of Kedesh. Don't you think that it would be better to leave the majority of our soldiers in this area since we are closer to Mount Tabor rather than to march them on a three-day journey to Kedesh?"

"At first, I thought about that. But after reconsideration, I came to another conclusion. As our soldiers march to Kedesh, the people will be encouraged seeing our growing numbers. The march will build physical stamina and discipline. Moreover, the new recruits will acquire the experience of taking orders from their regimental commanders. Most of all, Sisera's spy network keeps a close eye on our troop movements. And when they see us marching to the North away from Mount Tabor, this will disguise our true intentions."

"I have a question," said another of the elders. "How long will the war last?"

"Maybe the Prophetess, Deborah can answer that question," replied Barak, as he looked toward her.

"The main battle will last about a day, but after that, there will be pursuits after the fleeing enemy to other areas."

"Well, Deborah, you have been right in the past, I hope you are right this time, because we don't have the means to fight a prolong war," commented an elder who had not spoken until now.

After consultation with the elders, Barak began to end the discussion. "I want to thank all of you for your time and cooperation on behalf of our people during these terrible times. In addition, I want our honorable elders to treat this matter as top secret—especially the place where our army will meet. Again, I want to thank you for giving up your precious time."

Shortly after, the chief elder spoke up. "You are staying for the night aren't you?" he asked, rolling his eyes from side to side looking at both of them. At that moment, Deborah and Barak just smiled. "Good," the elder said. "We'll prepare supper and quarters for all four of you and your ten soldiers."

"Did we say we were staying elder?" asked Barak, scratching his head.

"No! Not in words, but your smile spoke for you. Why do you ask? You don't like our company?"

"Your company is just great ... elder," said Barak, shaking his head up and down.

When Barak, Deborah, and the elders had finished talking, they heard a commotion outside; and there was a knock on the door. One of the elders opened the door, and a crowd of people stood outside. A middle-aged woman stood there crying and exhausted. She began to speak: "My family they ..." She could not get all the words out because she was hungry, thirsty, and exhausted from running through the Zebulun hills.

"Calm yourself down my dear! What happened to your family?" asked one of the elders.

"Sisera and his ... soldiers came into our village during the night and killed everybody. All of my family is ... dead," she sobbed bitterly, dropping her head into her hands.

After that, Deborah and Barak approached her slowly. "What is your name? At what village did this slaughter take place?" asked Barak.

She raised her head slowly with tears running down her cheeks. "My name is Marah ... . Our village was located about five hundred cubits ... east of the City of Nahalol in the Zebulun hills."

"Come … ! Take a seat over here … will someone get her a skin of water," requested one of the elders.

Deborah brought over the water and comforted her. "We understand that you have been through a lot, and we are here to help you."

Barak came closer and sat next to Deborah. "Marah, I know that this is going to be hard for you, but we need to know—exactly what happened back there—everything!"

Marah looked at Barak with a long stare. "All right … . I'll try." Then she wiped the tears from her eyes with the sleeve of her torn beige dress. Marah began to tell them what happened about four days ago. She mentioned everything: including the coming of the noblemen pretending to want friendship, the Canaanites inviting the Hebrews to visit their city, and the Canaanite demanding the Hebrews to sacrifice their children to Baal. Finally, she told them about the Canaanite threat to retaliate against the Hebrews for showing disdain for the Canaanite gods.

While Barak listened to her story, he dropped his head; and he looked infuriated. Next, he raised his head and looked at her. "Are you sure that the leader of the soldiers was Sisera?"

"Yes," she said softly. "I am sure," answered Marah, looking directly into his eyes.

"How can you be so sure?"

"After the massacre, the leader asked one of his soldiers. 'Is everyone dead?' The soldier replied, 'I believe so, lord Sisera.' "

"All right, those words convinced me. Thank you Marah, you have been very helpful."

"When will we be delivered from the heavy yoke of Sisera?" asked Marah.

"This is why we are here. The Lord has heard the cry of our people, and He has sent Barak and me to rally together the army of Israel. For the Lord will destroy Sisera and his armies."

A man in the crowd shouted through the open door. "We heard that the Hebrews of Nahalol neither bowed down to the idol god, Baal, nor did they sacrifice their children. So why did they have to die?"

"The ways of the Lord are mysterious," Deborah said, as she turned and looked toward the crowd. "Your question is hard to answer, but if you be patient and seek the Lord in sincerity, He will reveal the secret things in His due time," she continued. "Sometimes, the Lord causes us to endure bitter pain in order to improve our character. We must look within ourselves for the answer."

"Deborah, you said that our deliverance will come soon, but it seems that we are suffering more now than before. Why?" asked Marah.

Deborah thought for a moment. "A new nation is soon to be born. Can a woman give birth without pain? Our people cannot give birth to a newborn freedom without suffering ... . From our grievous pain ... will come forth a deliverance and liberty which will echo throughout the centuries."

Marah spoke again with tears running down her cheeks and in a crying voice. "Sisera killed my entire family—even my son and daughter. I have nobody ... and I am ... am past childbearing age," she sobbed with exhaustion.

"I know how you feel, Marah," said Barak compassionately. "Sisera also murdered my mother."

"What can I do, Deborah? What?"

Deborah looked at her with compassion and a long stare. "Do you want the truth?"

"Yes ... ! The truth," answered Marah, wiping the tears from her blinking eyelids.

"Well then, here is the God-given truth: There are orphans among our people who don't have mothers or fathers. Adopt a son and a daughter and be a mother to them—raise them as your own and give them joy and love. Then in return—they will give you joy and love."

"But how can I raise children by myself without a husband?"

Deborah took her by the hand. "The Lord and I shall help you until you are able to find a husband. Until then, you can stay with me. Oh Marah, your dress is ripped in various places."

"I know. I tore it in several places when I ran frantically through the woods."

At that moment, Deborah turned toward the crowd, "Would someone ask around and see if the ladies have any clothes to spare?" Shortly thereafter, a group of ladies returned with some clothes for Marah; and Deborah gave them to her.

"Thank you Deborah, I trust you."

After that, several elders agreed to help Marah. Suddenly, a third elder looked at the General—then Barak nodded his head in consent. "Yes ... ! I shall help you also."

Meanwhile, Deborah turned away from the elders and faced Marah. "You see, the Lord has already made a way for you."

"Everything you say sounds pleasing to my ears," agreed Marah. "But I am older now, and what man is going to want me? I do not even have enough gerahs to purchase makeup."

Deborah then assured her, "You do not need any makeup. A good spirit and a genuine smile are inexpensive ways to improve your appearance."

Marah moved toward Deborah then embraced and kissed her. "You are truly a kind and wise lady. Thank you so much."

"Don't mention it. We are here on earth to help one another whether we realize it or not." said Deborah. "If we are not doing this, we are contributing to the problems of mankind by our neglect and selfishness."

Barak spoke up. "Deborah ... in light of what has happened to the village of Nahalol and to Marah, I think that you should take another swordsman with you for protection."

"I thank you Barak for being concerned about me; however, if there is any danger, the Lord will send his angels."

"Well ... I would feel a little better if you would take an extra guard anyway ... just in case the angels are a little bit late" he said, in a light-hearted way. Deborah received his words with mixed emotions and chose to remain silent.

CHAPTER 18

After enjoying the great hospitality from the elders of the City of Daberath, the next morning Deborah and Barak set out for the City of Kedesh. Traveling to Kedesh, she was concerned about her appearance and whether Barak's father would like her. This is where Barak grew up, and it was a special city from all other cities in the province of Naphtali. First, it was a special city because it was a fortified one. In addition to that, it was a Levite city and a city of refuge. Before Moses and Joshua died, they had designated six cities in the land of Canaan as cities of refuge where a manslayer could flee if he killed someone accidentally. At these cities, the manslayer could live without fear of the avenger of blood until his case came up in court. The City of Kedesh was located in upper Galilee, northwest of Lake Merom (now called Lake Huleh), not far from the Jordan River.

As Deborah and Barak traveled from the City of Daberath to Kedesh, Barak picked up two hundred and fifty soldiers from the Zebulun-Naphtali garrison to accompany him. On the third day after they left Daberath, just before they entered the city of Kedesh, they stopped at a spring and set up a tent so that they could freshen up and change clothes.

After they changed their clothes, they continued on their journey. Along the side of the road were many people waiting for the arrival of Deborah and Barak. They clapped their hands, made a yodel-like sound with their tongues, and chanted Barak, Barak, Deborah, Deborah, Barak, Barak, Deborah, Deborah. They chanted repeatedly.

The people came out in large crowds dressed in their best garments because they wanted to see their Prince, Barak, and the famous Prophetess, Deborah. He was their general who was fighting their enemies, the Canaanites. "I didn't expect to get a reception like this," said Deborah, looking at his medium blue tunic in admiration.

"This is how we do things here in Naphtali," he said bragging.

The men, women, and children continued to wave at Deborah and Barak as they passed. While they rode on their horses and donkeys, they returned the waves with enthusiastic smiles. As they rode along the main road, Deborah welcomed the joy of her people. In the background, there were the stately mountains of Naphtali laden with tall evergreen trees, and the fresh green grass of the springtime. On the right side of the road, they saw the green grass in the valley that led down to the Jordan River.

"Do you see the large house over against the mountain," asked Barak.

"Do you mean the white one to the left?"

"Yes … . That is where I live."

"It is beautiful, Barak. I like the courtyard that surrounds it and the side stairs that go up to the roof and terrace."

"Thank you. If I had more time, I would show you around my entire property."

"That is so thoughtful of you Barak, but there will be another time." Looking over into the distance, Deborah asked, "Who owns those sheep and goats over there?"

"They belong to me."

"Barak, how many do you have?"

"At the last count, there were 1,655 sheep, 945 goats, 53 horses, 20 camel, 15 asses, and 24 yokes of oxen. But tomorrow, I shall have even less because I am donating many to feed the soldiers."

She turned toward him. "That's so nice of you; you must have a lot of servants?"

"Twenty-three, all total," he said, passing by the crowd waving.

The bright warm day contributed to the turnout of a large number of people. As they approached closer to the city, the crowd grew larger; and the shrill blast of the trumpets became louder. "Is your father going to be in the city?" Deborah asked, hoping that she looked presentable enough.

"I think he will be there. He usually attends these kinds of functions."

"Well, being head of his tribe, I would think that he'd have to attend," she remarked, as they passed through the main gate. "By the way, do you think he'll like me?"

"Yes," Barak assured her. "He will love and adore you!"

"Oh ..." she remarked, expressing surprise as she continued to wave at the crowd.

Then they came to the open plaza where thousands of people were waiting. While the drummers continued to beat, they passed by many white stone buildings until they arrived at the Great Hall of the elders and judges. The elders and judges stood in line on the stone steps in front of the Hall waiting for the arrival of Deborah and Barak. When Barak came within ten cubits of the stone steps, he dismounted and went over to Deborah and helped her off the donkey. "Walk with me over to the lower steps and wait there. Then I shall ascend the steps to greet my father and the elders. Afterwards, I shall return to get you," he whispered.

"Yes Barak." Deborah stood there in her dark green dress with gold fringes on the borders, and on her head was a light green mantilla.

Barak walked up the steps. "Peace my father," he greeted, bowing at him and then to the rest of the elders and judges. Then he stepped closer to his father, embraced him, and kissed him on each cheek. "How have you been father?"

"Well, my son." Elder Abinoam's long flowing white beard covered most of his brown skin. He had a strong striking face that displayed wisdom and humor. His burgundy tunic hugged his small body and blended well with his white turban-like head wrap. "I see that the God of our ancestors has been taking good care of you," he replied, looking him over to see if he had any disfigured bones. Looking down at the bottom of the steps, he asked, "Is she the famous lady, Deborah?"

"Yes, she is," Barak answered, smiling as he shook his head up and down.

"Well! Bring her up! We would like to meet her."

Barak went down the steps, lined with beautiful green tropical plants and returned with Deborah. "This is my father, Abinoam."

"Peace be unto you," she greeted, bowing to him slightly.

"Peace be to you, my daughter. Barak, she is so beautiful and graceful. It is so nice meeting you. I have heard so much about you."

"Good things, I hope," she replied gently.

"Mostly good, but every person has some opposition; and that is to be expected."

"Now I can agree to that father."

After their meeting and greeting, Barak and his father introduced Deborah to the rest of the elders then went and had an afternoon meal. The people prepared roasted lamb, goat, and roasted beef. Deborah and Barak could smell the aroma in the spring air. They had ground corn, beans, fresh green vegetables, olives, dates, figs, raisins, apricots, pomegranates, wheat bread, and fish from the Sea of Galilee. The entire Hebrew community of Kedesh contributed the food, and there was plenty for everyone.

After Deborah and Barak finished the afternoon meal, they went to a special chamber in the Hall of the Elders. They briefed the elders concerning what the Lord told Deborah, and they were willing to supply thousands of men for the war against Jabin and Sisera. The elders agreed that they had enough of Sisera, and that he had become more brutal and intolerable. They said that they wanted to do something, and this was their opportunity. Now they received the endorsement of a Prophetess of the Lord, and He chose their tribal son, Barak, to lead the campaign. The elders of the people agreed to supply all the necessary food, horses, cattle, flocks, donkeys, camels, mules, tents, and slings and stones.

Deborah and Barak came out of the meeting about two hours after midday. The white stone plaza was still full with people. Some were still eating, some were talking, and others were singing spiritual songs. As soon as the people saw Deborah, Barak, and his father approaching the top of the steps, they began to yell for Deborah to speak.

"They want you to speak, Deborah. Do you feel up to it?" Elder Abinoam inquired.

The people yelled again, "Deborah, Deborah."

"All right," she said, knowing that she could not disappoint them.

"First of all, let me make a few remarks; and then I'll introduce you," he whispered.

The crowd was still shouting for Deborah when Elder Abinoam took two steps forward to speak. He raised his left hand for the crowd to stop. Once they became silent, he began to talk.

"Bless be the God of our ancestors who is merciful and just. I want to take this time to give my thanks to all the elders and judges who made the sacrifice to come here to our city on a moment's notice. Moreover, I want to welcome and thank all the soldiers and you citizens for putting forth your great effort. Many of you have heard why we are assembled here today. We have suffered under the yoke of the Canaanites for many years. Now the opportunity has arrived for us to be free. I am not going to talk long because Deborah will be speaking after me. The elders and I have heard what the Lord revealed to her, and our discussion confirms that she is a true prophetess. The Lord has declared all-out war with Jabin and his commander, Sisera; and He has appointed Barak, my son, as commander of the Hebrew army. Furthermore, the elders of the tribes of Naphtali and Zebulun have given their unselfish support for the war effort. May God be with us. In closing, I want to thank the elders of the tribe of Issachar who brought a company of men to help take care of the wounded. The Princes have special knowledge of the heavenly forces. These men have the understanding of the times, and know what Israel ought to do. They will consult with Deborah and Barak on all-important matters. Now at this time, I present to you Mother Deborah."

The crowd went wild shouting Deborah's name and gave the yodel praise-like sound with their tongues. As Deborah stepped forward, the crowd continued to shout her name. She raised her right hand for them to stop, but they continued for another two minutes to applaud her. She attempted to speak twice, but the cheers were too loud for her to speak. Then at last, the voices subsided. "I wish blessings and prosperity to all my brothers and sisters. In addition, may we continue to give praises and glory to our eternal God, the God of Abraham, Isaac, and Jacob. I ask our Lord to give peace and good health to all our great elders who made this long journey to come to this city in such a time as this."

Deborah spoke for what seemed like a half an hour. Revealing what God had told her, reminding them to keep all of God's commandments, she admonished them to deal righteously with one another. Then she began to relate a parable: "There was once a very poor man living in the famous City of Babylon who became a middle man and sold grains. After working hard for three years, he became a successful merchant and invested his savings in expensive jewelry. He learned all about the jewelry business—and after working for five years, he became even wealthier. Then a severe famine stuck the land; and multitudes of people came to him and begged for help; but he looked down on them and refused to give it. He told them to go out and work hard as he did. Many of the people became weak, some caught diseases, and others died.

"As time passed, the rich man also became sick and contracted a disease. Eventually, he became paralyzed from the neck down. He spent a lot of his money for doctors and nurses. He even hired workers to wash, clothe, feed, and to put him in and take him out of bed. His life became so unbearable; and he concluded, what good is it to have all of this money and the best doctors cannot heal me. He suffered and thought for many months:

*When there was a famine in our land,
the poor came to me for help and I
rejected them. Now I am in poor
health and my wealth cannot heal me
or make me happy.*

"Lying still and quiet on his bed one night, he reflected, 'what misery I brought on myself because of my selfishness.'" After she finished telling her parable, Deborah emphasized the following salient points: "It is cruel to see and know that the poor exist and refuse to give when you are able. Those that decline to share with others violate the laws and virtues of giving which are inherent in our traditions. When we do not give, we suffer retribution in this lifetime or in the next life. This means that we reap what we sow, and only the merciful will receive mercy. Giving accomplishes three things: One, it brings joy to the hearts of the needy. Two, the giver receives additional blessings. Three, the act of giving makes the world a better place for all of us. I want all of you to remember this from the scroll of Deuteronomy. When you become wealthy, don't say that 'my power and the might of mine hand hath gotten me this wealth. But thou shall remember the Lord thy God; for it is He that giveth thee power to get wealth … .' "

Her speech was interrupted four times by cheers and great applause. Then she began to end her speech. "Many of our ancestors didn't drive out the Canaanites. Therefore, many of us live among them. It is written in our holy books that God places temptation among us to see if we shall keep His commandments. Even though you live among the Canaanites, don't be tempted to copy after them because only the unaware and the misguided copy the bad traits of others to the detriment of themselves and to society. They worship idol gods, commit incest, cohabitate with animals, sacrifice and burn their sons and daughters in the fire to their gods, and they cut and make markings on their flesh. We must resist temptation and not become like them. Because they did these things, our God defeated them in the past and will defeat them again very soon."

"Continue Deborah!" shouted a man in the crowd.

"Now I have a few words about Sisera. Even though he oppresses us, remember that God raised him up to punish us for our disobedience. We should not put all of the blame on Sisera because some of the fault lies in ourselves. We can correct this by doing what is right. At this season, God has heard our prayers, and He has decided that twenty years of punishment is enough. In order to redeem you, God chose Barak and me to be your leaders. As I close, I want to remind you that when we go to war against Sisera and defeat him, the victory belongs to God. So let us give Him the glory, hallelujah."

"Hallelujah! Hallelujah! Hallelujah!" repeated the crowd.

When Deborah finished her speech, the crowd erupted in a great applause and began to cheer her enthusiastically. Finally, the crowd went automatically into groups of folk-like dances. They sang as they danced praising God for answering their prayer and for sending them Deborah and Barak. Not being able to resist the gaiety, Deborah and Barak joined in with a circle of dancers. They went around in a circle. They took two steps backward and two steps forward, and they danced to the rhythm of the drums and tambourines as they clapped. They looked at one another with joy in their hearts, smiling and teasing each other. It had been a long time since she had enjoyed herself with such jubilation.

They stopped dancing and walked away together from the crowd. "Oh, it was so wonderful," she remarked, looking up at him and panting from being out of breath.

"Yes, it has been years since I've danced like this. I believe it was at one of the Sukkoth festivals."

"You know, Barak; I've enjoyed myself from the time we arrived at the City of Daberath until now. The countryside is so beautiful. Your people have been very warm, friendly, and receptive. Even your father is sensitive and kind," she said, patting him on his chest softly with the palm of her hand.

"Well ... thank you, Deborah,"

"And you ... you've made me feel like I am 15 years younger, she admitted. "You have made me feel alive again."

"Well ... you know it doesn't have to end."

Then Barak looked over the crowd and both of them remained silent for a moment. Finally, he looked down at her and joy surged through him. He took her by the hand and said softly, "I love you, Deborah. I want you to be my wife, Deborah ... will you?"

"Oh Barak, you are a good man ... you came from a good family, but it is too early to think about marriage." Then she turned and looked away.

"You were going to marry Caleb ... and he is gone! Now what is there to stand in our way?" he asked, as he looked into her eyes.

"That was different ... . The war will be starting soon, and there are a few things that remain uncertain."

"In regards to my question, Deborah, is that a yes or no?" he inquired.

"It isn't a yes or a no. It is a go slow ... we don't have to make any definite promised right now. Do we?"

"No ... but I think we should be able to make a decision soon after the war."

"Now I can agree to that."

Deborah was glad that Barak asked her to marry him. It proved his good intentions, she thought; and her journey to his hometown showed a more positive side of his life that she liked. However, there was one thing that held her back from committing herself; she felt that his spiritual faith was questionable. In view of this, she wanted to give herself more time to see how that worked out.

The following day, Barak met with his regiment commanders. They made preparations and drew up plans for the journey. Then Barak sent an advance detachment of five hundred men to take control of Mount Tabor. After the priests, elders, and soldiers were ready, Barak shouted, "Tonight we march!" Moreover, the Princes of the tribe of Issachar were with Deborah and Barak when they arrived at Mount Tabor three days later.

CHAPTER 19

On the fourth day, after Barak departed from the City of Kedash, Sisera called an urgent meeting with King Jabin and his courtiers. When the King sent word to Sisera that he was ready to see him, he marched into the Grand Hall of the Canaanites at a rapid pace. Sisera was in full battle dress—with chest protection, a sword on his side, and a brass helmet on his head with a purple plume at its peak. He strutted in like a rooster.

"This better be urgent … for you to interrupt my meeting with the ambassadors," said the King, looking disturbed.

Bowing to the King, Sisera remarked, "Yes, it is, my lord! Our spies have reported to me that Barak and this … this woman Deborah have taken control of Mount Tabor."

"How many men are you talking about?" inquired the King, as he changed positions on his copper throne.

"Between ten and fifteen thousand."

"As my commander-in-chief of the Canaanite army, what do you make of this troop movement?"

"It is simply an act of war … my lord! It appears that Barak and Deborah want war!"

"Go on …" the King ordered, as he placed his elbow on the armrest of the throne.

"When Barak and Debora took Mount Tabor, this meant that they intended to attack our forces in the Jezreel Valley and endeavor to terminate our control there," said Sisera. It was twenty years earlier that Sisera conquered the Jezreel Valley. As a result, many Hebrews fled to the mountains and hills where they lived in the dens and caves. This easy conquest by his iron chariots enabled Sisera to divide the Hebrews north of the Jezreel from those of the south. In effect, his military operation helped contribute to the disunity and separation between the Hebrew tribes.

"Why do you think that Deborah and Barak took control of this particular mountain?" asked the Vizer.

"There are at least two reasons … . Tabor is a good place to assemble soldiers because it is a flat top mountain. Two, it is the highest mountain that overlooks the Jezreel Valley; and from it, they can keep an eye on all our troop movements."

"What?" The King switched positions on his throne and remarked. "It seems like Deborah and Barak are not so stupid after all. Furthermore, it appears that the rabbit has outfoxed the leopard," he said, leaning forward with his head facing toward Sisera. "If this mountain is such an important piece of real estate, and a good lookout post, why in the hell didn't you take control of it before Barak?"

Sisera stood there dumbfounded with a sheepish look on his face. "I never thought …"

"You never thought what …? Speak … ! Speak up General!" ordered the King.

"Well, they were just backwoods people from the mountain and cave … and I never thought that they would have the sense to organize an army of more than five hundred men."

The King sat back slowly. "I see … . In the future, I would suggest that you remember that even a jackass has a brain," said the King, looking down at him in disappointment.

"Our spies," said Sisera, "saw the Hebrew soldiers marching north, and they stopped at the City of Kedesh … ."

"Go on," prompted the King.

"Night fell, and the spies went to sleep. By the next morning, the spied learned that the Hebrews departed during the night and marched to Tabor, my lord the King,"

The King stood up and placed both hands on his hips and spoke, "We have the most powerful army in Canaan and have experts in every field of knowledge. In spite of this, we have been out-maneuvered by this so-called mountain boy and his consort, Deborah … . Now they can watch us like hawks watch their prey waiting for the first chance to pounce down on their victims. We, the mighty ancient Canaanite people will become the laughing stock of the civilized world."

Sisera made a gesture with his hand and attempted to speak. "My lord, the …"

But the King interrupted him and continued. "Barak and his woman have the best position they could want. Barak and his army have the protection on the north by the hills of Zebulun and the people of Naphtali. We look like fools … ! Like fools … Isn't this true, Sisera?" the King asked.

Sisera hesitated to answer the question because he knew that he dared not displease the King. At that moment, he lowered his head slowly and answered cautiously, "Yes … my lord the King."

Dressed in his purple tunic, which extended from his shoulders to his feet, the King turned around sharply in a stately fashion and sat down gracefully. "There is one thing that troubles me." The King rubbed his chin and closed his eyes for a moment. "Why would the Hebrew men want to go to war with such small numbers and without chariots?" he asked, raising his head slowly with piercing eyes looking in Sisera's direction.

Sisera looked surprised—he squirmed and struggled to speak. His head moved in several directions at once. "I ... I don't exactly know ... . Perhaps, they have armies hidden in the mountains north and south of the Jezreel and intend to surprise us."

"You know Sisera ... that I hate surprises! Barak will most likely attack us from the North; however, we shall need additional soldiers to protect our rear in case the Hebrews attack us from the South."

"I agree, my lord."

At that moment, the High Priest stroked his chin and appeared deep in thought standing there in the panoply of his office. He wore a dark green brocaded robe with a light green sash trimmed in gold and silver. On his head was a conical cap. "If it pleases the King ... may thy servant, the High Priest say a word or two?"

"You have my ear, oh servant of Baal."

"When I researched the history of the Hebrews, I discovered that one of their leaders, Moses, took a census of the men from twenty years of age who were able to go to war. At that time, there were more than one hundred and ten thousand men from the tribes of Zebulun and Naphtali alone, and this was one hundred and fifty years ago ... ."

"And just what is your point?" asked the King, showing a little impatience.

"My point is that I am sure that their numbers have increased. Therefore, isn't it good sense to conclude that they are able to muster far more than ten or fifteen thousand men?" asked the High Priest, as he extended his hand.

"Yes," said the King. "That makes sense. They must have reserve forces hidden away somewhere."

The King then turned toward his advisor, Kenaz, an expert on Egyptian and Nubian affairs. "Do you think we should send to Egypt for help?"

Kenaz threw his dark green tunic over one shoulder and spoke. "Not at this time, my lord."

"And why not?" asked the King, rising up suddenly.

"These are very unstable times in Egypt. From the reign of Rameses IX, Libyan marauders have threatened the Theban Capitol. Civil war has been rampant. Because the silver and the gold had been scarce, the economically distressed people have robbed the tombs of the kings and nobles. In view of this, the government at Thebes had to call in Nubian troops to restore order. As you can understand, my lord ... Egypt and our Hametic brothers are in no position to send us help."

"I don't want to be surprised by these Hebrews. To whom can we turn? There must be at least a token force that Egypt can send."

The grand Vizier stepped three paces toward the King. "There is no need, my lord to send to Egypt for help ... when we have friends nearby ..."

"Nearby? Continue!"

"We can summon help from the nations of the East, from Ammon, from Moab, and from Syria."

"What makes you think that they will send help?" asked the King.

Pointing toward the East, the Vizier explained, "These nations are the old enemies of Israel. They will be glad to get revenge because of their humiliating defeat over eighty years ago."

"Who was the Hebrew leader at that time?"

"Ehud, Ehud Ben Gera ... oh King, I think that we need to do three things immediately: One, call up the kings of the East. Two, summon all the Canaanite nations from Sidon down to the City of Dor. Three, unite with all the Canaanite city-states from Megiddo and Taanach to Beth Shean. Then we can confront and defeat Barak and his buzzing bumblebee, Deborah, in the Valley of Jezreel."

"Ummm," The King sat back on his throne and placed his finger on his chin. "This sounds like a splendid idea. Yes, we shall go with the Vizier's recommendation. From this day, I hereby appoint you responsible for the diplomatic negotiations to unite all of the aforementioned Canaanite nations."

"I will commence these efforts right away, my lord," the Vizier promised and departed.

Then the King commanded, "Approach the throne, General Sisera." Sisera came near, stopped at the bottom step, did a slight bow, and saluted the King by bringing up his right fist briskly to his chest and stood at attention.

"I am at your service, my lord, the King."

"General Sisera, many years ago, my father appointed you as commander-in-chief of his army because he saw skill and ability in you. However, within recent years, several events have made me wonder about you ... the loss of over five hundred elite soldiers and weapons at the Japhia Pass and now this spy debacle."

"My lord, but I was not present at the Japhia Pass."

"I know that ... ! Nevertheless, as commander-in-chief of my army, I hold you responsible for the conduct of your officers and soldiers. It is your duty to instruct your soldiers on how to behave in every situation. Is that understood?"

"Yes, my lord."

The King then asked Sisera to come closer to the throne because he had something to say to him in private. The King whispered, "Deborah and Barak outsmarted our spies and made us look like fools. Now after the war is over, make sure you do not have to return in humiliation. Can I depend on you, General?"

"Yes, my lord," said Sisera humbly, as he bowed.

Finally, the King gestured to him to return to his former place. "Oh, there is another matter. Do you think that we should attack Mount Tabor?"

"No, I do not, my lord."

"Why not?"

"Our losses would be too great … Barak, the mountain boy, has the advantage because he controls the high ground. This gives him the opportunity to roll down on us large boulders and hurl down rocks and stones like hail from heaven."

"Then what do you suggest?"

"We move our armies into the Jezreel Valley and wait for him to attack. When they do, we can use our charioteers and horsemen against them and crush them like ants. This way, we can annihilate the forces of Deborah and Barak in one central location."

"Oh! Your words are pleasing in my ears … you have my permission to take up your positions as soon as possible and keep me informed of everything," ordered the King.

"Yes, my lord."

"Furthermore, when you defeat the Hebrew army, I want you to bring Deborah and Barak to me … alive … I want them to stand before me ... in chains ... in chains. Is this clear, General?"

"Yes, my lord ... . You want them in chains," Sisera repeated, and snapped to attention. "There is one last thing. Deborah and Barak outwitted our spies and made us look like jackasses—Make sure that you do not return in disgrace with a defeated look on your face. Now you may leave."

As Sisera stood before the King, it irked him to entertain the thought that Barak, the mountaineer, and his female consort could defeat him. He asked himself, what kind of man was this that needed to hide behind the skirt of a woman. He dubbed Barak the mountain boy who dashed over rocks and cliffs and who was scared to come out and fight.

When the King finished speaking, the High Priest, Eved-Baal, said, "Oh King, for the success of the war, I think it is only befitting to offer special sacrifices to our god, Baal who needs to be pacified."

"Yes, I agree. When would you like to have the ceremony?"

"The sooner the better ... in a few hours would be good, my lord."

When the time came, the priests blew the trumpets to announce that a ceremony for a sacrifice was about to take place. For these ceremonies, the people gathered in the area of the temple; and next to the temple was a large statue of Baal. Before bringing up the sacrifices, the High Priest rendered his prayer: "Oh Baal, our god, lord of the world, we beseech thee to grant us victory over the Hebrews and their leaders Barak and Deborah."

The priests heated a large fire in the stomach of the idol, Baal. They brought in four victims for a sacrifice: two

Canaanite boys, and two Hebrew captives—one male and one female.

"Bring forth the two Hebrews," ordered the High Priest.

They brought the Hebrew male and female blindfolded with their hands tied behind their backs. The High Priest placed his hand on the head of the female and recited. "This sacrifice is offered to thee, oh lord, Baal, to grant us victory over the woman known as Deborah."

The face of Baal was about ten cubits wide and about twelve cubits high. He had thick lips and a broad nose. His stomach was open so that he could receive the human sacrifices. After they killed the Hebrew girl, they carried her over to the belly of Baal and cast her inside the hot flames.

They repeated the same ritual for the Hebrew boy. The only thing that was different was that his sacrifice symbolized the victory over Barak. Finally, they sacrificed two Canaanite boys so that their idol god, Baal, could be appeased enough to grant them victory over the Hebrew army.

When the High Priest finished the sacrificial ceremony, the King, Sisera, the Vizier, and the rest of the courtiers returned to the palace. Sisera gathered up his war instruments—charts, maps, and rode off with a detachment of soldiers to where his army was in bivouac.

Sisera had a surprise for Deborah and Barak. He was not about to let his soldiers be trapped between two Hebrew armies on both sides of the Jezreel Valley. He did not want it to be said that a woman and a mountain boy defeated him. Will Sisera succeed?

CHAPTER 20

The army of the Hebrews now occupied Mount Tabor, a flat top mountain excellent for mustering troops and high enough to observe much of Sisera's troop movements. Tabor is located on the northeast side of the Jezreel Valley not far from the southwest shore of the Sea of Chinnereth which was renamed the Sea of Galilee. From Mount Tabor, the highest mountain overlooking the Jezreel Valley, Deborah and Barak looked due south in the direction of Mount Gilboa. Also, from this vantage point, they could see Mount Carmel and Megiddo. They walked around the mountain to check the physical features. At the foot of the mountain on the northwest side, they noticed the spring of water that drained into the Kishon River to the southwest. The most common ascent to Tabor is on the northwest side. Barak's army took this route when they climbed to the summit; they ascended in a serpentine course. The path became steeper and narrower with hairpin turns, and a few people slipped and fell. They passed by beautiful varieties of grass, oak trees, evergreen trees, and green bushes. Tabor has lower peaks on the northwest side leading to the hills of Zebulun and the City of Nazareth. However, the City of Nazareth was not in existence in the time of Deborah and Barak.

On the second day that the Hebrew army encamped on Mount Tabor, the soldiers gathered rocks and stones to hurl at the enemy. The Hebrews did not have many swords and spears; in view of this, they used some slings and stones as weapons because the Canaanites had taken away their blacksmiths.

Before Barak reached Mount Tabor, he sent out various groups of spies to keep a careful watch on all the activities and movements of the Canaanites. Barak read scrolls on warfare used by other Hebrew generals and warriors to increase his knowledge in preparation for the big battle to come. One of the scrolls he perused was, *The Book of the Wars of the Lord*, mentioned by Moses. Everything was on a high war footing. Sisera increased his military presence in the Jezreel particularly on the main artery of the Kishon River northeast of the City of Megiddo. The Hebrews saw hundreds of chariots moving bristly up and down the Valley along with thousands of horsemen and tens of thousands of infantrymen. The Hebrews knew that it would be only a matter of days before all hell would break loose.

As Barak sat in his tent reviewing military matters, one of his guards entered. "General, a lieutenant is here to see you."

"Send him in," ordered Barak.

The lieutenant walked in and snapped to attention. "Our patrols have captured a group of people, General."

"How many?"

"Five. And I believe they are spies, General," commented the lieutenant.

"Oh? You do huh ... . That's up to me to decide what they are."

"They have the appearance of the heavenly moon."

"Now what makes you thing that they are spies?" Barak asked, gently tilting his head to one side.

The lieutenant extended his hand in gesturing. "Their kind is not from around here."

"Oh...? I see ... And if you visited their country, your kind would not be from around where they live ... would that make you a spy?"

"I ... I ... I ... guess ... not," he stuttered.

"Did you get their names?" asked Barak.

"The head man of the group said that his name ... I think, he pronounced it Demetius."

"Do you mean Demetrius?" asked Barak, as he recognized the name and smiled.

"Yes, that's it. Do you know him?" he asked, with surprise.

"Yes! I know him. Does this mean that Demetrius has returned?" he asked himself aloud, with joy and excitement. "Did you tie them up?"

"Yes General! I did according to standard orders."

"Good, now untie them ... and bring them to me!" Barak ordered forcefully.

A short while later, the lieutenant and a few of his soldiers escorted the Greeks to Barak's tent. As soon as Barak heard them coming, he stepped out from his tent with a big smile. "Peace be with you Demetrius. You have returned. You have returned to us." Then they embraced like old friends.

"Peace Barak ... you look good in your uniform." Barak wore a white tunic and a dark blue vest with gold embroidered borders.

"Thank you, is everyone well?"

"Yes, we are all here: my three medical assistants, my wife, Isis, and my daughter, Hatshepsut."

Everyone looked pleased and smiled at Barak for his warm greeting. After that, Barak excused the lieutenant.

"I want to apologize for any discomfort that my soldiers may have caused you," said Barak. "Come!" invited Barak. "Come into my tent! I have water and food for you to satisfy your hunger and thirst."

After his guest partook of the victuals, Barak asked the important question. "Oh Demetrius, did you return to us to help with our wounded?"

"Yes, that is true."

"May I ask what made you change your mind?"

"Well, it was the dream that I had on the night that we slept in the Canaanite City of Tyre. In my dream, the wolves attached my neighbor's sheep; and I did not help him. Then I ran away and I felt very sad. After discussing this dream with my wife, my daughter, and my medical assistants, I decided to return to help you, General."

"I am very happy that you decided to return," commented Barak.

"My wife always tells me that there is a deeper meaning to our dreams if we think about them and apply them to our everyday lives. I have listened to her advice in the past, and it has been very helpful to me."

"You are fortunate to have such a valuable wife," Barak said, looking at her. "Not only has her wisdom benefited you but also my people." Barak paused and lowered his head and thought for a moment. "Now I want to introduce you to my people." He looked directly at Demetrius to see if this met with his approval.

"Whatever you think is best is all right with us," commented Demetrius.

Then Barak called out aloud, "Guard!" The guard came in and snapped to attention. "Blow the ram's horn and assemble the people."

"Yes General."

A short while later, Barak and his guests went out of the tent and they stood on an elevated part of the mountain for everyone to see them. The news had spread like a windstorm that visitors were in the camp. As a result, the people were eager to assemble in order to learn what Barak had to say. The people were very quiet and pensive—not one soul moved. A few moments later, Deborah and the Princes of Issachar came up. Finally, Barak began to speak. "Sages, elders, priests, princes, Prophetess Deborah, officers, soldiers, and people of the Hebrew tribes, I greet you all with great love. Many of you know why I summoned you here today. For those of you who may not know, it is only befitting for me to inform you that earlier today; visitors came into our camp of their own free will. They came from Greece—a distant country west of the Hittite Empire."

"The Greek Islands," Demetrius whispered, softly in Barak's ear.

"Thank you," said Barak, and he continued. "For the last twenty years, they have been studying in Egypt and Nubia. Now that their studies are complete, they were returning to Greece. Deborah and I first met them in the City of Tirzah more than a week ago. Their knowledge and learning is of a high quality; and because of this, I felt that their service would be very useful to us. Therefore, I have asked them to remain with us for a fortnight."

Then Barak paused; and one of the elders said, "Go on, Barak, we want to hear more."

"The soldiers of the tribes of Zebulun and Naphtali are encamped on this mountain because we are expecting war any day now. Like any war, there will be injuries to our soldiers; and they deserve the best medical care that we can provide for them. Demetrius Lysimachus and his staff are standing to my right. They received expert training as doctors in Egypt— the most advanced nation in the world. His wife and daughter are both trained nurses. As of this moment, I have placed Demetrius as head over the hospital, and I want you to give him and his staff your greatest respect and cooperation. If I find anyone faltering, the court of the elders and I will deal with them. However, I know that you will conduct yourselves in the proper manner. If anyone has any questions or complaints, this is the time to utter them." Barak remained silent for a short while. When no one spoke up, he continued and said, in jest smiling. "There may be some children here who are old enough to remember Moses … when he stood on Mount Sinai," then the people laughed at Barak's humor. "At that time, Moses advised us with these words: 'Thou shall neither vex a stranger, nor oppress him: for ye were strangers in the land of Egypt.' " The crowd went wild, clapped their hands, shouted, and greeted the visitors with smiles and words of pleasantness. Moments later, the elders, priests, princes, and officers lined up and passed by the visitors saluting them and expressing words of welcome and gratitude.

Then Barak summoned a war council meeting of his staff officers and other officials. This group included the princesses, elders, priests, Deborah, and Demetrius. The officials scheduled the meeting in the large headquarters' tent at sunset.

After the reception for Demetrius, Deborah returned to her tent. She and her handmaids shared a tent together, and Nachshon had his own tent nearby. "Sarah would you and Marah mind going down to the watershed to get some water?" asked Deborah.

"Surely, my lady … right away."

"And take Nachshon with you!"

As Deborah sat in her tent alone, she reflected on the impending war. She knew that it had to come; but once it was over, she realized that things would be normal again. A little later, Deborah stood up in her tent; she looked through the opening and saw Barak talking to one of his officers. She wanted to go to him and embrace him because she felt deep down that he had almost everything she wanted in a man. Deborah was beginning to think of Barak as her man. After all, didn't the Lord ask her to send for him; and didn't the Lord remove Caleb from her life? There must be some special meaning in that.

At last, Sarah, Marah, and Nachshon returned with the water. "We were able to get three skin containers, my lady, and Nachshon helped us to fill all three," said Sarah. Then Marah and Nachshon looked at each other and smiled with interest.

"That's great. Oh Sarah, I have to go to a staff meeting with the officers, the elders, and with Barak. Would you like to walk over with me?"

"Sure, my lady," said Sarah smiling.

"Mother Deborah, I'll talk with Marah until Sarah returns," said Nachshon.

"Thank you, that's a good idea."

When Deborah arrived at the large tent of the military headquarters, she noticed three Terra-cotta lamps burning which provided the light in the tent. She greeted all the elders, princes, staff officers, and Barak. They smiled at one another, and Deborah was pleased. Barak was waiting for two more people. After they arrived, he opened the meeting. The head priest of the City of Kedesh opened the meeting with prayer and ended with the priestly three-fold blessing: "may the Lord bless thee ... ."

When the priest finished his prayer, Barak spoke. "We are here today to discuss plans for the war, and it is just a matter of a day or so before the war will breakout. By the way, my staff estimates that the enemy has us outnumbered five to one. Now I would like to hear the report from Captain David."

"General, all the food and water supplies are ready including all bandages and medicines for the wounded."

"Good … ! I want you to give all the medical supplies to Dr. Demetrius."

Dr. Demetrius turned to Barak and requested, "General Barak, I will need for you to designate about one hundred men to help bring the wounded soldiers to the hospital tent."

Then Prince Zaken, from the tribe of Issachar stood up and remarked, "I would like to offer a hundred men from my tribe to assist Dr. Demetrius and his staff."

"Thank you oh prince. This takes care of that. Now Captain Enoch, give us your report."

"The weapons, slings and stones, spears, and rocks are ready; and we have strengthened the ramparts that surround the top of this mount. Those men who do not have swords and spears, we have issued farming tools as their weapons."

"What about the training of the men?" inquired Barak, with concern?

"We trained them in all the body movements, riding horses, and how to take the enemy's swords and spears. And we taught them how to use them," explained Captain Enoch confidently.

"Captain Enoch, have you heard anything from our spies yet?"

"No General, but I am expecting a report any time now."

Barak remained quiet for a moment and appeared to be in deep thought. Then he asked, "Do any of you priests or elders have anything to say?"

"Yes," answered one of the elders. "Just before the battle, the priest must blow the trumpets and recite the conditions that exclude some soldiers from war duty."

"Thank you elder, are there any more questions?"

"Oh General Barak," said a senior priest. "We understand from your own words, that our forces are outnumbered five to one. "I heard a rumor that you refused help from Prince Abihu. Is this true?"

"Yes! However, it is also true … that I refused his help because he based his offer on harsh conditions. He wanted me to persuade the leaders of the northern tribes to accept his leadership; if they refused, he wanted to have them murdered. As a result, I refused to be a party to his scheme … ."

"Don't you think it would have been better to have had his soldiers so that they could help us get rid of Jabin and Sisera?" asked the priest.

"No! I do not. We must not trade one cruel master for another just to say that we have a Hebrew king … . The end does not justify the means. The scheme proposed by Abihu would have plunged the Hebrew tribes into civil war, and that is too risky. If civil war came, more people would die from our own hands, than by the swords of Sisera. I can take some cruelty from Sisera … but I shall not take … the oppression … and dictatorship of Prince Abihu," he argued, shaking his head from side to side in opposition.

Meanwhile, a young officer raised his hand and received recognition to speak. "Some of our elders tell us that we have enough men from the tribes of Zebulun and Naphtali to put in the field more than two hundred thousand soldiers. If this is true, why are we calling up only ten thousand men?"

"Deborah would you like to answer that question?" asked Barak.

"I'll be glad to answer … . The Lord asked for only ten thousand and no more."

At that instant, one of the guards outside of the tent handed Barak a letter from Sisera. Barak read the letter then read it to the counsels:

> *In the name of Jabin, King of the Canaanites, I, General Sisera, order you Barak and Deborah to surrender to me by noon tomorrow. If you do this, your soldiers will be allowed to go free. If not—our gods, Baal, Ashtaroth, and Mot will deliver you into our hands. Then some of you will be sold into slavery, and the rest of you will be sacrificed in the fire to our gods. Furthermore, don't think that your God will save you from our hands. He hasn't delivered you during the last twenty years, and He will not save you now. This is the only warning you will receive.*
> *General Sisera*

"You have heard the letter; shall we send him an answer?"

Everyone remained silent. At last, Elder Ram spoke, "If no one has anything to say, I do," he informed them, looking to one side of the tent and then to the other. He raised his chin high "General Sisera has the gall … to ask Barak and Deborah to surrender to him … . Then he insults our intelligence further by telling us that our soldiers will go free … . His words are only lies … lies … lies … . Let's not honor him by giving him an answer," he pleaded, looking around the tent. "But let him wait and sweat … until the water runs down into his breeches," he urged, as the people laughed in agreement.

"Does anyone else have anything to add?" asked Barak.

A young officer raised his hand. "When will we attack?"

"I … don't really know. I guess, Prophetess Deborah … will give us that information," Barak answered, slowly and cautiously.

"When do we start taking instructions from a woman?"

"Listen young man! If I don't question her, don't you."

"Thank you Barak," Deborah interrupted. "I would like to speak for myself." She spoke softly and calmly: "I would like to remind my brother that you received your first instructions from a woman, and she, no doubt, was your mother or another woman. In addition, you probably have heard that some say that I am a prophetess, but I am not the first one. Miriam, the sister of Moses, was a prophetess, and that is not all my young brother," she said calmly. She spoke to him the way a mother would speak to her own son. "Have you not heard that Abraham, our father, listened to his wife, Sarah, in the matters of Ishmael; and the Lord agreed that she was right. Furthermore, have you not heard from the elders that the Lord revealed himself to Rebecca, the wife of Isaac, and told her that twins were within her? Now, the Lord has revealed to me, my brother, what we must do to defeat Sisera … and if you have a problem in accepting this, then you are not rejecting me; but you are rejecting the Lord."

"Very well put, Deborah," said one elder.

"You handled yourself very well," remarked another elder.

After Deborah finished speaking, Barak gave her a compliment. "The manner in which you presented yourself was great, and I sincerely hope my officers have learned something from you," he commented, as he looked over at the young officer.

Deborah was proud of Barak because he wanted to speak up on her behalf. In addition, she wanted to keep the respect of the officers, princes, and elders based on her own wits and merits and not just on what Barak could say for her. For many years, Deborah fervently hoped that the Lord would put an end to the Canaanite oppression. For this purpose, she prayed—day after day, month after month, and year after year—encouraging her people to do the same. Now, her hopes were coming closer to fruition.

The Lord had revealed Himself to Deborah and told her what to do. There were three major phases to the command of the Lord. The first one was to call Barak, and this she did. The second phase was to tell him that the Lord commanded him to take ten thousand men from the tribes of Zebulun and Naphtali and bring them to Mount Tabor, and this they accomplished. There remained one final phase not yet accomplished, and that was the victory over the enemy in battle. Deborah had come to that final moment, and she was very hopeful that her people would be free at last.

She admired Barak more and more, and she prayed to the Lord that He would help Barak to increase his spirituality and trust in Him. Deborah concluded that once he had arrived at that spiritual level, she would be ready to accept his marriage proposal without hesitation. She knew that he would have to go through more trials and tests before he would be ready to accept a higher spirituality. He was almost there but not quite, she thought. Nevertheless, she was optimistic. Because she wanted him, she was beginning to feel that he belonged to her.

Returning to the war agenda Barak said, "I have something to add. We will divide our army into two segments. Each segment will contain five thousand men. I shall lead the frontal attack, and Captain Enoch will head the second segment. Captain Enoch, you will remain about five hundred cubits behind me. Your men will act as a reserve unit to protect my rear against any surprise attack. Deborah and the elders will remain here on Mount Tabor; and if they have any information to relay to us, they can do it by flag signals or by horse messengers."

When Barak finished explaining his point, Deborah spoke, "If we have completed the most important matters of this meeting, I would like to be excused to leave." Everyone nodded his head in consent, and Deborah departed.

CHAPTER 21

A little while after Deborah departed from the meeting; a man approached one of the guards at the rear of the tent and whispered in the ear of the guard. The guard then waived to General Barak who was talking at the front of the tent.

"Captain Enoch, will you see what that man wants who is standing next to the guard."

"Yes General!" As the Captain went out the opening of the tent, he could see that the man was the chief of his spy network. The man whispered something in the ear of the Captain. "Are you sure?" asked the Captain. "Did you check your information?"

"Yes! I got the same report from all four of my spy units," he said confidently.

"Thanks chief," commented the Captain. "The General will want to know this."

The Captain walked back into the tent. He stood at the front but to the side of the tent and waited for Barak to finish talking. After Barak had finished explaining a point, he turned to the Captain.

"Yes, Captain Enoch?" The Captain walked over to General Barak and whispered in his ear. Barak opened his eyes wider and looked extremely solemn. Then the Captain returned to his place. "Alas!" Barak grimaced, as he took a deep breath and exhaled suddenly with deep concern.

All the officers, princes, and elders in the tent were tense and silent. You could discern by the glances on their faces, that they were wondering what was happening.

"What is the problem now?" Someone inquired.

"People of the Hebrew nation, I have ... sad tidings." Barak breathed with a slow deep voice. "There has been a great change in the number of men, horsemen, and chariots in Sisera's army. Two weeks ago, we knew that he had about nine hundred chariots, ten thousand horsemen, and thirty thousand footmen. At that time, he had us outnumbered about five to one. Now, everything has changed."

"Changed?" echoed the other officials.

"Yes. The chief of our spy network has reported to me that Sisera now has three thousand chariots, fifteen thousand horsemen, and fifty thousand footmen. These new numbers give Sisera sixty-eight thousand men arrayed against our small ten thousand. This situation is compared to a fight between the lion and the chicken, and we are the chicken."

"Alas! Alas! Alas!" said the various elders, as they looked at one another and shook their heads with grief and disbelief.

Then Barak continued. "It was bad enough when they had us outnumbered five to one; now, they have us outnumbered ... almost seven to one" he pointed out, as he gestured with his hands.

"General, are you sure that the numbers in Sisera's army are correct?" asked one of the priests.

"Yes, I am. They are very close estimations. The report that we have is that more than fourteen kings have joined up with Sisera. Even if our numbers are off by as much as ten thousand, and I don't think they are; the fact remains that

Sisera would still have fifty-eight thousand soldiers—and that is a lot of men," he emphasized, looking around the tent at the solemn faces.

"General Barak, from whence came these great numbers?" asked Captain David.

"Two large armies came across the Jordan from the nations of Ammon and Moab. Moreover, our spies have sighted a third army moving south from Tyre and Sidon. Finally, a fourth army marched down from Syria," said Barak, pointing at a map.

"General, what do you make of this large horde that Sisera arrays against us?" asked Captain Enoch.

"I am not sure … but it could be that he thinks that we are going to marshal all the twelve tribes of Israel against him."

"What do you think we should do General?" inquired one of the elders.

"You want the truth?"

"Yes … ! I want the truth!"

"I will be honest about it! I think that we should call off the attack," said Barak, looking stern as he stared at the elder. There was complete silence in the tent; and many of the officers, princes, and elders seem shocked and confused.

"Call off the attack?" asked another elder, as he stood up. "Our people have been waiting in great anticipation for this moment."

"Yes, waiting in anticipation for victory—but not in anticipation for defeat … . I am not willing to sacrifice the lives of our twenty-one year old young men against Sisera's superior odds. If we go into a war with Sisera and lose, all of our young men, who do not die in battle, will be captured and sacrificed in the fire to the Canaanite god, Baal. I cannot support a war wherein the enemy has the advantage of seven to one ... . It is as though all the surrounding nations have risen up against us." After Barak's words, the elder sat down.

Elder Ram raised his hand and began to speak. "General Barak, priests, officers, princes, and elders," he said, as he struggled to his feet slowly needing the support of the man next to him. As he arose, his dark blue dashiki-like garment became more visible. Gold and silver thread accentuated the neckline and sleeves. "My father was a young man when Joshua was alive," he reminded them, as he leaned on his stick and rubbed the side of his face. "My father would tell me stories of how Joshua was outnumbered by the Amorites ... and other nations; yet, he was victorious. I remember when the deliverer, Ehud, fought the Moabites; and they outnumbered us. But for now ... I say let's take a poll, and see how many are for war, and how many are not." Barak and the entire body agreed that they should take the poll. They took the poll; and it was deadlocked, nine for and nine against.

"Barak is the General, why don't we let him decide," suggested a younger elder.

One of the Princes of Issachar made a counter proposal. "Let's not be hasty—my brothers," he said, adjusting the white turban on his head. "It is getting late and I think we need to do two things: One, close out this meeting right now. Two, continue this meeting tomorrow morning when Deborah can be here."

"Yes, yes, yes!" Everyone stood up in agreement.

At the end of the meeting, Captain Enoch approached Barak. "General, we have to check the fortification on the northwest spur before it gets too dark."

"Oh that's right ... let ... let me have a word with the Princes of Issachar, then I'll be ready to go." Barak walked over to the Princes. "Peace be unto you my brothers."

"Peace, Brother Barak."

"If it isn't too much trouble, I would like to ask a favor of you. I have to check the fortifications before it gets too dark. Would you be so kind as to inform Deborah about everything that was discussed at this meeting?"

"We shall be glad to do this for you, Barak. May God be with you until we see you in the morning."

After everybody had departed, the Princes of Issachar sent for Deborah to meet with them in the headquarters' tent. Deborah came with her handmaid, Sarah. When Deborah arrived, the Princes of Issachar explained to her everything that she had missed. They told her about the spies who brought the bad news and about the fourteen kings that had joined up with Sisera. This gave him overwhelming odds of seven to one. Furthermore, they told her that Barak said that he would not take his men into battle and be slaughtered by Sisera's all-powerful force. They also informed her that the meeting would continue tomorrow morning.

After Deborah heard this depressing news, the Princes departed; and Deborah hung her head in grief. She sat there for a short while and reflected on the bad news. Then Barak came. He saw her sitting in the tent with her head lowered in grief, and he asked. "Why has thy countenance fallen, Deborah?"

She raised her grief-stricken head slowly and looked at him. "What is this I hear that you have called off the attack?"

"I did it because I felt that it would be suicide to go up against Sisera's overwhelming numbers," he replied, as he walked towards her.

"Where is your spirituality? Where is your trust in God? Where is your belief in me? Where is it Barak?" she demanded.

He stood there silently starring at her. Then he labored to speak. "I … am responsible for the lives of my men."

"When you came to my house that last time, you said to me, 'if thou will go with me, then I will go: but if thou will not go with me, then I will not go.' Is this not true Barak?" she inquired, with trembling in her voice.

"Yes ... . It is true," snapped Barak, with a little anger.

"At that time, I agreed to go with you, and I kept my word. Now, you ... are refusing to go into battle! Doesn't your word mean anything?"

"Of course it does! But the situation has changed."

"Changed ... ? But the Lord has not changed," she retorted, as tears ran down her cheeks. "Barak I've had enough. You have rejected the Lord and disappointed me. There will be no marriage. I cannot live with a man who has no trust in God to deliver his people from Sisera," she reminded him frantically, as she marched out of his presence broken-hearted.

Barak stood there and watched her leave. Finally, he walked to the opening of the tent and yelled to her, "A man must do what he has to. You are just like a woman. You blow off steam—just like a hot water pot."

Deborah went to her tent. It had gotten dark, so Sarah, her handmaid, lit a small lamp. Then Deborah sank her head into the palms of her hands as she sat down. Soon thereafter, Sarah asked, "Is there something that I can do for, my lady?"

"No thank you, Sarah ... . I just want to be alone with my thoughts."

Deborah reflected on how she came with Barak to Mount Tabor with great hope. A hope about how their relationship developed from one stage to another, from the first time they met until now. She thought about those warm romantic moments at the City of Kedesh when he danced with her and made her feel alive again. There, he asked for her hand in marriage.

When she agreed to go with Barak to Mount Tabor with the Hebrew army, she had great hope that he would put his trust in the Lord. Now, the man whom she was coming to love had refused to lead the Hebrew army and refused to trust in the Lord and even to believe in her. In essence, he shattered all her hopes; and she felt empty in her stomach. She tried to forget him, but the pain gnawed in her chest.

Sarah put out the oil lamp, and Deborah prepared to go to sleep. However, sleep would not come. She thought about when she departed from the outskirts of Bethel and went to Tirzah, Daberath, Kedesh, and now to Tabor. She had come a long way; met many people, and raised their hope. Now it seemed that all was in vain. As time passed, she sank into deep despair; and her future with Barak seemed very uncertain. As a spiritual woman, she knew that she could never have any harmony with any man who did not trust in the Lord. It was during the middle of the second night watch, and still, there was no sleep. Barak's actions weighted heavily upon her interrupting her rest. She could not even discuss it with her handmaid, Sarah, because it was too disturbing. During the night, she tossed and turned and got only about an hour and a half of sleep. She seemed to be fearful to think of what the next morning would bring. The only consolation she got was when she prayed to her Lord. Finally, she resigned herself to the fact that at sunrise, the decisive breakup would come.

Chapter 22

The next morning, not long after sunrise, the officers, princes, priest, and elders continued their meeting in the large headquarters' tent. The atmosphere was solemn, tense, and uncertain. When the officials came in, they moved slowly; and they were ready to deal with the deadlock. Everyone was present except Deborah.

"Can we start the discussion?" asked one elder.

Elder Ram said, "Let's give Deborah a little more time to get here." Shortly thereafter, Deborah arrived. They reviewed all of the issues that they had discussed in the previous meeting, including General Sisera's overwhelming numbers. "General Barak, have you changed your thinking?" asked Elder Ram.

"I am not sure what my position is at the present time. I have mixed feelings," he confessed. "I need more discussion."

One of the young officers raised his hand to speak. "Yesterday, I asked Prophetess Deborah why we recruited only ten thousand men when we are very capable of mobilizing over two hundred thousand men. Would you be so kind to explain this to me in more in detail?"

"Yes, I shall be glad to explain. If the Lord had told us to select more than two hundred thousand men for war, and we became victorious; then our people would say that it was because of our might that got us this victory. However, instead of this number, the reason Lord chose only ten thousand men is, when we win, we cannot say that we gained this victory by our strength, and not even by our great numbers—but we can surely say that only by the help of God did we win this war," she said, as she noticed the smiles of approval on the faces of the men.

"Are there any more questions or comments?" asked Elder Ram.

Deborah realized that if she was going to win over the elders and princes, she had to take the initiative and keep it. Then she raised her hand.

"Deborah, you may speak,"

"I stand before you elders, priests, and officers of the Hebrew nation. There is no need to fear the great numbers of our enemy. All we need to do is to keep God's word, be righteous, and trust in Him. I want to remind you that Moses wrote the following: 'When thou goes out to battle against thine enemies and seest horses and chariots, and a people more than thou—be not afraid of them—for the Lord thy God is with thee ... .' This ... I swear in the name of the Eternal One, and in the spirit of our ancestors. For after tomorrow, Sisera will not breathe another breath," she assured them, as she held out her hand in gesturing.

"I hope you are right my dear, because ... if you are not," emphasized Elder Ram, "some of the people will want to bring charges against you."

"Elder Ram, on the words that the Lord had spoken to me, I stake my honor, reputation, and my life."

At that moment, Deborah stepped forward three feet. She closed her eyelids and she remained perfectly still. During this moment of silence—she received a revelation. Her face shined radiantly and the power of her aura permeated throughout the entire tent. She opened her eyes and turned toward the General. "I have a message from the Lord for you Barak; you can no longer afford to tarry in your safe position on this mountain: 'Up! For this is the day in which the Lord has delivered Sisera into thine hands: is not the Lord gone out before thee?' " she asked, with tears in her eyes.

Everyone present, including Deborah, fixed their eyes on Barak. No one spoke a word. They waited patiently to see what his reactions would be. It was obvious from the look on his face that he was under much emotional pressure. He took a deep breath and said, "All right, we shall put all battle plans into operation and let's meet on the lower northwest spur." Suddenly, Barak grabbed a spear from the corner of the tent and held it high above his head. "Oh ye officers of the Hebrew nation … follow me!" he shouted, as he marched bristly out of the tent.

The priests blew the ram's horn to assemble all the soldiers, priests, elders, and princes. They met on the northwest ridge of Mount Tabor. This ridge was the lowest section of the mountain and the easiest to ascend and descend. As the Hebrews assembled, they could see the army of Sisera doing their maneuvers off in the distance.

When everybody had arrived and all plans were prepared, Elder Ram stepped forward and said a prayer: "Hear, oh Israel, the Lord our God the Lord is one. Oh Eternal spirit of the universe and of all flesh, we gather here today to go out against our enemy who has persecuted us for the last twenty years. We place our trust in Thee, be merciful to us and give us the victory in the time of our need because we go up against an enemy, who far outnumbers us, is better trained and armed. All of us thank Thee and we give You the glory, amen."

Soon after the prayer, Elder Ram spoke. "We shall have the recitation of the words of encouragement."

One of the priests began to recite from the sacred laws of the Hebrews, " 'Hear Oh Israel, ye approach this day unto battle against your enemies: let not your hearts faint, fear not and do not tremble, neither be ye terrified because of them; for the Lord our God is He that goeth with you, to fight for you against your enemies, to save you.' "

After the priest finished, Elder Ram turned to Deborah and asked? "Are there any more formalities, Prophetess Deborah?"

Deborah lowered her head, thought, and squeezed her nose on both sides with her index finger and thumb. "Oh yes! Now we must have the reciting of the exemptions for the soldiers," she reminded him, raising her head.

"Thank you, Prophetess Deborah; I knew that you wouldn't forget anything."

Next, Elder Ram called for one of the military officers to recite the exemption rights to their men, "Now hear this ... oh ye host of Israel: 'What man is there that hath built a new house, and has not dedicated it? Let him go and return to his house, lest he dies in battle, and another man dedicates it. And what man is he that hath planted a vineyard, and hath not yet eaten of it? Let him also go and return unto his house, lest he dies in battle, and another eats of it. And what man is there that hath betrothed a wife, and hath not taken her? Let him go and return unto his house, lest he dies in battle and another man takes her.' "

Next, another officer recited the psychological conditions to the men; "What man is there that is fearful and faint-hearted? Let him go and return unto his house, lest his brethren's heart faint as well as his heart."

Elder Ram spoke up once more. "With the authority given to me by the princes of the tribe of Issachar, the priests, and the elders, I confirm Barak to be the general of the Hebrew army as spoken by the Lord through the Prophetess Deborah. Moreover, we grant Barak the authority to designate his deputy and his staff of officers. May God be with us, even though we are like rabbits going up against crocodiles."

After all of the introductory formalities were completed, Barak divided his army into two segments—each under the head of a captain with five thousand men. Then he appointed Captain Enoch to be his first officer of the army and his next in command to succeed him. "Captain Enoch, I want you to organize the soldiers into battle formation," Barak said. "Line up all of the men facing the southwest in the direction of Sisera's army and stand by for further orders."

"Yes General."

They brought up the standards of the tribes of Naphtali and Zebulun which had the images of a deer and a ship embroidered on them, respectively. Afterwards, the Levites came up with the ram's horn and the drummers. They blew the horns, and they beat the drums.

Boom! Boom! Boom! This sound became the beat for the marching army, and they repeated it over and over and over. Barak bade farewell to the princes, elders, and to Deborah.

"God be with you," Deborah exclaimed.

Finally, he turned his horse away and waived. "Take care of yourself, Deborah, I shall return."

Deborah smiled frostily, understanding in his words the intention to pursue her. She knew in her heart that his decision to go into battle resulted only from her encouragement and from the indirect pressure of the elders. In light of this, she knew that Barak did not have any deep faith in God. Therefore,

Deborah resigned herself to the fact that Barak would not be an appropriate mate; even though, he was a man of high social standing, and temptingly handsome.

The army continued to march to the beat of the drums. Barak could see the armies of Sisera across the Jezreel Valley. The army camp of Sisera was about nine miles southwest of Mount Tabor. This camp was between the City of Megiddo and the Kishon River. The Kishon River flowed northwest at this point and the calm waters of the surrounding mountains fed into it.

***

Just outside the City of Megiddo, stood Sisera, the General of the army of Jabin, King of Canaan. He welcomed and addressed the allied kings and soldiers who came to support him in the war effort against the Hebrews. Sisera stood on a six-foot boulder and saluted the kings as they drove by in their iron chariots. He said, "Thank you oh kings of Taanach, Dor, Megiddo, Ibleam, Beth-Shean, Kitron, Nahalol, Acre, Sidon, Ahlab, Aphik, Ammon, Moab, Syria, Beth-Shemesh, and Beth-Anath." Sisera continued. "As you know, the Hebrews came into this land over one hundred and fifty years ago, under the leadership of that notorious Joshua, the son of Nun. Since they have been here, they have destroyed our gods and altars. Furthermore, these Hebrews have become a danger to our way of life, and we came here today to put an end to this threat. There is no doubt that we can win. Our numbers far exceed theirs, and we control the Jezreel Valley with over three thousand iron chariots. We have divided the Hebrew nation by our control of the Jezreel.

"In addition, Barak and that—that—woman associate of his made their worst mistake when they took their army up to Mount Tabor. Because of their actions, this gives us the opportunity to destroy them in one central location."

The soldiers then hit their swords against their shields to express applause. Clang! Clang! Clang! Then Sisera called up the High Priest, Eved-Baal. "It is with great pleasure that I take this opportunity to come before all of you kings of majesty, princes, and soldiers of the Canaanite nations. We thank you for your cooperation and unity. Let us pray: Oh beloved Baal, our sun-god, giver of light and life, god of fire and summer heat, we ask thee to be with us in our fight to destroy our enemies, the Hebrews." The High Priest spoke for fifteen minutes, and he concluded by saying that Baal can be appeased only with human sacrifice by fire. Then he called the custodians to bring forth one young male and a female as a sacrifice. After the sacrifices, the parade began.

Every army of each nation passed in review. They passed onward by hundreds, and by thousands marching in cadence with the trumpets blaring and the drums emitting the rhythmic booming sound: Boom … Boom … Boom … Boom … . "General Sisera, our soldiers look just magnificent in their new uniforms," complimented General Kara. "Their red tunics and kilts were made by our best weavers."

"Yess … and they look very neat in their army uniforms with their brass leggings and coats of mail. Their brass helmets glow in the bright sunshine. That alone—is enough to terrify the enemy," emphasized Sisera. The armies put on a great show of pomp and pageantry changing into right and left flanks. They performed the rear march; companies combined with others to form one unit; then the units separated again and again. It was a great show of well-trained disciplined spectacular troops with horses and camels prancing, soldiers waving their spears and swords and the flags fluttering by the force of the gales.

Finally, Sisera received the news which he eagerly expected. One of his staff officers, Kara, reported. "General, the enemy has been sighted approaching from the north."

"How many would you say are out there?"

"I would say between ten and fifteen thousand, General."

"What fools they are to come against our mighty force," commented Sisera, smiling wickedly. "This will be an easy victory!"

"General, do you think that they have more soldiers hidden in the mountains of Zebulun?"

"I don't believe so. If they do, they better not come down into the Jezreel," he concluded. "Prepare the soldiers for battle and pass the word down that I want Deborah and Barak brought to me alive—that's an order!"

"Yes, my lord Sisera, and what units shall we use for the first attack," asked General Kara.

"We'll use five thousand horsemen, and five thousand foot soldiers—all new recruits. This will give the new recruits a taste of battle on an easy prey," said Sisera, as he stepped down the ladder leaning against the boulder.

When General Kara came down the ladder, he asked Sisera, "Are you going to use any of our charioteers against the enemy?"

"Not at first, but we will hold our charioteers in reserve." With General Kara standing nearby, Sisera began to mumble, "We finally meet here in the plain of Jezreel—you and I, Barak—you and that associate of yours have caused me enough problems. I shall put an end to you forever."

***

It was a bright and sunny day. After Barak and his army marched for four miles, they stopped to rest; and they could see the Canaanite army in full battle dress. A little later, Barak and his army continued to march southwest, staying not far from the Zebulun hills, just in case they needed the advantage of the high ground. The Hebrew army was now about five miles from Mount Carmel; then Barak turned and marched due south. Now Barak's position was between the City of Shimron on the north and Megiddo on the south. When he came within one mile of the Kishon River, Barak and his officers could see Sisera's army maneuvering in the distance because it was clear weather.

"What do you think of the situation?" asked Captain Enoch.

The General leaned forward over the long white mane of his horse and gazed into the distance. "It seems that the bulk of Sisera's charioteers are in the center. The horsemen are on both sides of the charioteers, and the foot soldiers are out in front," commented Barak, as he drew back and sat erect.

"I would agree, General," Captain Enoch added. "If Sisera attacks us with his charioteers first, we shall suffer rapid and very heavy losses; but if he uses his footmen first, we shall have a better chance, however, that chance would only be temporary."

"Yes, that seems logical," said Barak.

"General, look at Sisera's forces," Captain Enoch pointed out. "They are lined up like tidal waves—ready to overrun us."

"Yes, I see Captain."

At that moment, Captain David came up from the rear to talk to Barak. "General Barak, there are about ten horsemen approaching from our rear. Furthermore, the men are getting restless because of Sisera's large numbers; and there is talk of some of them turning back."

"I thank you Captain for your report."

"Shall I return to my unit?"

"No! Wait here until the horsemen arrive." As Barak and his officers waited for the horsemen to arrive, they saw dark clouds coming out of the north from the rear of their soldiers. At the same time, they could hear Sisera's band blowing their trumpets and beating their drums. There was no stop to the beating of the drums, and they continued the repetition.

Finally, the horsemen arrived. It was Deborah with the three Princes of Issachar, her handmaid, Sarah, and her bodyguard, Nachshon. "Barak, we came because we felt that the soldiers needed our moral support," said Deborah.

"I guess only a prophetess or prophet would know that. I am glad that you came. It was so considerate of you."

Then a prince of the tribe of Issachar said to Barak, "We have read the signs of the stars and heavens, and they are favorable for you."

"This is good news, thank you," said Barak.

"If it is pleasing to you, on the way back, we would like to ride between the ranks of the soldiers and encourage them," she said, as she looked over his shoulder and refused to give him direct eye contact."

"This is all right with me." Then he turned to Captain David. "You may accompany Deborah, as you return to your unit, Captain."

"Yes Sir, General," he saluted, nudging his horse forward.

At last, Deborah and the Princes of Issachar began to speak. "Hear oh warriors of Israel; be not afraid of the numbers of our enemies for God is with us to fight our battles. Direct your hearts, souls, and minds unto the Lord; trust in Him, and He will give us the victory."

When Deborah repeated these words in the ears of the men, Barak and his soldiers became emboldened. Then she returned to Mount Tabor.

CHAPTER 23

The Hebrew army continued to march southwest toward the Kishon River. At this time, small drops of rain began to fall. The Kishon was just a small stream; and during very hot spells, it became like a dried-up creek or wadi. However, during the rainy season, it overflowed its banks and became a mighty torrent fed by the waters running down from the nearby mountains.

The Valley of Jezreel or sometimes called the Great Plain of Esdraelon extends across central Canaan (Israel) from the Mediterranean Sea to the Jordan River in the East. On the northwest side of the valley stands Mount Carmel and just to the east are the hills of Zebulun and Mount Tabor not far from the Jordan. Across from Tabor, going 12 miles south, is Mount Gilboa. Finally, there is Mount Megiddo about 10 miles due south of Mount Carmel on the southwest side of the valley. Altogether, the Jezreel Valley spans a distance of 35 miles wide and about 12 miles north and south.

Here in this wide open plain, General Sisera mobilized his army. His chariots could maneuver well at great speed in this area. The army of Sisera was arrayed in battle formation just south of the Kishon River and north of the City of Megiddo.

Boom! Boom! Boom! As Sisera's drummers continued to beat, dark clouds overcast the entire valley. Then the drummers stopped beating. The Hebrew army also came to a halt. There was complete silence in the dark cloudy valley. "Oh God help us," pleaded Barak.

Suddenly, that quiet tense moment gave way to an eerie feeling. Pow! Pow! Pow! Powerful sudden cracks of thunder and lightning seemed to shake the foundation of the entire valley. In an instant, as if by divine intervention, Barak shouted, "Charge men!"

Barak dashed forward with the Hebrew army with him. He reacted as though the thunder and lightning was his signal from God to begin the attack.

When Sisera saw the Hebrews advancing, they charged toward the Kishon River, footmen in front and horsemen behind.

"I cannot understand," said Barak, "why Sisera is putting his footmen into action first."

"Perhaps the Lord is confusing his mind," said one of the junior officers.

As Barak's army came within one hundred cubits of the Kishon, hail began to fall. Thunder and lightning in repeated succession flashed forth, and harsher rain and wind ensued. The rain and wind was at the backs of the Hebrews, but it blew in the faces of the Canaanites and blinded them. In light of this, the Canaanites were not able to use their arrows, spears, or swords. The Canaanite army reached the Kishon first. By this time, the entire central valley north of the City of Megiddo became a marshland and extremely muddy. Horses ran into each other and slipped and fell because the hail and rain blinded them.

"Use your slings men," yelled Barak, as he approached within fifty cubits of the enemy. The slings were very useful to the Hebrews, because the rocks remained airborne longer,

278 Mary L. Windsor and Dr. Rudolph R. Windsor

with the wind behind them pushing them forward. Barak then ordered his soldiers to take up defensive positions along the Kishon. The Hebrews then seized the spears and swords of the dead and wounded Canaanites.

As time passed, it was still raining. Finally, Sisera put his charioteers into action. Seeing the lightening and hearing the thunder, the frighten horses that were attached to the chariots sped down the slope. Onward and onward, the mighty monster machine raced, as the Hebrews watched in astonishment, undaunted by the spontaneous power and fierce onslaught of the racing iron chariots. The horses and chariots were slipping and sliding in the mighty torrent. The rain and the hail continuously beat down in the faces of the Canaanites and blinded them. As a result, the horsemen and charioteers ran over their own soldiers causing them to drown. Not long after, the swift torrent of the Kishon River swept them away.

***

Meanwhile, back at Mount Tabor, Deborah prayed in her tent. She knew that her people would get the victory; in view of this, she prayed that the Lord would keep the causalities low. After she finished her prayer, she went outside to join the rest of the people as they watched the battle.

It was raining a little on Mount Tabor as they watched; the day turned into semi-darkness.

"Did you see that lightning bolt?" asked Demetrius. "It struck down into the heart of the Canaanite army and split some chariots into pieces."

"Yes," said Deborah, "The heavens are fighting for us, and a mighty angel is with us."

"Does that angel have a name?" inquired Elder Ram.

"Yes, it is Michael, the Arch Angel who appeared unto Moses and Joshua at various times in seemingly human form. This angel stands up for the children of thy people when they are righteous."

The bolts of lightning struck in repeated succession, creating havoc, confusion, and destruction on the Canaanite army. Other chariots became aflame and the horses ran around frantically pulling fiery chariots behind them. The lightening lit up the sky like daylight. It was only during the time when the lightening flashed, that Deborah and the elders could get a good glimpse of what was happening out there—in the valley.

"Deborah, you were so right when you said that the Lord would fight our battle. You are truly a servant of the Lord."

"Thank you, Elder Ram."

As Deborah and the elders watched the battle, they began to sing praises to the Lord because they were greatly inspired and thankful.

***

Back at the front line, the army of Sisera became very confused and began to scatter. Then Captain Enoch looked to the right and saw a man dressed in a very majestic uniform riding in his chariot. At that moment, one of the Hebrew soldiers threw a spear at the man in that chariot and missed. Instead, the spear struck the horse in the neck. The horse fell down to its knees and did not move.

"General Barak! Look at that fancy chariot over to your left," said Captain Enoch.

"Yes, I see, that could be General Sisera."

"He is dismounting from his chariot and running away. Do you want me to pursue him, General?"

"No, I need you here. I will get that crocodile eventually. Right now, the destruction of his crocodile army is more important."

"Yes General."

"Captain Enoch, I am going to pursue after the rest of Sisera's army. It seems like they are fleeing toward the City of Harosheth-ha-goiim near Mount Carmel. Can you and your men hold this line?"

"We'll hold, General—at the risk of our lives," said the Captain confidently.

"If the enemy takes off and runs, pursue them and look after my nephews. In the meantime, while I am near the City of Harosheth, I am going to see if I can locate my third nephew named Joseph if he is still alive."

Barak and his men then pursued after the chariots and the remainder of Sisera's army; they fought and pursued them all the way up to the gates of the City of Harosheth which was located on the east side of Mount Carmel. As Barak led his men, he remembered the words of Deborah, "the Lord hath delivered Sisera into thine hands: is not the Lord gone out before thee?" Barak then became more encouraged and shouted, "Hallelujah."

The City of Harosheth soon fell quickly because several bolts of lightning struck it, and the attack of Barak and his men was furious. Then his soldiers gathered up the spoils of the city and liberated the Hebrews who were working at hard labor in the Canaanite stone quarries.

But Barak didn't fine his nephew, Joseph. As he rode along the trail near the mountain, he saw a group of Hebrews walking slowly and looking weak. When Barak and his soldiers came near them, one man spoke up. "Bread, sir, would you be so kind to give us some bread?" he pleaded, holding out his hands. "We have not eaten in two days."

Then Barak turned around to his soldiers and spoke loudly, "You heard the man, give them some bread!" After they ate the bread like hungry ducks, Barak asked them, "Do you know or have you seen a young man about seventeen years old by the name of Joseph?"

The men stared at each other with a puzzled look, shook their heads from side to side and said, "We don't know him. Every month, someone dies or is sacrificed. He may not even be alive." At that moment, Barak looked disappointed and turned away. The man spoke again, "And who might you be?"

Barak faced toward the man and hesitated then answered, "I am Barak, General Barak"

Various men looked at each other with surprise and repeated his name. "Barak, Barak." The man that did most of the talking spoke again. "We want to thank you for your victory and for saving us from the Canaanites taskmasters."

"Don't thank me thank God, your Creator, and give Him the glory. Is there another place where the Canaanites keep Hebrew laborers?"

"Yes, there is another labor camp about 300 cubits down the road."

After that conversation, Barak galloped away hoping to find his nephew alive. It became a life and death struggle for him. Then he uttered the words: "Oh Lord, if I have found favor in Thy sight, let my nephew Joseph be found alive." Barak pressed onward with great speed because he wanted to find Joseph and return to the front line. As Barak rode by the eastern side of Mount Carmel and the swollen Kishon River, he came to another Canaanite labor camp where some Hebrews were being held. When the Canaanite guards saw Barak and his soldiers, they fled. Barak approached the Hebrew laborers, "You are free now. You can return home or you can join up with us."

"We will join up with you."

"Good, have you seen a young man by the name of Joseph?"

"We know of a young man we call Jo; the Canaanites put him in a deep pit three days ago because he attempted to escape."

"Where is this pit?"

"Come, we will show you. But we better hurry up because the pit fills up quickly with water running down from the mountain; he might already have drowned." They ran frantically to the pit on this cloudy day. The pit was seven feet by seven and twelve feet deep. They looked into the pit, but they could only see the top of Jo's head because the water had reached his mouth. It had not yet come up to his nose.

Barak realized that he had to act quickly and he ordered, "Bring me that rope that hanging on the side of my horse; I'm going down into the pit." One of the soldiers brought over the rope which Barak got from Deborah's estate about a week ago; Barak tied the rope around his chest and the men lowered him into the pit. The water now reached Jo's nostrils and he was gasping for air. Barak grabbed Jo by the waist and ordered, "I have him, pull me up quickly." As they were pulled up out of the pit, Barak could see that it was his nephew Joseph but he was now unconscious. "Thank God I have found him," he muttered.

The soldiers laid Joseph on his stomach and turned his head to one side. The soldiers could see from his appearance that Joseph was a handsome boy with milky skin and white wooly hair. Then one soldier pressed the palms of his hand against Joseph's lower rib cage and forced out some water but there was no response. Barak then said, "Breathe boy and talk to us, God is with you." All of a sudden, there was a gush of water and air that came from his mouth. Joseph coughed and expelled more water several times. He opened his eyes slowly and looked delirious. Barak then kneeled over him and said, "I am your uncle, Barak. We are at war with Sisera's army. I must return now to the front line. I will leave some soldiers here to look after you."

Joseph smiled and said, "Thank you God and you Uncle Barak for saving me," and they embraced each other affectionately.

After Barak found his nephew Joseph, he returned to Captain Enoch at the front line. When Barak arrived, he learned that fresh troops from the tribes of Issachar and Ephraim had joined up with the Captain because the Canaanites had threatened their territory and were penetrating southward. The Captain pursued the Canaanites all along the Kishon River from Megiddo to the City of Taanach.

"Captain Enoch, congratulations! You have done a splendid job here! I see that the Lord has been with you."

"That is true General Barak, and lot of the credit must be given to our soldiers who fought with valor."

"I see that you have things under control here, so I'm going to take fifty men with me and pursue Sisera before I lose his trail entirely.

"Do you have any idea of his whereabouts?"

"Not exactly, but I think he is headed for the City of Damascus. I had heard some time ago that he was born not far from there."

The rain had stopped and Barak rode off into the twilight. The night came, and they camped not from the City of Beth-Shean to sleep. However, before Barak could retire, he received a message from his other nephew, Joel who was injured in battle.

Then Barak placed his hand on his forehead in emotional agony and commented, "Ah, I saved one nephew from a hell hole and now I have another one on the verge of death in a hospital tent. I can imagine what his mother will say to me now; she will berate me to no end"

The next morning as Barak pursued Sisera toward the Sea of Galilee, he changed his mind and decided to visit and check on the welfare of his nephew, Joel who was lying on a table in a hospital tent on Mount Tabor in severe pain. Someone discovered him alive beneath two dead Canaanites with a broken leg and an arrow wedged below his right shoulder. Joel sent for Barak after they had taken him from the battlefield.

***

In the hospital tent, Joel was writhing in pain and hollering for his uncle. Mud and blood covered his entire body. The doctors wanted to give him a sleeping potion; but he refused all care until his Uncle, Barak, arrived.

Then Demetrius, the head doctor, came into the operation tent. He lifted the cover from Joel's legs and his facial appearance changed with shock. "We cannot delay," he uttered. The boy tried to resist, but they restrained him. "If you continue to move, you could rupture a blood vessel or puncture your lung," warned Demetrius.

"No! No! Not right now! I must see him first," yelled Joel.

Demetrius looked at his leg again. Then he leaned over his chest and spoke, "We cannot delay forever, Joel." Everyone looked down at him and remained silent.

As they held Joel down, he turned his head from side to side in defiance and shouted. "I sent for my Uncle Barak. I know he will be here. He is coming! He is coming!" Demetrius looked at his leg once more and pleaded, "If you want us to save your leg, we have to work on you right away. Do you understand?"

"I must talk to him first!" he emphasized strongly. As his head was facing the tent opening, he saw his uncle walking in slowly. "He has arrived!" Joel informed them.

Everyone stopped what they were doing, turned around quickly, and looked at General Barak with awe. "Congratulations General Barak on your victory," said Demetrius.

"Thank you." Barak walked slowly toward the mutilated body of his nephew, and looked down at him with tears in his eyes. He raised his head with a grimace on his face and then lowered it again in emotional agony. "I promised your mother—that I would take care of you; and it seems that I have failed," said Barak, as he held Joel's hand with tenderness and love.

"I know—" He struggled to speak with labor, and Barak heard the sound of pain in his voice. "She told me that you would. I am glad that you came. Oh Uncle, are they going ... to cut off my leg?" he asked, gritting his teeth in pain.

Barak glanced at his leg. Then he looked at the doctor. "What do you think, Dr. Demetrius?"

"Well, the arrow is not that close to his vital organs; and it did not penetrate very deep; so it shouldn't be any problem in that area. However, we are concerned about his leg. The tibia bone is fractured; and it will have to be reset," he said quite frankly, leaning his head to one side.

"Doctor Demetrius, what could prevent him from having a complete recovery?"

"There are a number of things—poor blood circulation, infection, and leg movement. We will have to stabilize the leg to prevent it from moving. Any movement will hamper the fractured bone from binding together. To help prevent infection, we need to go to work right away!" he urged.

"I shall not keep you much longer. How long will it take for him to walk again?"

"It can take anywhere from four to eight months. But before we can start to work on him, he needs to cooperate with us and take the sleeping potion. Without it, he will not be able to endure the pain.

Barak then turned to Joel. "I want you to cooperate with the doctors and take the potion."

"But ..."

"No buts in it," Barak interrupted. "Do it for your mother! Do it for me; and above all, do it for you!" admonished Barak, as he leaned over him and held his hand tightly.

"Yes ... Uncle Barak," he said softly. "I wanted you to be here, so that I would know ... that I am in good hands."

Barak lowered his head. "You are in good hands." Then he let go of Joel's hand. "I'll pray for you," he promised.

Finally, one of the doctors gave Joel the sleeping potion; and within a short while, the herb-like drug put him into a state of deep unconsciousness. As the doctors began to work on Joel, Demetrius turned his head toward Barak. "I'll contact you and let you know how he is progressing." Then he continued with his work.

"I am not leaving ... just yet."

"Not leaving—? Huh—?" Demetrius paused and turned towards Barak again. "I can understand how you feel about your nephew, General; however, did not you appoint me as head over this hospital?"

"Yes ... that is true!"

"Well, by your authority ... and as head ... I must ask you to give us the privacy to do our work. We are perfectly capable of taking care of your nephew and saving his leg ... ." They both looked at each other. "If Deborah was here, I am sure she would tell you the same thing."

Barak looked at him and smiled. After that, the Hebrew medical assistants looked at Barak and nodded their heads in agreement. Barak began to walk away slowly. Finally, he stopped and turned around. "I can see that they trained you very well in Egypt, and I know that you will do your best. May peace be with you."

"Peace," said Demetrius. "Your nephew is young and strong. He should recover without any problems."

The operation lasted for a couple of hours. Afterwards, Demetrius looked pleased with the success of the operation. As he washed and dried his hands, he gave instructions to his assistants. "When he wakes up, give him some of that herb tea called, Ginseng which I bought from the merchants coming from China. It will help in the healing process."

After Barak departed from Mount Tabor, he joined up with his men near the Sea of Galillee to continue the search for Sisera.

***

In the early afternoon, Barak sent out three men in an advance party to inquire if anyone had seen Sisera, and if not, to be on the lookout for him. They went to many places—

towns, villages, fields, woods, hills, and caves—from sunrise to sunset; but they found no Sisera.

On the second day of his search, Barak and his men arrived at Lake Merom about eleven miles north of the Sea of Galilee. As Barak was searching for Sisera, a fast riding horseman rode up and shouted, "I have a letter for General Barak."

"I am Barak! Who sent the letter? "

"It is from the Prophetess, Deborah."

"Oh! It is?" asked Barak, with surprise. Barak took the leather pouch and opened it eagerly. He wondered what she wanted in light of their last breakup on Mount Tabor. He read:

> *Peace ye warriors of Israel. Hallelujah! Praise the Lord for the great victory that He gave to us this day.*
>
> *To General Barak, your officers, and gallant soldiers who jeopardized your lives unto death in the high places and fields of the valleys. We invite you to a victory celebration of praise to the Lord. This celebration will take place at the City Daberath, seven days from the 2nd of this month. We look forward to your presence.*
>
> *Deborah and the elders.*

After Barak read the letter, he informed his men of the contents, and they were jubilant to hear about the good news.

"Are ladies going to be there?" asked one soldier.

"Yes, many ladies," answered Barak.

"Hurrah, hurrah, hurrah," expressed the soldiers, with cheer and excitement.

"All right men, it is time for us to continue our search for Sisera." They began to search the area west of Lake Merom, and came to a place of the great oak tree of Zaanannim not far from Kedesh. As Barak and his men advanced toward a tent which belonged to a woman named Jael, she came out to meet Barak and greeted him. "Peace be with you, General Barak. Come! and I will show thee the man whom thou seekest."

As Barak approached the tent, he drew out his sword, entered the tent cautiously, and behold, Sisera lay dead with a tent nail in his temple. "Did you do all of this?" he asked, looking astonished as he scratched his head.

"I did!" she answered softly. "Now I got my revenge."

"What revenge were you seeking? Why did you kill him?"

"After my husband and I separated, Sisera killed my sons. My sons had lived not far from here, and when they were not able to pay their taxes, Sisera carried them off and had them sacrificed to Baal, his god."

Then Barak walked slowly around the tent inspecting everything. He picked up a jawbone of an ass, and an ox goad and inspected them. "This jawbone has had a lot of use," he said, looking at Jael. "It has cracked many skulls, and this goad has pierced the bodies of mighty warriors. To whom did they belong?"

"They belonged to Shamgar, the warrior, who slew six hundred Philistines and some Canaanites—he was a powerful man."

"Did you know him?" asked Barak.

"Yes General! After my first husband, Shamgar died, I married Heber. Shamgar and I fought the Canaanites and the

Philistines, a long time, before you came on the scene. Barak, you finished the great work that we didn't complete."

"I thought King Jabin, and your previous husband, Heber, had a treaty."

"My husband had a treaty with King Jabin, not I—"

"Oh how I wanted the revenge of capturing this man ... and I forgot that Sisera was supposed to be given into the hands of a woman."

"A woman's hands?" asked Jael.

"Yes. When Deborah called me to undertake this mission, I said to her, if thou will go with me, then I will go: but if thou will not go with me, then I will not go. And she said, 'I will surely go with thee: notwithstanding the journey that thou takest shall not be for thine honor; for the Lord shall give Sisera into the hands of a woman,' " Barak informed Jael.

Then Jael asked, "So that which I did was a result of a prophecy?"

"Yes! Oh Deborah, oh Deborah, I cannot escape thee; your prophecy is fulfilled before my very eyes. Thanks Jael for helping us to capture Sisera."

"May I keep the sword of Sisera?" asked Jael.

"Yes! It is your conquest! Now it is your sword!"

Barak looked down once more at the corpse, and tears ran down his cheeks. "Why do you shed tears for Sisera, General?" asked a soldier.

"I am not shedding tears for him, but only for my dear mother who he murdered," he said, as he wiped the teardrops from his eyes. Barak turned to walk out of the tent; then he stopped. "Bury him!" he commanded his soldiers and walked out of the tent with a feeling of satisfaction.

When Barak left the tent of Jael, he wasn't far from his family estate. He stopped by to check with his overseer about personal affairs and to take care of the needs of his soldiers. Also, his overseer gave him a letter which he opened and read:

> *To Barak, Deborah, and the elders: all of the nobles of the tribe of Judah, and I want to congratulate all of you on account of your great victory. There is no doubt, in our minds, that the Lord fought for you on such an occasion as this. Furthermore, I want to take this time to inform you that Prince Abihu has been removed from office and he is now in exile. As of this month, I, Malak Ben Judah, am the chief prince of my tribe. I wish you and Deborah well, and we are looking forward to a cordial relationship with you."*
> *Malak Ben Judah.*

After two day's rest, he set out for the City of Daberath to attend the victory celebration. He wondered what Deborah's reaction would be in view of their last confrontation.

CHAPTER 24

Finally, the day of the victory celebration came. While Barak was away searching for Sisera, Deborah and her retinue stayed at the guest quarters of one of the elders in the City of Daberath. Her retinue now included three persons, Sarah, Nachshon, and Marah. Arising early that morning, the ladies prepared themselves for the special celebration. After Marah finished bathing and dressing, she came into Deborah's presence. "How do I look Deborah?" Deborah stood still and stared at Marah. "What is the matter Deborah? You look like you've seen a ghost!"

Deborah hesitated and thought for a moment, not wanting to hurt her feelings. "The dress...the dress is too revealing below the neckline."

"Well, I just want to be admired. Is anything wrong with that?"

"No, but …" Deborah said slowly.

"My husband used to admire me often," she sniffled, lowering her head, "now he's … he's gone, and he can't say those nice things to me anymore."

"Oh my dear troubled soul, a man doesn't have to see your bare skin to know what you have and to admire you. When a woman has a nice figure, it will show through her clothes. Now, come Marah, I have a dress I believe you will like."

She took Marah by the hand and escorted her over to a small chest. Deborah opened it and took out a long orange linen dress with a sash and gold borders. Marah opened her eyes and mouth wide and could not resist commenting. "Oh Deborah, it is so beautiful."

"Put it on and see how it fits."

After Marah put on the dress, she smiled. "I love it."

"I knew you would, we are about the same size," said Deborah, looking at herself, and then at Marah.

"You see Marah, this dress isn't revealing and any man can see that you have a fine shape. It is not too loose and not too tight. It is just right. Marah, I want you to make me a promise that you will be a good example to our young girls who are growing up to be ladies. You must understand Marah, that most people will not be convinced by things we say and teach, but by what we do."

"Yes Deborah, I promise."

"One last thing Marah, it is easy to earn a few gold shekels, but harder to make a difference in life. By this, I mean, as you become more successful and fortunate, remember to reach back and help someone else. This is how we make a difference in the world, and make it a better place. Now, we must be on our way to the victory celebration. Barak and his soldiers will also be there."

***

It was a little passed midday when Barak and his soldiers rode into the City of Daberath. Everyone could see the clear blue sky interspersed with some white clouds. The city was crowded with men, women, children, and soldiers carrying palm branches. Soldiers, who fought bravely and had listened to the encouragement of Deborah, came to thank the Almighty and to celebrate their victory. Most people waived the branches of the palm trees as a symbol of celebration, victory, and joy. It was a beautiful majestic sight to behold the unity and to hear the hymns of praise. As they marched into the city, they passed by shops, vending stands, and houses; some of these houses had two stories. From the rooftops, the ladies and children threw down fresh flowers to the soldiers.

Captain Enoch and Captain David rode on their horses behind Barak with their troops brandishing their latest weapons captured from the enemy. The Levites blew the ram's horns, the trumpets, and beat the drums. The people rejoiced in their victory and yelled, "Hallelujah." You could see smiles on the faces of everyone.

Barak, Captain Enoch, and Captain David stopped in front of the reviewing stand and saluted the elders, priests, princes, and other dignitaries. The viewing stand was made of wood, and the railing was decorated with palm branches along the rear, and the sides. Barak caught the eye of Deborah, and they gazed at one another as if they wanted to talk but it was not the right time.

Then there was a yell from the crowd: "Where is Sisera?" Barak turned and looked at the man.

Before Barak could answer, another man shouted: "Yes Barak, we want to know … . What happened to Sisera?"

"He was killed by a woman," commented Barak, as he turned toward the man.

Another man asked, "Barak, are you saying … that you didn't capture Sisera?"

"That is right. I did not capture Sisera. A woman named Jael killed Sisera in her tent. She took a tent nail and drove it through his temple with a hammer."

Men and women turned to those standing nearby and asked: "Did you hear that?" "Sisera killed by a woman?" "Yes, Sisera killed by a woman," another man repeated. "Can you believe it?" interrupted an older woman. "The mighty Sisera killed by a woman!" The news spread like wildfire throughout the city. Then the women began to chant: "Sisera stood tall before his fall: the Lord delivered Sisera into the hands of a woman." Everyone began to dance in the streets and in the open places. They danced to the music of the flutes, cymbals, tambourines, and drums praising the Almighty for their victory.

As the people moved to the beat of the music, they pulled Barak into the dance. "Come Barak! Come....Let's see if you are as good a dancer as you are a soldier," urged a pretty woman smiling seductively. Different women grabbed him by the arm as they danced in a circle. They took two steps backwards and then two steps forward as they clapped their hands to the rhythm of the folk music.

Barak appeared caught up in the joy of the moment, and it was difficult for him to break loose. As he danced, he looked up and caught Deborah's eyes and he attempted to go to her; but the women continued to pull him around the circle. One lady said to him, "come on and enjoy yourself ... . You act like you are in a daydream."

Finally, Barak broke loose from the women and approached the platform. As he approached, the soldiers snapped to attention, and raised their right fist to their chest. On all sides of the platform, stood the soldiers with their weapons captured from the Canaanites. A few moments later, Elder Ram whispered to Barak. "It is your time to speak next ... . I have spoken already and Deborah will speak after you. I'll introduce you."

"This is all right with me, Elder Ram."

When Elder Ram walked to the center of the platform, the large crowd was still dancing and singing. He raised his hands high over his head to indicate to the crowd to stop dancing and singing. The music stopped. The people slowly became quiet, and the crowd became attentive. "Oh people of Israel, I stand here before you again not to give a speech, but to introduce to you a man who has dedicated twenty years of his life fighting for you … . The Prophetess Deborah told us that the Lord had chosen him for this mission … and without further delay, I bring to you, Barak Ben Abinoam, our liberator."

Barak went to the center of the platform to speak. As he walked, his eyes fell upon Deborah standing at the opposite side with Demetrius, his family, and his medical assistants. The multitude went wild with applause chanting his name, clapping their hands, and making the yodel sound with their tongues. The applause lasted for a long time, and then finally stopped when he raised his hands. "Hebrew citizens … !" shouted Barak with a loud base voice, looking over the entire crowd. The crowd went wild again with applause, but the voices soon subsided. "Hebrew citizens … ! I welcome you to this victory celebration in the name of our God, in the name of our elders … and in the name of Deborah, the Prophetess," explained Barak, as he looked over the crowd to the right and then to the left. "Today … we dedicate this great victory to the glory of our God … and to the glory of Israel which we all belong. Let us honor our brave soldiers … who sacrificed their lives unto death for the freedom of our people. When our soldiers captured the City of Harosheth-ha-goiim, they killed King Jabin and liberated thousands of our people who are now free from hard labor. They have now returned home to their wives and children."

Again, the crowd applauded like thunder, and chanted his name: "Barak, Barak, be our judge; Barak, Barak be our judge."

Barak quieted the crowd again with his upraised hands and continued. "This celebration would not be complete without special recognition given to our friends who came from a far land. These visitors have been with us for more than a week. As some of you know, Demetrius and his associates have been trained in Egypt as physicians. They have rendered their services unselfishly for the healing of our soldiers. As a result, they have saved many lives! At this time, I'm going to ask Dr. Demetrius to come up front." After he came up, Barak said, "Dr. Demetrius, we salute you." Then the drums and trumpets sounded and the soldiers snapped to attention. After the salute, Barak presented Dr. Demetrius with a golden medallion which Barak placed around his neck. Barak also instructed two of his soldiers to bring up a chest of gold coins.

Demetrius' eyes lit up and he smiled. "This is so nice of you General Barak—but—I cannot—accept this," he stuttered, flustering.

"Yes! But we want you to have this because of your great generosity and untiring service," explained Barak, as he moved the chest closer to him. "We know how you, your family, and associates spent many sleepless nights caring for the wounded."

"Well—if you insist. We shall use the money to help build a hospital and a medical school back home. This is truly a blessing." he said. Demetrius then looked at the chest of gold coins again in amazement.

Barak once again looked up at Demetrius. "Have you anything more to say? We want to honor you by allowing you to speak to us for a short while," explained Barak, as he smiled.

"Oh ... ! Yes, yes, surely," he uttered, as he squirmed to gain his composure. "But I'll need more time—because I want to praise you and your God!"

"Well, in that case—then take all the time you need, just long as you finish before tomorrow morning."

"I'll finish before night," Demetrius smiled, turned around slowly, and the crowd became very quiet. "This is truly a surprise. It is with great honor that I stand here before you today. I want to thank you General Barak, Deborah, the princes, the priests, the elders, and all of you good people for your hospitality and kindness," he choked with emotion, as he wiped the tears from his eyes with the sleeve of his tunic. "I am gratified to share with you these few moments of your great victory. It was more than two weeks ago that I first met your commander at the City of Tirzah. At that time, he informed me that he was going up against Sisera with only ten thousand soldiers. I told him, that it was suicide ... and surely you don't expect to win. However, little did I know that the stars and the God of Heaven would fight on your behalf. The windows of heaven opened up; thunder and lightning terrified the enemy. A fierce storm broke out with heavy rain and hail that obscured the vision of the Canaanites."

"That's right," said Barak.

"Now, it is befitting, at this time, for me to relate to you a true story: The great king of Egypt, Thutmose III, led seventeen military campaigns into Canaan and Syria and he won by his strategy, his numbers, and his great war machine. Oh Israel ... you didn't have these luxuries. You won by the spirit of right and not by might! The sages of the pyramids and temples of Egypt taught that there was nothing more powerful than the idea of freedom when its time has arrived. Oh Israel, your time has arrived," he emphasized, pointing his outstretched hand toward the heavens. "And this is evident by your great victory. In closing, I want to thank Barak and Deborah for asking me to remain here to attend to the wounded. Their request gave me the rare opportunity to gain additional practical medical skill and to experience a victory unique in the annals of military science. I saw—with my own eyes—the manifestation and intervention of God on behalf of a people lacking military might. Now—my work here is almost complete—and I will be returning home in a few days to join my people and my relatives. Peace be with you."

After that momentous and timely speech, the crowd went into a frenzy and roared with applause. It was very inspiring to the people to hear those words coming from a Greek. When Demetrius turned around and faced Barak, the General spoke, succinctly: "Well done Dr. Demetrius! I couldn't have done better myself." Finally, Barak embraced him and patted him on the back. Right at that moment, Demetrius' wife and daughter wiped the tears from their eyes because they were overcome with great emotion. After Demetrius finished his speech, Barak beckoned for the three medical assistants to come forward. "We want to honor you also for your great service you have rendered to our wounded soldiers." Barak then placed a gold medallion around the neck of the three medical assistants.

"We thank you for the medallions and your kind words. It was a pleasure to serve your people."

Meanwhile, the three medical assistants returned to the back of the platform, and at the same time, Elder Ram beckoned to Deborah to come forward. When she came to the front of the stage, the multitude gave her an exceptionally prolonged ovation. She attempted to speak several times, but could not.

"Oh people of Israel—Oh people of Israel—" but the crowd continued to applaud her. Finally, she proceeded to speak and the ovation subsided. "Oh people of Israel—the previous speakers have spoken very well; and what I would add, on the most part, would be repetition. Therefore, I am going to be brief. I am asking you to love and forgive one another for any wrongs. Hatred is like a parasite or disease; it gradually destroys and eats away the vital organs of the human body. When we forgive one another, we stop the cycle of hate; we lift a heavy burden from our shoulders. Then together we can make progress for the improvement of our world. Show mercy and patience to each other, when you do this, you will receive mercy when you need it the most. If you do this, you will make me very happy. Will you do this?"

"Yes! Yes!" answered the crowd.

"I can't hear you. Will you do this?" she repeated.

"Yes! Yes! Mother Deborah!" The crowd answered much louder.

Then Deborah and Barak began to sing a song:

> Praise ye the Lord for the
> avenging of Israel, when
> the people willingly offered
> themselves.
>
> Hear, O ye kings; give ear,
> O ye princes; I even I,
> will sing unto the Lord
> I will sing praises to the
> Lord God of Israel.

....

Blessed above woman shall
Jael the wife of Heber the
Kenite be, blessed shall
she be above women in
the tent.

Then Deborah turned around and called for the wife and daughter of Demetrius to come forward. They looked at each other with surprise and walked slowly up to Deborah. Demetrius stood nearby and gave the translations into the Hebrew and the Greek languages. Deborah began to speak slowly: "In appreciation of your devoted service to our wounded soldiers, I present to both of you these valuable necklaces." As Deborah placed the necklaces around their necks, she kissed both of them on their cheeks. The ladies were very touched by the gifts and by Deborah's warm smile.

Isis, the wife of Demetrius, stood there in her pink silk dress. "This is truly a surprise," she commented. "We didn't expect this. However, we do thank you so much."

At last, Hatshepsut, the daughter of Demetrius stepped forward. "Deborah, we shall never forget your kindness." After she finished speaking, Hatshepsut hugged Deborah warmly and kissed her on the cheek. As Deborah returned to the back of the platform with the ladies, she noticed a woman placing a chaplet of flowers around Barak's neck and kissed him on both cheeks and hugged him.

When she departed, Barak conversed with the various dignitaries on the platform. After that, he looked around casually for Deborah; but she was nowhere in sight. Later, he saw his first officer. "Have you seen Deborah, Captain Enoch?"

"Not recently. The last time I saw her, she was standing with the dignitaries," he replied, looking worriedly toward the viewing stand.

"I know that Captain, tell me something I don't know!" he snapped, harshly looking around for her. The Captain looked startled momentarily with disbelief, and then gazed around the crowd. "Excuse me Captain for being snappy. Would you take some soldiers and look for her?"

At that moment, Captain David approached Barak. "The elders want to see you, General."

Barak returned to the platform and saluted the elders. Elder Ram approached Barak smiling and said, "The people and the elders want you, along with Deborah, to be our judges and rulers. Since she is already a judge, do you accept?"

"Well, this is ... a surprise."

"Do you accept Barak?"

"Well ... Yes. Yes Indeed."

"Where is Deborah?" asked the Elder.

"I don't know," answered Barak looking worried. "She just—just disappeared," he remarked, shaking his head.

"Disappeared!" repeated the Elder, with disbelief on his face. "Well, come with me! It is time for me to swear you in as ruler of the people."

"I'll be right behind you Elder."

When the both of them reached the center of the platform, Barak stood with his eyes fixed directly on Elder Ram. Then Elder Ram recited the oath of office: "Do you Barak swear to uphold the commandments of the Lord and to protect the Hebrew tribes from all their enemies whether they be foreign or home born?"

"Yes! I do swear," answered Barak, with a stern look on his face.

"I now pronounce you judge and ruler." At that moment, all the people cheered and shouted with great joy. Finally, Elder Ram informed the people that the formalities were finished; and he encouraged them to enjoy themselves by eating, dancing, and singing praises to the Lord.

Not long after, Barak turned around toward the crowd and shouted, "Hebrew citizens! Let the celebrations begin!" Then a group of ladies and men began to sing Hebrew spiritual songs.

As Barak walked to the other side of the platform, he noticed Elder Ariel, the chief elder of the Council of the Seventy Elders. The Elder looked up at Barak, and said, "Congratulations on your appointment as judge and ruler of the people."

"Thank you Elder. I am glad you were able to come to the celebration."

"Oh Barak—I have some advice for you. Now that you are ruler of the people—remember—that you are mortal, that you must serve the people, and that you must serve not for your own personal gain. In order for you to be a good leader, you must love the people. And in order for you to help and to save the people from social decline, you must serve the people and work for their personal welfare," said the ninety year old elder in a deep bass voice, as he touched Barak's arm. "Walk humbly before God and before your fellow man in righteousness and with justice. Remember this: Justice, a helping hand and righteousness elevates a race; but sin and violence is a total disgrace and a downfall to any people." At that moment, he looked around the platform. "By the way, where is Deborah?"

"I don't know—she just disappeared," answered Barak, throwing his hands in the air.

Elder Ariel stared at Barak, and repeated, "You don't know?" The elder had a thoughtful look on his face and concluded. "When an eligible woman who is not spoken for runs away from a handsome eligible man in the glory of his hay day, rest assured, she wants to be pursued. This is especially true when she doesn't have anyone else in mind. Now, go—! Find her. Find Deborah and join up with her. She will help you—and together, the both of you can govern the people and save them from self-destruction, social decay, and hopelessness."

"Yes Elder, I'll go. I'll go find her," Barak intimated with determination. The soldiers looked around the city and checked the roads and asked about Deborah but they were not able to locate her. After Barak finished meeting with the elders, he returned to Captain Enoch. "Did your men locate Deborah, Captain?"

"No General! She just vanished like a young doe among the thickets," he responded, shaking his head in disbelief. "Have you had any harsh words with her lately?"

"Yes, but that was the night before the battle. She was very angry with me because I suggested to the Council of the Elders that we should call off the war. She said that I had no trust in God, and no belief in her. She ended the conversation by saying that there will be no marriage and stormed away with tears in her eyes."

"Marriage? You asked her to marry you?"

"I did. And what's wrong with that?"

"Not a thing, General. Nothing at all. It's just—just the first time I've heard of this. When did you ask her—and what was her answer?"

"She said that she would consider it after the war. I cannot understand it. She sent me an invitation to attend the victory celebration, and then she just disappeared like a gazelle in the wheat field."

"I think she is interested in you, General. I could tell by the way she looks at you."

"I think so too; then she got so angry at me; we haven't had any long conversations since." There was a silence; and after a few moments, Barak spoke. "Well—I think I'll go visit her next week, and see where I stand."

CHAPTER 25

For seven days, Deborah thought about Barak. She wondered how he was doing and what he was doing. Would he come to visit her; was he still interested in her; did he have another woman in mind. She remembered the woman who kissed him at the City of Daberath. Then Deborah recalled that on his first visit he said that he would pursue her. As a result, she wanted to hear from him; she felt unsure of where they stood and she had some questions.

It was on a late cloudy dreary morning one week later that Barak arrived at Deborah's estate. As Barak looked through the gate, he could see Nachshon and Marah talking and holding hands. He could discern from the expressions on their faces that they were serious about each other. Barak knocked on the gate and Nachshon, came and opened it. "Congratulations, Prince Barak on your victory!"

"Thank you. Peace be to you Nachshon, I came to see Deborah. But first, I want to talk to the little boy, Ben. Would you be so kind to call him and tell his mother that I would like to speak to her also?"

"My pleasure, I'll do it right away, Prince Barak."

After a little while, Nachshon returned with Ben and his mother. When Ben saw Barak, he ran to him eagerly with a big smile on his face. Barak stooped down and they embraced warmly. Ben said, "I miss you so much, Prince Barak." Ben wiped the tears from his eyes. "I was afraid that you would not return."

"God was with us. Is this your mother?"

"Yes, her name is Leah."

"It is my pleasure to meet you, Leah," said Barak.

"I have heard," said Leah, "a lot about you from Ben, Deborah, and other people. You come highly regarded and the people look up to you."

"Thank you, your son wants me to be something like a father to him. Do you approve?"

"Do I have a choice? Barak, you stole the hearts of the people and now you have stolen the heart of my only son! What else do I have left Prince Barak?"

"You are his mother; you will always be his mother; in addition, he loves you. When you allow him to be attached to me, he will love you even more."

"I am not sure whether Ben is old enough to decide what he wants."

"Ben is old enough to know if he wants a father figure in his life to guide him. He needs a good father image and he wants it. Can he stay at my estate for certain periods of time...?" Barak paused, "I promise you that I will be a good father to him as my father was to me."

Leah stared at him in silence... then said, "Very well, you have my consent. I want the best for my son."

"Good, you are a wise woman. Also, I came here to visit Deborah and to express my sincere affection for her. I hope to win her love"

"Well good luck to you, Barak, and God is with you," she smiled, and both Leah and Ben departed. After the conversation, Nachshon escorted Barak to the back courtyard where Deborah sat under her palm tree.

"Peace be with you Deborah," said Barak.

"Well, this is a surprise, Barak. What seeketh thou?" She asked with her back to him denying him the privilege of face-to-face contact.

"I seek thee!"

"There are many women in Galilee, why thou seeketh after me?"

"I'll get right to the heart of the matter," he said, standing five cubits behind her. "When you were at the City of Daberath, I wanted to see you."

"You did see me," she said, looking over her shoulder.

"I meant—I meant I wanted to talk with you."

"Why didn't you Barak? I was there."

"I was busy celebrating our victory with the people of the town."

"Oh. I understand," she drew in her lips. "You were very busy with the ladies."

"Yes, and when I looked around again, you were gone." Barak then raised both of his hands, leaned forward, and asked, "Why did you disappear?"

"I left because I didn't want to interfere with your happiness."

"But, you are my happiness," he interrupted.

"And the second reason I left was because I had completed my work there. Therefore, I felt no need to linger."

"I see … my dear," observing all of her reactions.

"Now since you know why I left the City of Daberath, what are the real reasons you came down here?"

"The first reason is I wanted to talk with little Ben and his mother. She has agreed to let her son visit me for certain periods of time."

"That was a wise move on your part, Barak. Now what is the second reason you came?"

"I've made war—and that is over. Now I want to make peace with you!"

"To make peace, first, I need you to answer a few questions," she said, turning around slowly.

"This is pleasing in my eyesight," Barak remarked.

"When you were at the War Council meeting on Mount Tabor, you told the elders that the attack should be called off. What made you change your mind?"

"After thinking about the situation for several hours that night finally, I had to admit the truth that our people would not be better off without the war because Sisera was making our lives a living hell. I could continue to be a good mountain fighter leading a few hundred men; however, I realized that if I did not take advantage of the moment, it would be even harder in the future to gain the support of the elders and the masses. In addition, you did make a strong appeal for me to take action on the following morning."

"Barak, I want you to know that on that very night on Mount Tabor—you put me through a lot of pain. I promised my people that they would be free, and you almost make a liar out of me."

"That was not my intension. I get no pleasure out of hurting you or anyone else. I thought that I was doing the right thing for my men and for my nephews."

"You had nephews in the war?"

"Yes, there were two."

"Did they survive?"

"Yes ... but not without injury."

"I'm so sorry to hear about the injury," she said, with deep concern raising her head.

Barak continued to speak. "If they had not survived, I don't know how I would have revealed the bad news to their mother. As it was, I did have an opportunity to see and speak with my sister at the victory celebration; and at that time, she put a chaplet of flowers around my neck, kissed me, and thanked me for looking after Joel."

"Oh, I did not know that your sister was there."

"Yes, my sister told me that my nephew, Joel, was doing just fine. In addition to thinking that I was doing the right thing for my men, I didn't realize the truth until after the war?"

"What truth?"

"It was after the war that I realized that the Divine Creator could have chosen another man instead of me. After the battle, I understood that I was wrong about you, wrong about God, and wrong about spiritual things...."

"Go on."

"The war became a revelation to me. I must confess ... that when I first marched into battle, I did not believe that we could win against those great odds. I guess I didn't believe," he scratched his eyebrow as he spoke slowly; "because I didn't know how we would win the victory."

"I didn't know either," commented Deborah. "Excuse me for interrupting, would you please continue."

"But when I saw the heavy rain beat down into the eyes of the enemy and blinded them, then I became connected with God and convinced that the Almighty was fighting our battle. When I heard the thundering and saw the lightening, I instinctively gave the command to my soldiers to charge forward. It was as though God, the lightening, and I became one at the same moment."

"I can assure you Barak that you were born for this task; and as you know, your name means lightening one," she explained. "Are you finished Barak?"

"No. After God fought our battle and after the victory; then I realized the importance of all the spiritual things you had been telling me all along."

"This is wonderful Barak," she said smiling. "In view of the fact that war has many horrible consequences, I am glad that it had, at least, a spiritual awakening for you."

It was a dreary cloudy morning when Barak first arrived. As he continued to converse with Deborah, he gazed up into the heavens. The thick dark clouds started to break up, and the bright warm sun began to shine through bringing hope and promise of a better day. "Deborah, everything seems to have come to a complete circle."

"A complete circle? What do you mean?" she inquired, with a puzzled look on her face.

"Well." Barak took one step to the side and looked down. Then he gazed up at her as he walked. "I mean ... our first meaningful conversation began here. We went to many places together; now that the war is over, here is where I return." At that moment, Barak turned around, faced the courtyard wall, and raised his hand to his mouth and eyes, as if he was preoccupied with deep thoughts. Then he turned to her and spoke. "We came through peacetime, war time, and now peacetime again. Where do we stand Deborah?"

"We?"

"Yes! You and I."

Deborah lowered her head smiling, and then she looked up. "I am waiting for the right man."

312 Mary L. Windsor and Dr. Rudolph R. Windsor

"Well! I believe that you have found him. I am the right man," he said with confidence.

"Oh! You think so? What makes you so sure?" she inquired, sensing a little arrogance.

"I think that the Lord meant for us to be together ... from the beginning." Barak paused. "If this was not meant to be, your deceased brother-in-law, Caleb, or another man would be standing right here—where I am standing, my dear."

Deborah smiled slightly and for a moment, she could not speak. Then she mustered enough energy. "Since you've been here today, I haven't heard how you feel ... ."

"How I feel about you?" asked Barak, finishing her unspoken words.

"Yes! How do you feel about me?" she asked vigorously, staring into his dark brown eyes.

"My feelings are very strong for you Deborah. They haven't changed since the dance and our conversation at the City of Kedesh where I introduced you to my father." He moved closer to her and took hold of both of her hands. He said to her softly. "I love you ... Deborah and I want you to be my wife."

She wanted to shout hallelujah, but she retained her composure. Then she looked away and smiled. "Are you sure it's love or is it passion?"

"Oh Deborah, I am sure. When I say love, I do not mean passion. I mean spiritual love—from the depth of my heart—and from the depth of my sacred inner soul. I could have had plenty of passion. I ran away from passion to find you!"

"You have really changed, Barak."

"In what way?"

"I remember the times when you were reluctant to say the Divine name or to talk about spiritual matters."

"I know. The war changed all of that. It was just no way we could have won without the Heavens fighting for us."

Barak looked into her dreamy eyes and drew her up on her feet, placing his arms around her shoulders. His strong chest pressed gently against her well-defined figure. She sensed a feeling of peace and harmony. She began to feel wanted, loved, and alive again.

Then Barak lowered his head and kissed her on her cheek. "Will you be my wife, Deborah?" he asked again in a whisper.

She raised her small soft right hand to his face and stroked the side of his cheek affectionately as she looked into his eyes. She choked for the words, "Yes! Yes! Yes!" she said in a whisper. "I'll be your wife Barak. I'll be your—"

He interrupted her last word and kissed one cheek and then the other; staring into her eyes, he gently pressed his lips against hers lingering for a few seconds. Abruptly, she pulled away.

"What's wrong Deborah? Why did you pull away?" he asked, with the feeling of a loss.

"It's a woman's ... thing," she said turning her back to him. "Barak, do you have any idea when you want to get married?"

"Just as soon as we can make all of the arrangements."

"Good, because if you want to be around me, I suggest we start making plans right away."

"That's fine with me. You want to begin right now?"

"Yes! We can start right now because we are going to have a lot of preparations to make."

They decided to have the wedding in six months at Deborah's estate. When the time came, hundreds of people attended the wedding ceremony from all parts of the Hebrew nation, including priests, princes, elders, and businessmen with their families.

Following the wedding, Deborah and Barak settled down to as much of a normal life that public servants could expect. They decided to spend their lives together partly in the City of Kedesh and partly at Deborah's estate outside of Bethel.

After the wedding, Deborah reminded Barak: "We must live by being good examples and to teach the people to give and share with one another. This is how we can make the world a better place in which to live for the benefit of future generations. When we share our wealth, this act builds love and helps to remove disease, greed, and hunger from the earth."

"Yes, I agree. I am ready to support this concept."

Many people continued to come to her to seek advice and judgment. She became a mother in Israel. Moreover, Deborah and Barak judged and ruled Israel for forty years and the land rested in peace.

Other Available Books by Dr. Rudolph R. Windsor

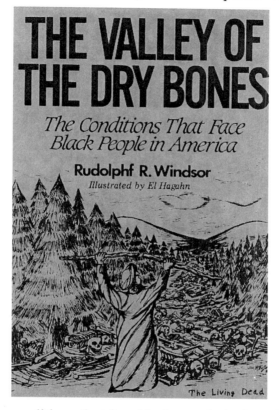

The conditions that face black people in America.
Paperback, 162 pages. $13.95

website: windsorgsgoldenseries.com

For speaking engagements,
lectures, or book signings write to:

Windsor Golden Series
P.O. Box 310393
Atlanta, GA 31131-0393
email:windsorgs@comcast.net

Other Available Books by Dr. Rudolph R. Windsor

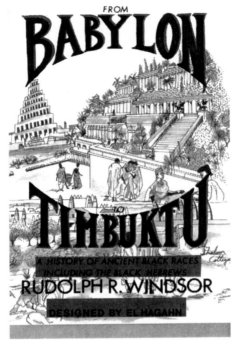

Africa and the Middle East was the seat of highly developed dark skin people and civilization. Dr. Windsor's treatment of black culture and the migration of the black Hebrews to all parts of Africa are edifying.

Paperback, 151 pages. $13.95

website: windsorgsgoldenseries.com

For speaking engagements,
lectures, or book signings write to:

Windsor Golden Series
P.O. Box 310393
Atlanta, GA 31131-0393
email:windsorgs@comcast.net

CPSIA information can be obtained at www.ICGtesting.com
Printed in the USA
LVOW130522211112

308258LV00001B/67/P